Exercises in Dynamic Macroeconomic Theory

Exercises in Dynamic Macroeconomic Theory

**Rodolfo E. Manuelli
and
Thomas J. Sargent**

Harvard University Press
Cambridge, Massachusetts
and London, England
1987

Library of Congress Cataloging-in-Publication Data

Manuelli, Rodolfo E.
    Exercises in dynamic macroeconomic theory.

    Contains answers to: Dynamic macroeconomic theory by
Thomas J. Sargent.
    Bibliography: p.
    Includes index.
    1. Macroeconomics—Mathematical models.
2. Equilibrium (Economics)—Mathematical models.
I. Sargent, Thomas J.   II. Sargent, Thomas J. Dynamic
macroeconomic theory.   III. Title.
HB172.5.S27 1987 Suppl.   339′.0724   86-25767
ISBN 0-674-27476-8 (pbk.: alk. paper)

Preface

This book provides scrimmages in dynamic macroeconomic theory. It contains answers to the exercises in *Dynamic Macroeconomic Theory,* by Thomas J. Sargent (Cambridge, Mass.: Harvard University Press, 1987).

Modern macroeconomics treats an equilibrium as a sequence or, more generally, as a probability distribution over sequences for prices and quantities. The sequences are indexed by time, so that an equilibrium is a probability model for economic time series. An equilibrium model provides a mapping from parameters of preferences, technologies, endowments, and "rules of the game" (parameters that are meaningful to economists) to the probability model for time series. By "inverting" this mapping, economists interpret observations on economic time series. The rigor of the logical connection between theory and observations that the mapping provides is an attractive feature of dynamic equilibrium, or "rational expectations," models.

Models of this kind, however, are new and unfamiliar to most economists. Someone who is accustomed to doing macroeconomics by shifting IS and LM curves is not used to thinking in terms of models in which the sequences of endogenous variables in general depend on the entire sequence of exogenous variables. Furthermore, the mapping mentioned above is complicated and has also often delivered conclusions that have seemed paradoxical to people who approach things armed with an intuition developed from long practice with Keynesian, or monetarist, macroeconomics. The intuition exercised, say, by users of the static IS-LM model is not innate but represents the cumulative effects of long hours spent doing experiments that entail shifting IS and LM curves. (If you think otherwise, find a smart physical scientist or high school geometry student who has studied no economics, and try to explain how government open-market exchanges of one kind of paper asset for another will affect the price level and aggregate output as they do in the IS-LM model.)

Our purpose in presenting the exercises in this book is to provide a vehicle for the practice of dynamic macroeconomic theory on problems of manageable dimensions. The exercises in *Dynamic Macroeconomic Theory* call for variations and extensions of the analyses contained in the text. By working these exercises, the reader will, we hope, acquire the ability to put the theory to work in a variety of new situations. The exercises are intended to build technical skill, to give the reader experience in fruitful ways of setting up problems, and to provide an appreciation for cases in which problems are well posed and cases in which they are not. Modern dynamic macroeconomics has troubled some people because it has altered the kind of questions that we regard as interesting and answerable and has caused us to consider some of the questions that are routinely studied using IS-LM curves as simply ill posed. The use of systems incorporating foresight and strategic interdependence to study macroeconomic questions, however, inevitably meant that such questions would be reconstituted.

We have tried to make the answers set forth in this book relatively self-contained and have therefore tolerated a certain amount of repetition in the sense that similar results are derived in the answers to different exercises. We have likewise forgone the temptation to shorten our answers by repeatedly referring to arguments in the text.

In some of the problems the answers can be attained by approaches different from the ones we have described. We sometimes ignore the hint given in the statement of the problem, for example, and follow a different line of attack. In such cases the reader will usually be able to follow the hint independently to reach the answer by an alternative route. Also we occasionally give solutions for general classes of functional forms of which the specific example in the problem is a special case.

We had much help in writing this book. We received excellent services in typing and manuscript preparation from Judy Andrew, Linda Dixon, Nancy Muth, and Wendy Williamson. Wendy Williamson also helped us research references and edit the text. Eugene Yun helped by reading and criticizing much of the text.

We also thank the Federal Reserve Bank of Minneapolis, where both of us worked part-time during the period over which this book was composed. We are grateful to Preston Miller and Arthur Rolnick, the leaders of the Research Department of the Bank, for their encouragement and support. The Bank provided an ideal environment for thinking about many problems in macro-economics and monetary economics, including those addressed in the exercises. Kathy Rolfe and Phil Swenson of the Minneapolis Federal Reserve Bank drew the graphs accompanying the present text, for which we thank them.

In a real sense this book results from a collaborative enterprise undertaken jointly with several generations of graduate students in macroeconomics at the University of Minnesota. Almost every problem set forth on these pages was written for and tested upon Minnesota students. We feel privileged to have taught macroeconomics at the graduate school in Minnesota. The attitude taken toward macroeconomics there has been that the subject is very unfinished and that teachers of courses are not experts but merely slightly more experienced students. We too have learned by wrestling with many of these problems and from having students question us and correct us.

Contents

Exercises in
Dynamic
Macroeconomic
Theory

The abbreviation *DMT,* used throughout the exercises and solutions, refers to *Dynamic Macroeconomic Theory,* by Thomas J. Sargent (Cambridge, Mass.: Harvard University Press, 1987).

1 | Dynamic Programming

EXERCISE 1.1   Brock-Mirman (1972)

Consider the Brock-Mirman problem of maximizing

$$\sum_{t=0}^{\infty} \beta^t \ln c_t, \qquad 0 < \beta < 1,$$

subject to $c_t + k_{t+1} \le A k_t^{\alpha}, 0 < \alpha < 1, k_0$ given. Let $v(k)$ be the optimal value function. Use recursions on Bellman's equation (1.27), starting from $v_0(k) \equiv 0$ to show that

$$v(k) = (1 - \beta)^{-1} \left[\ln A(1 - \alpha\beta) + \frac{\alpha\beta}{1 - \alpha\beta} \ln A\beta\alpha \right] + \frac{\alpha}{1 - \alpha\beta} \ln k.$$

SOLUTION

One of the most useful results in Chapter 1 (*DMT*) is that the sequence of value functions of finite-horizon problems converges uniformly to the value function of the infinite-horizon problem. As a result we can proceed by solving the $j = 1, 2, \ldots, n$, period-truncated versions of it. For each j, we can compute the corresponding value function. The limit as the horizon j goes to infinity of these value functions is the "correct" value function for the infinite-horizon problem.

The purpose of this exercise is to show how such a procedure can be applied. We first note that this problem does not quite fit the structure for which Bellman's principle of optimality was claimed to apply. In particular, the return, or objective function, ln c, is not bounded. Generally, when this assumption is violated, there may be many solutions to Bellman's equation, with only one being the "true" value function. Moreover, even if we know the value function, the decision rules that attain the maximum on the right-hand side of Bellman's equation may not be optimal. For the present technology, however, there is a maximum sustainable capital stock $\bar{k}$. As long as $k_0 \in [0, \bar{k}]$, the return function is bounded, and the techniques presented in Chapter 2 (*DMT*) apply.

Define $v_j(\,\cdot\,)$ as the value function when the planning horizon ends j periods ahead. We will find a sequence of value functions $\{v_j(\,\cdot\,)\}$ and compute $v = \lim_{j \to \infty} v_j$, where v satisfies Bellman's equation.

1. Computation of $v_1(\,\cdot\,)$

By Bellman's equation we have that

$$v_1(k) = \max_{c,k'}\{\ln c + \beta v_0(k')\},$$

subject to $c + k' \leq Ak^\alpha$. The function $v_0(\,\cdot\,)$ can be any bounded continuous function. For example, a convenient choice is $v_0 \equiv 0$. To motivate this choice, recall that $v(k')$ gives the value of a given stock of capital next period if the planner behaves optimally. When the planning horizon is one period, however — the world ends this period — the value of carrying over some capital to provide for consumption tomorrow and in subsequent dates is zero.

Given our choice of v_0, the maximization problem has a trivial solution, namely $k' = 0$ and $c = Ak^\alpha$. Therefore $v_1(k) = \ln A + \alpha \ln k$.

2. Computation of $v_2(\,\cdot\,)$

Again, Bellman's equation is

$$v_2(k) = \max_{c,k'}\{\ln c + \beta v_1(k')\},$$

subject to $c + k' \leq Ak^\alpha$, where $v_1(k') = \ln A + \alpha \ln k'$, as found in the previous step. Solving the maximization problem on the right-hand side gives the optimal choices of c and k' as a function of k. For this step the optimal choices are

$$c = \frac{1}{1 + \beta\alpha} Ak^\alpha, \qquad k' = \frac{\beta\alpha}{1 + \beta\alpha} Ak^\alpha.$$

Substituting these optimal values into the objective function, we get

$$v_2(k) = \ln\left(\frac{A}{1 + \alpha\beta}\right) + \beta \ln A + \alpha\beta \ln\left(\frac{\alpha\beta A}{1 + \alpha\beta}\right) + \alpha(1 + \beta\alpha)\ln k$$

or $v_2(k) = v_0^2 + v_1^2\ln k.$

3. Computation of $v_3(\cdot)$

We proceed exactly as before to solve

$$v_3(k) = \max_{c,k'}\{\ln c + \beta v_2(k')\}$$

subject to $c + k' \le Ak^\alpha$, where $v_2(k') = v_0^2 + v_1^2\ln k$ was found in step 2. The optimal values of c and k' are given by

$$c = \frac{1}{1 + \beta\alpha + \beta^2\alpha^2}\, Ak^\alpha, \qquad k' = \frac{\beta\alpha + \beta^2\alpha^2}{1 + \beta\alpha + \beta^2\alpha^2}\, Ak^\alpha.$$

The value function is

$$v_3(k) = \beta \ln\left(\frac{A}{1 + \beta\alpha}\right) + \beta^2\ln A + \beta^2\alpha \ln\left(\frac{A\beta\alpha}{1 + \beta\alpha}\right)$$
$$+ \ln\left(\frac{A}{1 + \beta\alpha + \beta^2\alpha^2}\right) + \beta\alpha(1 + \beta\alpha)\ln\left(\frac{A\beta\alpha(1 + \beta\alpha)}{1 + \beta\alpha + \beta^2\alpha^2}\right)$$
$$+ \alpha(1 + \beta\alpha + \beta^2\alpha^2)\ln k$$

or $v_3(k) = v_0^3 + v_1^3\ln k.$

4. Computation of $v_4(\cdot)$

In this step we find $v_4(\cdot)$ by solving the standard maximization problem

$$v_4(k) = \max_{c,k'}\{\ln c + \beta v_3(k')\}$$

subject to $c + k' \le Ak^\alpha$, where $v_3(k') = v_0^3 + v_1^3\ln k'$ was found in the previous step. The optimal c, k' are given by

$$c = \frac{1}{1 + \beta\alpha + \beta^2\alpha^2 + \beta^3\alpha^3}\, Ak^\alpha,$$

$$k' = \frac{\beta\alpha + \beta^2\alpha^2 + \beta^3\alpha^3}{1 + \beta\alpha + \beta^2\alpha^2 + \beta^3\alpha^3}\, Ak^\alpha.$$

The corresponding value function is

$$v_4(k) = \ln\left(\frac{A}{1 + \beta\alpha + \beta^2\alpha^2 + \beta^3\alpha^3}\right) + \beta \ln\left(\frac{A}{1 + \beta\alpha + \beta^2\alpha^2}\right)$$
$$+ \beta^2\ln\left(\frac{A}{1 + \beta\alpha}\right) + \beta^3\ln A$$
$$+ \beta\alpha(1 + \beta\alpha + \beta^2\alpha^2)\ln\left(\frac{A\beta\alpha(1 + \beta\alpha + \beta^2\alpha^2)}{1 + \beta\alpha + \beta^2\alpha^2 + \beta^3\alpha^3}\right)$$
$$+ \beta\left[\beta\alpha(1 + \beta\alpha)\ln\left(\frac{A\beta\alpha(1 + \beta\alpha)}{1 + \beta\alpha + \beta^2\alpha^2}\right)\right]$$
$$+ \beta^2\left[\beta\alpha \ln\left(\frac{A\beta\alpha}{1 + \beta\alpha}\right)\right] + \alpha(1 + \beta\alpha + \beta^2\alpha^2 + \beta^3\alpha^3)\ln k$$

or $v_4(k) = v_0^4 + v_1^4\ln k.$

5. *Generation of the Conjecture*

So far we have five elements of the sequence of functions $\{v_j(\cdot)\}$, which we know converges to the "true" value function for the infinite-horizon problem. All the elements of the sequence take the form $v_j(k) = v_0^j + v_1^j\ln k$. It is natural, then, to guess that the limit of these functions takes the form $v(k) = v_0 + v_1\ln k$, where $v_i = \lim_{j\to\infty} v_i^j$, $i = 0, 1$. Therefore we need only "discover" these limits. It is very simple to do so for the sequence $\{v_1^j\}$, because each term takes the form $v_1^j = \alpha(1 + \beta\alpha + \cdots + \beta^{j-1}\alpha^{j-1})$, and hence

$$v_1 = \lim_{j\to\infty} v_1^j = \frac{\alpha}{1 - \alpha\beta}.$$

On the other hand, the sequence $\{v_0^j\}$ can be regarded as the sum of two sequences $\{a^j\}$ and $\{b^j\}$ where

$$a^j = \sum_{t=0}^{j-1} \beta^t x_t^j$$

and $x_t^j = \ln \dfrac{A}{1 + \beta\alpha + \cdots + \beta^{j-1-t}\alpha^{j-1-t}},$ $b^j = \sum_{t=0}^{j-2} \beta^t y_t^j$

and $y_t^j = \beta\alpha(1 + \beta\alpha + \cdots + \beta^{j-2-t}\alpha^{j-2-t})$
$$\cdot \ln\left(A\beta\alpha \frac{1 + \beta\alpha + \cdots + \beta^{j-2-t}\alpha^{j-2-t}}{1 + \beta\alpha + \cdots + \beta^{j-1-t}\alpha^{j-1-t}}\right).$$

Notice that $\lim_{j\to\infty} x_t^j = \ln[A(1 - \beta\alpha)]$ for all t and that convergence is monotone. Similarly,

$$\lim_{j\to\infty} y_t^j = \frac{\beta\alpha}{1 - \beta\alpha} \ln(A\beta\alpha),$$

and the series is also monotone. These two properties are sufficient to establish that

$$\lim_{j\to\infty} a^j = \lim_{j\to\infty} \sum_{t=0}^{j-1} \beta^t x_t^j = \lim_{j\to\infty} \sum_{t=0}^{j-1} \beta^t \ln[A(1 - \beta\alpha)]$$
$$= (1 - \beta)^{-1} \ln[A(1 - \beta\alpha)]$$

and
$$\lim_{j\to\infty} b^j = \lim_{j\to\infty} \sum_{t=0}^{j-2} \beta^t y_t^j = \lim_{j\to\infty} \sum_{t=0}^{j-2} \beta^t \frac{\beta\alpha}{1 - \beta\alpha} \ln(A\beta\alpha)$$
$$= (1 - \beta)^{-1} \frac{\beta\alpha}{1 - \beta\alpha} \ln(A\beta\alpha).$$

Therefore we have shown that

$$\lim_{j\to\infty} v_0^j = (1 - \beta)^{-1} \{\ln[A(1 - \beta\alpha)] + \frac{\beta\alpha}{1 - \beta\alpha} \ln(A\beta\alpha)\}.$$

Then the value function for the infinite-horizon problem is

$$v(k) = (1 - \beta)^{-1} \{\ln[A(1 - \beta\alpha)] + \frac{\beta\alpha}{1 - \beta\alpha} \ln(A\beta\alpha)\} + \frac{\alpha}{1 - \beta\alpha} \ln k.$$

EXERCISE 1.2 Howard Policy: Improvement Algorithm

Consider the Brock-Mirman problem: to maximize

$$E_0 \sum_{t=0}^{\infty} \beta^t \ln c_t,$$

subject to $c_t + k_{t+1} \leq A k_t^\alpha \theta_t$, k_0 given, $A > 0$, $1 > \alpha > 0$, where $\{\theta_t\}$ is an i.i.d. sequence with $\ln \theta_t$ distributed according to a normal distribution with mean zero and variance σ^2.

Consider the following algorithm. Guess at a policy of the form $k_{t+1} = h_0(A k_t^\alpha \theta_t)$ for any constant $h_0 \in (0, 1)$. Then form

$$J_0(k_0, \theta_0) = E_0 \sum_{t=0}^{\infty} \beta^t \ln(A k_t^\alpha \theta_t - h_0 A k_t^\alpha \theta_t).$$

Next choose a new policy h_1 by maximizing

$$\ln(Ak^\alpha\theta - k') + \beta E J_0(k', \theta'),$$

where $k' = h_1 Ak^\alpha\theta$. Then form

$$J_1(k_0, \theta_0) = E_0 \sum_{t=0}^{\infty} \beta^t \ln(Ak_t^\alpha\theta_t - h_1 Ak_t^\alpha\theta_t).$$

Continue iterating on this scheme until successive h_j have converged.

Show that, for the present example, this algorithm converges to the optimal policy function in one step.

SOLUTION

Under the policy $k_{t+1} = h_0 Ak_t^\alpha\theta_t$, we have

$$\ln k_t = \ln(Ah_0)\frac{1 - \alpha^t}{1 - \alpha} + \ln \theta_t + \alpha \ln \theta_{t-1}$$
$$+ \cdots + \alpha^{t-1}\ln \theta_0 + \alpha^t\ln k_0.$$

Substituting this expression into the objective function and simplifying, we have

$$J_0(k_0, \theta_0) = H_0 + H_1\ln \theta_0 + \frac{\alpha}{1 - \alpha\beta} \ln k_0,$$

where H_0 and H_1 are constants. The policy h_1 is then chosen to maximize

$$\ln(Ak^\alpha\theta - k') + \beta E \left(H_0 + H_1\ln \theta' + \frac{\alpha}{1 - \alpha\beta} \ln k'\right).$$

The first-order condition for this problem is

$$-\frac{1}{Ak^\alpha - k'} + \frac{\alpha\beta}{1 - \alpha\beta}\frac{1}{k'} = 0.$$

This is identical with the optimal solution of the original problem, which appeared in Exercise 1.1 and in *DMT*. Further iterations would evidently result in the very same policy function.

EXERCISE 1.3   Levhari-Srinivasan (1969)

Assume that

$$u(c) = \frac{1}{1 - \alpha} c^{1-\alpha}, \qquad \alpha > 0.$$

Assume that R_t is independently and identically distributed and is such that $ER_t^{1-\alpha} < 1/\beta$. Consider the problem

$$\max E \sum_{t=0}^{\infty} \beta^t u(c_t), \qquad 0 < \beta < 1,$$

subject to $A_{t+1} \leq R_t(A_t - c_t)$, $A_0 > 0$ given. It is assumed that c_t must be chosen before R_t is observed. Show that the optimal policy function takes the form $c_t = \lambda A_t$ and give an explicit formula for λ.

Hint. Consider a value function of the general form $v(A) = BA^{1-\alpha}$, for some constant B.

SOLUTION

The utility function $[1/(1 - \alpha)]c^{1-\alpha}$ does not quite fit into the framework of this chapter, because it is not bounded. It is possible to show that the condition $E(R^{1-\alpha}) < \beta^{-1}$ guarantees that the value function is the solution to Bellman's equation and that the policy that achieves the maximum is indeed the optimal policy (see Lucas, Prescott, and Stokey, forthcoming). Then we conjecture that $v(A) = BA^{1-\alpha}$. If so, it must be the case that

$$BA^{1-\alpha} = \max_{c \geq 0} \left\{ \frac{c^{1-\alpha}}{1 - \alpha} + \beta B(A - c)^{1-\alpha}E(R^{1-\alpha}) \right\}.$$

Inasmuch as the right-hand side is a standard concave programming problem, the first-order condition is necessary and sufficient. This is simply $c^{-\alpha} = \beta B(1 - \alpha)E(R^{1-\alpha})(A - c)^{-\alpha}$, which implies

(1) $$c = \frac{k^{-1/\alpha}}{1 + k^{-1/\alpha}} A,$$

where $k \equiv \beta B(1 - \alpha)E(R^{1-\alpha})$.

Substituting the optimal policy (1) into the right-hand side of Bellman's equation, we get

$$BA^{1-\alpha} = \left[\frac{1}{1 - \alpha} \left(\frac{k^{-1/\alpha}}{1 + k^{-1/\alpha}} \right)^{1-\alpha} \right.$$
$$\left. + \beta B E(R^{1-\alpha}) \left(\frac{1}{1 + k^{-1/\alpha}} \right)^{1-\alpha} \right] A^{1-\alpha}.$$

After some manipulations it can be verified that the unique value of B that satisfies the previous equality is given by

$$B = \frac{\{1 - \beta^{1/\alpha}[E(R^{1-\alpha})]^{1/\alpha}\}^{-\alpha}}{1 - \alpha}.$$

This result verifies our conjecture about the form of the value function. Given the value of B, it is immediately possible to compute the optimal policy using (1). It is indicated by

$$c = \{1 - \beta^{1/\alpha}[E(R^{1-\alpha})]^{1/\alpha}\}A.$$

EXERCISE 1.4 Habit Persistence: 1

Consider the problem of choosing a consumption sequence c_t to maximize

$$\sum_{t=0}^{\infty} \beta^t(\ln c_t + \gamma \ln c_{t-1}), \qquad 0 < \beta < 1, \qquad \gamma > 0,$$

subject to $c_t + k_{t+1} \leq Ak_t^\alpha$,
$A > 0$,
$0 < \alpha < 1$,
$k_0 > 0$, and c_{-1} given.

Here c_t is consumption at t, and k_t is capital stock at the beginning of period t. The current utility function $\ln c_t + \gamma \ln c_{t-1}$ is designed to represent habit persistence in consumption.

a. Let $v(k_0, c_{-1})$ be the value of $\sum_{t=0}^{\infty} \beta^t(\ln c_t + \gamma \ln c_{t-1})$ for a consumer who begins time 0 with capital stock k_0 and lagged consumption c_{-1} and behaves optimally. Formulate Bellman's functional equation in $v(k, c_{-1})$.

b. Prove that the solution of Bellman's equation is of the form $v(k, c_{-1}) = E + F \ln k + G \ln c_{-1}$ and that the optimal policy is of the form $\ln k_{t+1} = I + H \ln k_t$, where E, F, G, H, and I are constants. Give explicit formulas for the constants E, F, G, H, and I in terms of the parameters A, β, α, and γ.

SOLUTION

a. The state vector of this problem is the pair (k_t, c_{t-1}), with the transition equation for the first component given by the technology constraint, whereas the transition equation for the second component is a simple function of the decision variable, namely c_t. Then Bellman's equation is

$$v(k, c_{-1}) = \max_{c,k'}\{\ln c + \gamma \ln c_{-1} + \beta v(k', c)\},$$

subject to $c + k \leq Ak^\alpha$.

b. We conjecture that the value function takes the form $v(k, c_{-1}) = E + F \ln k + G \ln c_{-1}$. To verify this conjecture we must find a triplet (E, F, G) such that the corresponding value function satisfies Bellman's equation, that is,

(1)
$$E + F \ln k + G \ln c_{-1} =$$

$$\max_{c,k'} \{\ln c + \gamma \ln c_{-1} + \beta E + \beta F \ln k' + \beta G \ln c\}$$

subject to $c + k' \le Ak^{\alpha}$. The first-order condition of the maximization problem on the right-hand side is, after the constraint has been imposed at equality,

$$\frac{1}{c} + \frac{\beta G}{c} = \frac{\beta F}{Ak^{\alpha} - c},$$

which implies that consumption is given by

(2)
$$c = \frac{1 + \beta G}{1 + \beta G + \beta F} Ak^{\alpha}.$$

Substituting this expression for c in the right-hand side of (1), we get

$$(1 + \beta G)J_1 + \beta E + \beta F J_2 + [(1 + \beta G + \beta F)\alpha] \ln k + \gamma \ln c_{-1},$$

where $J_1 = \ln \dfrac{(1 + \beta G)A}{1 + \beta G + \beta F}$

and $J_2 = \ln \dfrac{\beta F A}{1 + \beta G + \beta F}.$

Then in order to verify the conjecture, we impose

$$E = (1 + \beta G)J_1 + \beta E + \beta F J_2,$$
$$F = (1 + \beta G + \beta F)\alpha,$$
$$G = \gamma.$$

It follows that $F = (1 + \beta\gamma)\alpha/(1 - \beta\alpha)$, that E can be computed from

$$E = (1 - \beta)^{-1} \left[(1 + \beta\gamma)J_1 + \frac{\beta\alpha(1 + \beta\gamma)J_2}{(1 - \beta\alpha)} \right]$$

and that J_1 and J_2 depend just on F and G, which in turn are functions of the "deep" parameters A, β, α, γ.

Substituting into (2) the values of F and G, we get $c_t = (1 - \beta\alpha)Ak_t^{\alpha}$. From the production function it follows that $k_{t+1} = (\beta\alpha)Ak_t^{\alpha}$. Taking the logarithm on both sides, we get $\ln k_{t+1} = \ln(\beta\alpha A) + \alpha \ln k_t$, which determines H and I.

EXERCISE 1.5 Habit Persistence: 2

Consider the more general version of the preceding problem, to maximize

$$\sum_{t=0}^{\infty} \beta^t u(c_t, c_{t-1}), \qquad 0 < \beta < 1,$$

subject to $c_t + k_{t+1} \leq f(k_t)$, $k_0 > 0$, c_{-1} given, where $u(c_t, c_{t-1})$ is twice continuously differentiable, bounded, increasing in both c_t and c_{t-1}, and concave in (c_t, c_{t-1}), and where $f'(0) = +\infty$, $f' > 0$, $f'' < 0$.

a. Formulate Bellman's functional equation for this problem.

b. Argue that in general, the optimal consumption plan is to set c_t as a function of both k_t and c_{t-1}. What features of the example in the preceding problem combine to make the optimal consumption plan expressible as a function of k_t alone?

SOLUTION

a. As in the previous exercise, the state vector can be chosen to be $x_t = (k_t, c_{t-1})$, because, given these two objects, the productive possibilities and the way that current outcomes are ranked are completely specified. The variables to be chosen—that is, the controls—are k_{t+1} and c_t. Bellman's equation is

(1) $$v(k, c_{-1}) = \max_{c,k'}\{u(c, c_{-1}) + \beta v(k', c)\}$$

subject to $c + k' \leq f(k)$.

b. The optimal consumption plan is the solution to the maximization problem on the right-hand side of (1). In general, different values of c_{-1} affect the marginal utility of current-period consumption and, consequently, its optimal level for any fixed k. In the preceding problem, utility is separable in current and lagged consumption, and in particular the marginal utility of consumption is independent of c_{-1}. Because the choice of c involves a comparison of the loss involved in increasing investment as measured by current marginal utility and the gain in terms of increased future consumption, the fact the marginal utility is independent of c_{-1} explains why this component of the state does not influence the choice of c.

EXERCISE 1.6 Lucas and Prescott (1971) and Kydland and Prescott (1982) Meet a Linear Regulator

Consider a linear quadratic version of a Lucas and Prescott (1971) model that has been modified to incorporate a rich time-to-build structure, à la Kydland and Prescott (1982). We first describe the model in terms of lag operators and then show how it can be mapped into a linear regulator problem.

The equilibrium of the model is supposed to solve the following problem:

(1)
$$\max E_0 \sum_{t=0}^{\infty} \beta^t \{ (A_0 - A_1 Y_t + v_t) Y_t - J_t i_t - [d(L)K_t][g(L)K_t] \},$$

$$1 > \beta > 0, \qquad A_0 > 0, \qquad A_1 > 0,$$

subject to

(2)
$$Y_t = a(L)K_t$$
$$K_{t+1} = (1 - \sigma)K_t + z_t^0, \qquad 0 < \sigma < 1,$$
$$z_t^l = z_{t-1}^{l+1}, \qquad l = 0, 1, \ldots, S - 1$$
$$\alpha(L)J_t = \epsilon_{Jt}$$
$$\xi(L)v_t = \epsilon_{vt}$$
$$i_t = \sum_{j=0}^{S-1} \tau_j z_t^j$$

where

(3)
$$a(L) = a_0 + a_1 L + \ldots + a_N L^N$$
$$d(L) = d_0 + d_1 L + \ldots + d_N L^N$$
$$g(L) = g_0 + g_1 L + \ldots + g_N L^N$$
$$\alpha(L) = 1 - \alpha_1 L - \ldots - \alpha_p L^p$$
$$\xi(L) = 1 - \xi_1 L - \ldots - \xi_q L^q,$$

where N, M, R, p, and q are all nonnegative and finite. In (2), ϵ_{Jt} and ϵ_{ut} are fundamental white noises for J_t and u_t, respectively. At time t, variables dated t and earlier are observed.

In (1), Y_t denotes output, c_t is investment expenditures, J_t is the price of new capital goods, K_t is the stock of capital, and v_t is a random process disturbing demand. The technology potentially incorporates two sorts of time-to-build delays. First, output Y_t is a distributed lag, $a(L)K_t$, of the capital stock K_t that is in place. As a result, given the capital stock, the one factor of production, it requires time to produce output. Second, time elapses between the moment when investment decisions z_t^s are made at time

t and the moment when the machines can be used as capital, z^0_{t+s}, at time $(t + s)$; z^j_t is interpreted as the number of machines in stage j available at time t. Only machines in stage 0 can increase the capital stock.

One interpretation of the parameters τ_j is that they represent the fraction of the total cost of a machine that is incurred when it is in stage j. Total expenditures in this concept, $\sum_{j=0}^{S-1} \tau_j z^j_t$, therefore correspond to investment at time j. It is also possible to think of the parameters τ_j as representing payments to another firm that "builds" the machines. In this sense they can reflect financing arrangements. The firm or industry also faces generalized costs of factor adjustment, which are represented by the cost term $[d(L)K_t][g(L)K_t]$.

This problem can be interpreted in a variety of ways. First, it can be interpreted as the solution of a monopoly problem, where the demand curve facing the monopolist is $p_t = A_0 - A_1 Y_t + v_t$, where p_t is the output price. Second, it can be interpreted as the solution of a rational expectations competitive equilibrium where the demand curve is $p_t = A_0 - 2A_1 Y_t + v_t$. Third, it can be interpreted as the outcome of a particular kind of Nash equilibrium (see Hansen, Epple, and Roberds 1985).

a. Show how this general problem can be mapped into the structure of the optimal linear regulator problem. Specify the vector of states and controls and the matrixes R, Q, A, and B.

b. Display the solution in feedback form, and show the difference equation that governs the state under the optimal rule.

SOLUTION

a. Define the following vectors:

$$
\begin{aligned}
&\bar{K}_t = (K_t, K_{t-1}, \ldots, K_{t-N})^T, && (N+1) \times 1 \\
&\bar{z}_t = (z^0_t, z^1_t, \ldots, z^{S-1}_t)^T, && S \times 1 \\
&a = (a_0, a_1, \ldots, a_N), && 1 \times (N+1) \\
&d = (d_0, d_1, \ldots, d_N), && 1 \times (N+1) \\
&g = (g_0, g_1, \ldots, g_N), && 1 \times (N+1) \\
&\tau = (\tau_0, \tau_1, \ldots, \tau_{S-1}), && 1 \times S \\
&e_{1l} = (1, 0, \ldots, 0), && 1 \times l, \quad l = p \text{ or } q \\
&\alpha = (\alpha_1, \ldots, \alpha_p), && 1 \times p \\
&\xi = (\xi_1, \ldots, \xi_p), && 1 \times q \\
&\bar{J}_t = (J_t, \ldots, J_{t-p+1})^T, && p \times 1 \\
&\bar{v}_t = (v_t, \ldots, v_{t-q+1})^T, && q \times 1
\end{aligned}
$$

With these definitions the problem can be written as

(1) $$\max E \sum_{t=0}^{\infty} \{(A_0 + \bar{v}_t^T e_{1q}^T)a\bar{K}_t - \bar{K}_t^T(A_1 a^T a + d^T g)\bar{K}_t - \bar{J}_t^T e_{1p}^T \tau \bar{z}_t\}$$

subject to

$$
\begin{bmatrix} \bar{K}_{t+1} \\ \\ \bar{z}_{t+1} \end{bmatrix} =
\left[
\begin{array}{c:ccc}
(1-\sigma) & 0_1 & 1 & 0_2 \\
C_{N+1} & & & 0_3 \\
\hdashline
0_4 & 0_5 & I_{S-1} & \\
& & 0_6 &
\end{array}
\right]
\begin{bmatrix} \bar{K}_t \\ \\ \bar{z}_t \end{bmatrix}
+
\begin{bmatrix} 0_7 \\ \\ 1 \end{bmatrix} z_t^s
$$

or, more compactly, as

$$
\begin{bmatrix} \bar{K}_{t+1} \\ \bar{z}_{t+1} \end{bmatrix} =
\begin{bmatrix} \underline{A}_{11} & \underline{A}_{12} \\ \underline{A}_{21} & \underline{A}_{22} \end{bmatrix}
\begin{bmatrix} \bar{K}_t \\ \bar{z}_t \end{bmatrix}
+
\begin{bmatrix} B_1 \\ B_2 \end{bmatrix} z_t^s,
$$

where the matrixes have the following dimensions (the term 0_k refers to a zero matrix):

(i) 0_1 is $1 \times N$, 0_2 is $1 \times (S-1)$, 0_3 is $N \times S$, 0_4 is $S \times (N+1)$, 0_5 is $(S-1) \times 1$, 0_6 is $S \times 1$, and 0_7 $(N+S) \times 1$.

(ii) I_k is an identity matrix of dimension k, whereas C_k is the $(k-1) \times k$ "companion matrix" given by

$$
C_k = \begin{bmatrix}
1 & 0 & 0 & \cdots & & 0 \\
0 & & & & & 0 \\
\vdots & & & & & \vdots \\
0 & & \cdots & & 1 & 0
\end{bmatrix}.
$$

To map the problem into the linear quadratic regulator framework, define the state vector x_t as $x_t = (1, \bar{K}_t^T, \bar{z}_t^T, \bar{J}_t^T, \bar{v}_t^T)^T$ and the control as $u_t = z_t^s$. Then (1) is equivalent to

$$\max E \sum_{t=0}^{\infty} \beta^t \{x_t^T R x_t + u_t^T Q u_t\}$$

subject to $\quad x_{t+1} = A x_t + B u_t + \epsilon_{t+1},$

where R, Q, A, and B are given by

$$
R = \begin{bmatrix}
0 & \dfrac{A_0 a}{2} & 0 & 0 & 0 \\[2ex]
\dfrac{a^T A_0}{2} & -(A_1 a^T a + d^T g) & 0 & 0 & \dfrac{a^T e_{1q}}{2} \\[2ex]
0 & 0 & 0 & \dfrac{-\tau^T e_{1p}}{2} & 0 \\[2ex]
0 & 0 & -e_{1p}^T \dfrac{\tau}{2} & 0 & 0 \\[2ex]
0 & e_{1q}^T \dfrac{a}{2} & 0 & 0 & 0
\end{bmatrix}
$$

is $(N + S + p + q + 2) \times (N + S + p + q + 2)$, $Q = 0$, and

$$
A = \begin{bmatrix}
1 & 0 & 0 & 0 & 0 \\
0 & \underline{A}_{11} & \underline{A}_{12} & 0 & 0 \\
0 & \underline{A}_{21} & \underline{A}_{22} & 0 & 0 \\
0 & 0 & 0 & \dfrac{\alpha}{C_p} & 0 \\
0 & 0 & 0 & 0 & \dfrac{\xi}{C_q}
\end{bmatrix}
$$

is $(N + S + p + q + 2) \times (N + S + p + q + 2)$,

$$
B = \begin{bmatrix}
0 \\
\underline{B}_1 \\
\underline{B}_2 \\
0 \\
0
\end{bmatrix}, \quad \text{is } (N + S + p + q + 2) \times 1,
$$

and

$$\epsilon_{t+1} = \begin{bmatrix} 0 \\ 0 \\ 0 \\ \bar{\epsilon}_{Jt+1} \\ \bar{\epsilon}_{vt+1} \end{bmatrix}, \quad \text{is } (N+S+p+q+2) \times 1,$$

where $\bar{\epsilon}_{Jt+1} = (\epsilon_{Jt+1}, 0, \ldots, 0)^T$ is $(p \times 1)$, and $\bar{\epsilon}_{vt+1} = (\epsilon_{vt+1}, 0, \ldots, 0)^T$ is $(q \times 1)$. As before, zero represents a zero matrix.

b. The solution of this problem is a feedback rule of the form $z_t^s = u_t = -Fx_t$, or

$$z_t^s = -F \begin{bmatrix} 1 \\ \bar{K}_t \\ \bar{z}_t \\ \bar{J}_t \\ \bar{u}_t \end{bmatrix},$$

where F is given by $F = \beta(Q + \beta B^T P \beta)^{-1} B^T PA$, and P solves the matrix Riccati equation

$$P = R + \beta A^T PA - \beta^2 A^T PB(Q + \beta B^T PB)^{-1} B^T PA.$$

Under this optimal rule, the system evolves according to the "closed loop" $x_{t+1} = Ax_t + Bu_t + \epsilon_{t+1}$ or

$$\begin{bmatrix} 1 \\ \bar{K}_{t+1} \\ \bar{z}_{t+1} \\ \bar{J}_{t+1} \\ \bar{v}_{t+1} \end{bmatrix} = (A - BF) \begin{bmatrix} 1 \\ \bar{K}_t \\ \bar{z}_t \\ \bar{J}_t \\ \bar{v}_t \end{bmatrix} + \epsilon_{t+1}.$$

EXERCISE 1.7   Interrelated Factor Demand

For another illustration of a problem that can readily be mapped into the linear regulator framework, consider the interrelated factor demand problem, to maximize

$$-E \sum_{t=0}^{\infty} \beta^t \{ y_t^T F y_t + [G(L)y_t]^T [H(L)y_t] + J_t^T y_t \}$$

where $\quad y_t = \begin{pmatrix} y_{1t} \\ y_{2t} \end{pmatrix}, \quad J_t = \begin{pmatrix} J_{1t} \\ J_{2t} \end{pmatrix},$

F is positive semidefinite; $G(L) = G_0 + G_1 L + \ldots + G_m L^m$, $H(L) = H_0 + H_1 L + \ldots + H_m L^m$, where G_j and H_j are each (2×2) matrixes. It is assumed that $G_0^T H_0$ is positive definite.

Here J_t denotes a (2×1) vector of factor costs, y_t denotes a (2×1) vector of factors of production, and $[G(L)y_t]^T H(L)y_t$ denotes generalized costs of adjustment. The maximization is subject to a Markov law for J of the form $J_{t+1} = \alpha_1 J_t + \ldots + \alpha_{p+1} J_{t-p} + \epsilon_{t+1}$, where ϵ_{t+1} is a (2×1) vector white noise. At time 0, y_{t-j-1} and $J_{t-j}, j \geq 0$, are taken as given.

a. Specify this problem as a linear regulator by defining the states and controls x_t, u_t as well as the matrixes A, B, Q, and R.

Hint. It is easier to map the problem into the following more general version of the linear regulator problem.

$$\max E \sum_{t=0}^{\infty} \beta^t \left\{ (x_t^T, u_t^T) \begin{bmatrix} \overline{R} & \overline{W} \\ \overline{W}^T & \overline{Q} \end{bmatrix} \begin{pmatrix} x_t \\ u_t \end{pmatrix} \right\},$$

subject to $x_{t+1} = \overline{A}x_t + \overline{B}u_t + \epsilon_{t+1}$.

The following well-known argument indicates that there is no loss of generality — when Q is nonsingular — in restricting ourselves to the case in which $W = 0$. Simply note that the previous problem is equivalent to the following

$$\max E \sum_{t=0}^{\infty} \beta^t \{ x_t^T (\overline{R} - \overline{W}\overline{Q}^{-1}\overline{W}^T)x_t + v_t^T \overline{Q}v_t \},$$

subject to $x_{t+1} = (\overline{A} - \overline{B}\overline{Q}^{-1}\overline{W}^T)x_t + \overline{B}v_t + \epsilon_{t+1}$, where $v_t = \overline{Q}^{-1}\overline{W}^T x_t + u_t$. Therefore, defining R, Q, A, and B by

$$R = \overline{R} - \overline{W}\overline{Q}^{-1}\overline{W}^T$$
$$Q = \overline{Q}$$
$$A = \overline{A} - \overline{B}\overline{Q}^{-1}\overline{W}^T$$
$$B = \overline{B}$$

gives us the standard version of the problem.

SOLUTION

Define $u_t = y_t$, $x_{1t} = [y_{t-1}^T, y_{t-2}^T, \ldots, y_{t-m}^T]^T$, and $x_{2t} = [J_t^T, J_{t-1}^T, \ldots, J_{t-p}^T]^T$. We are going to use the vector $x_t = [x_{1t}^T, x_{2t}^T]^T$ as our state and the vector u_t as the control variable. Notice that

$$G(L)y_t = \sum_{k=0}^{m} G_k y_{t-k}$$
$$= [G_0, G_1, G_2, \ldots, G_m][y_t^T, y_{t-1}^T, \ldots, y_{t-m}^T]^T$$
$$= [G_{-0}, G_0][x_{1t}^T, u_t^T]^T,$$

where $G_{-0} = [G_1, G_2, \ldots, G_m]$ is a $2 \times 2m$ matrix. Similarly, we can write $H(L)y_t = [H_{-0}, H_0][x_{1t}^T, u_t^T]^T$, where $H_{-0} = [H_1, H_2, \ldots, H_m]$ is a $2 \times 2m$ matrix. The term $J_t y_t$ can be written as $J_t^T y_t = x_{2t}^T K u_t + u_t^T K^T x_{2t}$, where K is a $2(p+1) \times 2$ matrix given by

$$K = \frac{1}{2}\left[\frac{I}{0}\right],$$

I being the 2×2 identity matrix and 0 a $2p \times 2$ matrix of zeros. Finally, denote $-F = \bar{F}$.

With this notation the original problem is to maximize

(1) $E \sum_{t=0}^{\infty} \beta^t \left\{ u_t^T \bar{F} u_t - (x_{1t}^T, u_t^T)\left[\begin{array}{c} G_{-0}^T \\ G_0^T \end{array}\right][H_{-0}, H_0]\left(\begin{array}{c} x_{1t} \\ u_t \end{array}\right) - x_{2t}^T K u_t - u_t^T K^T x_{2t} \right\},$

subject to $x_{t+1} = \bar{A}x_t + \bar{B}u_t + \xi_{t+1},$

where $\bar{A}$ can be decomposed as:

$$\bar{A} = \left[\begin{array}{cccc} \bar{A}_1 & \bar{A}_3 & \bar{A}_2 & \bar{A}_3 \\ C_{2m-1} & \bar{A}_4 & \bar{A}_5 & \bar{A}_4 \\ \bar{A}_1 & \bar{A}_3 & \bar{A}_2 & \bar{A}_3 \\ \bar{A}_6 & \bar{A}_7 & C_{2p+1} & \bar{A}_7 \end{array}\right].$$

Each $\bar{A}_i$ is a zero matrix of the following dimensions: $\bar{A}_1$ is $2 \times (2m-1)$, $\bar{A}_2$ is $2 \times (2p+1)$, $\bar{A}_3$ is 2×1, $\bar{A}_4$ is $(2m-2) \times 1$, $\bar{A}_5$ is $(2m-2) \times (2p+1)$, $\bar{A}_6$ is $2p \times (2m-1)$, and $\bar{A}_7$ is $2p \times 1$. The C_s matrixes are $(s-1) \times s$ companion matrixes (for a definition, see the previous exercise). $\bar{B}$ is given by

$$\bar{B} = \left[\frac{I}{0}\right],$$

where I is a 2×2 identity matrix, and 0 is $(2m + 2p) \times 2$ zero matrix. The vector ξ_{t+1} is given by

$$\xi_{t+1} = \left(\begin{array}{c} 0_1 \\ \epsilon_{t+1} \\ 0_2 \end{array}\right),$$

where 0_1 and 0_2 are, respectively, $2m \times 1$ and $2p \times 1$ vectors of zeros.

Denote by N the following matrix

$$N = \left[\begin{array}{c} G^T_{-0} \\ \hline G^T_0 \end{array}\right][H_{-0}, H_0] = \left[\begin{array}{c|c} G^T_{-0}H_{-0} & G^T_{-0}H_0 \\ \hline G^T_0 H_{-0} & G^T_0 H_0 \end{array}\right]$$

$$= \left[\begin{array}{c|c} N_{11} & N_{12} \\ \hline N_{21} & N_{22} \end{array}\right].$$

With this notation, (1) can be written as

(2) $$E \sum_{t=0}^{\infty} \beta^t \left\{ (x_t^T, u_t^T) \left[\begin{array}{c|c} R^* & W^* \\ \hline V^* & Q^* \end{array}\right] \binom{x_t}{u_t} \right\},$$

subject to $x_{t+1} = \bar{A}x_t + \bar{B}u_t + \xi_{t+1},$

where $$R^* = \left[\begin{array}{c|c} -N_{11} & R^*_1 \\ \hline R^*_2 & R^*_3 \end{array}\right]$$

is a $[2m + 2(p + 1)] \times [2m \times 2(p + 1)]$ matrix and the R^*_i's are zero matrixes of dimensions $2m \times 2(p + 1)$, $2(p + 1) \times 2m$, and $2(p + 1) \times 2(p + 1)$, respectively. In addition,

$$W^* = \left[\begin{array}{c} -N_{12} \\ \hline -K \end{array}\right]$$

is a $[2m + 2(p + 1)] \times 2$ matrix,

$$V^* = [-N_{21}, -K^T]$$

is a $2 \times [2m + 2(p + 1)]$ matrix, and

$$Q^* = [\bar{F} - N_{22}]$$

is a 2×2 negative definite matrix.

Next, recall that, if the matrix defining a quadratic form is not symmetric, there is no loss of generality in replacing the original matrix by a symmetric matrix. This point can be seen directly as follows: consider the quadratic form $y^T D y$ where D is not necessarily symmetric. Define $D^* = (D + D^T)/2$. Then because $y^T D y = y^T D^T y$, it follows that, for all vectors y, $y^T D y = y^T D^* y$. With this result in mind, we define

$$\bar{R} = \frac{R^* + R^{*T}}{2}, \qquad \bar{W} = \frac{W^* + V^{*T}}{2}, \qquad \bar{Q} = \frac{Q^* + Q^{*T}}{2}.$$

The maximization problem becomes

$$\max E \sum_{t=0}^{\infty} \beta^t \left\{ (x_t^T, u_t^T) \begin{bmatrix} \overline{R} & \overline{W} \\ \overline{W}^T & \overline{Q} \end{bmatrix} \begin{pmatrix} x_t \\ u_t \end{pmatrix} \right\},$$

subject to $x_{t+1} = \overline{A}x_t + \overline{B}u_t + \xi_{t+1},$

where $\overline{Q}$ is negative definite because our assumptions imply that Q^* is negative definite. Now, following the hint, this problem can be transformed into a linear regulator problem.

EXERCISE 1.8   Two-Sector Growth Models

a. Consider the following two-sector model of optimal growth. A social planner seeks to maximize the utility of the representative agent given by $\sum_{t=0}^{\infty} \beta^t u(c_t, l_t)$, where c_t is consumption of good 1 at t, whereas l_t is leisure at t.

Sector 1 produces consumption goods using capital, k_{1t}, and labor, n_{1t}, according to the production function $c_t \leq f_1(k_{1t}, n_{1t})$. Sector 2 produces the capital good according to the production function $k_{t+1} \leq f_2(k_{2t}, n_{2t})$. Total employment, $n_t = n_{1t} + n_{2t}$, and leisure, l_t, is constrained by the endowment of time, $\bar{l}$, and satisfies $l_t + n_t \leq \bar{l}$. The sum of the amounts of capital used in each sector cannot exceed the initial capital in the economy, that is, $k_{1t} + k_{2t} \leq k_t$, $k_0 > 0$ given. Formulate this problem as a dynamic programming problem. Display the functional equation that the value function satisfies, and clearly specify the state and control variables.

b. Consider another economy that is similar to the previous one except for the fact that capital is sector specific. The economy starts period t with given amounts of capital k_{1t} and k_{2t} that must be used in sectors 1 and 2, respectively. During this period the capital-good sector produces capital that is specific to each sector according to the transformation curve $g(k_{1t+1}, k_{2t+1}) \leq f_2(k_{2t}, n_{2t})$. Display the Bellman's equation associated with the planner's problem. Specify which variables you choose as states and which as controls.

SOLUTION

a. Notice that at the beginning of the period the stock of capital available, k, completely summarizes all the production possibilities of this economy. Therefore we choose it as the state. The controls are the allocation of that stock of capital between the two sectors (k_1, k_2), employment in each sector (n_1, n_2), leisure, l, consumption, c, and the capital stock that the economy decides to carry into the next period, k'.

Bellman's equation is

$$v(k) = \max_{c,n_1,n_2,l,k_1,k_2,k'} \{u(c, l) + \beta v(k')\},$$

subject to $\quad c \leq f_1(k_1, n_1), \qquad k' \leq f_2(k_2, n_2),$
$$n_1 + n_2 + l \leq \bar{l}, \qquad k_1 + k_2 \leq k.$$

b. In this case the state is given by the vector (k_1, k_2), because in this economy the distribution of capital across sectors determines the productive possibilities. Notice that in the previous economy we could have distributed the available stock of capital between the two sectors and used the vector of capital stocks as the state variable. We would have had a state variable of higher dimension (a vector in R^2 rather than a scalar) without gaining anything; when capital is fully shiftable between the two sectors, only the total amount matters. In this economy, however, the total does not give enough information about the amount of each good that can be produced. It is necessary to know the amount of capital each sector has available in order to determine the output that can be generated by alternative levels of employment. The controls are c, n_1, n_2, l, and the stocks of capital that each sector will have available next period, k_1' and k_2'.

Bellman's equation is

$$v(k_1, k_2) = \max_{c,n_1,n_2,l,k_1',k_2'} \{u(c, l) + \beta v(k_1', k_2')\},$$

subject to $\quad c \leq f_1(k_1, n_1), \qquad g(k_1', k_2') \leq f_2(k_2, n_2),$
$$n_1 + n_2 + l \leq \bar{l}.$$

EXERCISE 1.9 Learning to Enjoy Spare Time

A worker's instantaneous utility, $u(\cdot)$, depends on the amount of market-produced goods consumed, c_{1t}, and also on the amount of home-produced goods, c_{2t} (for example, entertainment, leisure). In order to acquire market-produced goods, the worker must allocate some amount of time, l_{1t}, to market activities that pay a salary of w_t, measured in terms of consumption good. The worker takes wages as given and beyond the worker's control. There is no borrowing or lending. It is known that the market wage evolves according to the law of motion $w_{t+1} = h(w_t)$.

The quantity of home-produced goods depends on the stock of "expertise" that the worker has at the beginning of the period, which we label a_t. This stock of "expertise" depreciates at the rate δ and can be increased by allocating time to nonmarket activities. To summarize the problem, the individual agent maximizes

$$\sum_{t=0}^{\infty} \beta^t u(c_{1t}, c_{2t}), \qquad 0 < \beta < 1,$$

subject to $\quad c_{1t} \leq w_t l_{1t}$ [budget constraint]

$\qquad\qquad\quad c_{2t} \leq f(a_t)$ [production function of the home-produced good]

$\qquad\qquad\quad a_{t+1} \leq (1 - \delta)a_t + l_{2t}$ [law of motion of the stock of expertise]

$\qquad\qquad\quad l_{1t} + l_{2t} \leq \bar{l}$ [restriction on the uses of time]

$\qquad\qquad\quad w_{t+1} = h(w_t)$ [law of motion for the wage rate]

$\qquad\qquad\quad a_0 > 0$ [given].

It is assumed that $u(\cdot)$ and $f(\cdot)$ are bounded and continuous. Formulate this problem as a dynamic programming problem.

SOLUTION

We choose the vector (a, w) — the initial stock of expertise and the current wage — to be the state variables. They completely summarize the consumption possibilities of both goods that the worker has. The controls are the number of hours allocated to market activities, l_1, the amount of time allocated to nonmarket activities, l_2, and consumption of each good c_1, c_2. The functional equation that the value function satisfies is

$$v(a, w) = \max_{c_1, c_2, l_1, l_2} \{u(c_1, c_2) + \beta v(a', w')\},$$

subject to $\quad c_1 \leq w l_1, \qquad c_2 \leq f(a), \qquad a' \leq (1 - \delta)a + l_2,$

$\qquad\qquad\quad w' \leq h(w), \qquad l_1 + l_2 \leq \bar{l}.$

EXERCISE 1.10   Investment with Adjustment Costs

A firm maximizes present value of cash flow, with future earnings discounted at the rate β. Income at time t is given by sales, $p_t \cdot q_t$, where p_t is the price of good, and q_t is the quantity produced. The firm behaves competitively and therefore takes prices as given. It knows that prices evolve according to a law of motion given by $p_{t+1} = f(p_t)$.

Total or gross production depends on the amounts of capital, k_t, and labor, n_t, and on the square of the difference between current ratio of sales to investment, x_t, and the previous-period ratio. This last feature captures the notion that changes in the ratio of sales to investment require some reallocation of resources within the firm and consequently reduce the level of efficiency. It is assumed that the wage rate is constant and equal to w. Capital depreciates at the rate δ. The firm's problem is

$$\max \sum_{t=0}^{\infty} \beta^t \{ p_t q_t - w n_t \}, \qquad 0 < \beta < 1,$$

$$\text{subject to} \quad q_t + x_t \le g\left[k_t, n_t, \left(\frac{q_t}{x_t} - \frac{q_{t-1}}{x_{t-1}} \right)^2 \right]$$

$$k_{t+1} \le (1 - \delta)k_t + x_t, \qquad 0 < \delta < 1$$

$$p_{t+1} = f(p_t)$$

$$k_0 > 0, \quad \frac{q_{-1}}{x_{-1}} > 0 \quad \text{given.}$$

We assume that $g(\cdot)$ is bounded, increasing in the first two arguments and decreasing in the third. Formulate the firm's problem recursively, that is, formulate Bellman's functional equation for this problem. Identify the state and the controls, and indicate the laws of motion of the state variables.

SOLUTION

The state variable is the vector that includes the beginning of the period capital stock, k, the previous period ratio of sales to investment, which we label z, and the current price of the good, p. Notice that, although w—the wage rate—affects the returns, the fact that it stays constant over time implies that we need not include it as an element of the state. The optimal decision rules will depend on the level of w, but this dependency does not differ from the way the optimal values depend on other parameters of the problem, for example, the discount factor or the depreciation rate. The controls are sales, q, investment, x, and employment, n.

Bellman's equation is

$$v(k, z, p) = \max_{q,x,n} \{ pq - wn + \beta v(k', z', p') \},$$

$$\text{subject to} \quad q + x \le g\left[k, n, \left(\frac{q}{x - z} \right)^2 \right], \qquad z' = \frac{q}{x}$$

$$k' = (1 - \delta)k + x, \qquad p' = f(p).$$

The last three constraints are the laws of motion for the vector of state variables.

EXERCISE 1.11   Investment with Signal Extraction

Consider a firm that maximizes expected present value of dividends. It is assumed that the price of the good produced by the firm is constant and equal to one. Production requires the use of a single input: capital that is firm specific. Total production, $f(k_t)$, is divided between sales, q_t, and investment, x_t. Revenue from sales is taxed at the rate τ_t. At time t, τ_t is known, as is z_t—a variable that is related to τ_{t+1} by the function $\tau_{t+1} = g(z_t, \epsilon_{t+1})$, where ϵ_{t+1} is an i.i.d. random variable that is not observed at t but whose distribution is known to the firm. Notice that, given z_t, the function g induces a conditional distribution of τ_{t+1} that we denote $F(\tau_{t+1}, z_t)$. The stochastic process $\{z_t\}$ is Markov with transition function $H(z', z) \equiv \text{prob}\{z_{t+1} \leq z' | z_t = z\}$. The capital stock depreciates at the rate τ. The problem faced by the firm is

$$\max E_0 \sum_{t=0}^{\infty} \beta^t (1 - \tau_t) q_t, \qquad 0 < \beta < 1,$$

subject to $\quad q_t + x_t \leq f(k_t)$
$$k_{t+1} \leq (1 - \delta) k_t + x_t, \qquad k_0 \text{ given}, \qquad 0 < \delta < 1.$$

It is assumed that $f(k)$ is increasing, concave, and bounded.

Formulate the firm's problem as a dynamic programming problem (that is, display Bellman's equation).

SOLUTION

The state vector contains k, the initial stock of capital; τ, the current tax rates; and z, the observed value of z_t. Notice that the first two elements directly influence the returns or profits in the current period, whereas z_t appears neither in the objective function nor in the constraints. We make z an element of the state because it helps predict future tax rates, which in turn affect future returns. Inasmuch as z_t belongs to the state, current decisions— q_t and x_t—are, in general, functions of it. This setup captures the effect that some "announcements" about future events may have on current decisions. It also illustrates here that variables not specifically related to a given industry—for example, z_t may be some measure of the fiscal deficit—can influence decisions made by the firm as information variables. Any variables that help forecast future values of variables that are of direct interest—in the sense that they affect future returns—belong in the state vector. The decision variables or controls are investment, x, and sales, q.

Bellman's equation for this problem is

$$v(k, \tau, z) = \max_{q,x}\{(1 - \tau)q + \beta \iint v(k', \tau', z')F(d\tau', z)H(dz', z)\},$$

subject to $k' \leq (1 - \delta)k + x, \qquad q + x \leq f(k).$

References and Suggested Readings

Basar, Tamer, and Geert Jan Olsder. 1982. *Dynamic Noncooperative Game Theory.* New York: Academic Press.

Bellman, Richard. 1957. *Dynamic Programming.* Princeton, N.J.: Princeton University Press.

Bellman, Richard, and Stuart E. Dreyfus. 1962. *Applied Dynamic Programming.* Princeton, N.J.: Princeton University Press.

Benveniste, Lawrence, and Jose Scheinkman. 1979. On the differentiability of the value function in dynamic models of economics. *Econometrica* 47(3): 727–732.

Bertsekas, Dimitri. 1976. *Dynamic Programming and Stochastic Control.* New York: Academic Press. (Esp. chaps. 2, 6.)

Bertsekas, Dimitri, and Steven E. Shreve. 1978. *Stochastic Optimal Control: The Discrete Time Case.* New York: Academic Press.

Brock, William A. 1982. Asset prices in a production economy. In *The Economics of Information and Uncertainty,* ed. J. J. McCall, pp. 1–43. Chicago: University of Chicago Press.

Brock, William A., and Leonard Mirman. 1972. Optimal economic growth and uncertainty: the discounted case. *Journal of Economic Theory* 4(3):479–513.

Cagan, Phillip. 1956. The monetary dynamics of hyperinflation. In *Studies in the Quantity Theory of Money,* ed. Milton Friedman, pp. 25–117. Chicago: University of Chicago Press.

Calvo, Guillermo A. 1978. On the time consistency of optimal policy in a monetary economy. *Econometrica* 46(6):1411–1428.

Cass, David. 1965. Optimum growth in an aggregative model of capital accumulation. *Review of Economic Studies* 32(3):233–240.

Chow, Gregory. 1981. *Econometric Analysis by Control Methods.* New York: Wiley, 1981.

Hansen, Lars P., Dennis Epple, and Will Roberds. 1985. Linear-quadratic duopoly models of resource depletion. In *Energy, Foresight, and Strategy,* ed. Thomas J. Sargent, pp. 101–142. Washington, D.C.: Resources for the Future.

Hansen, Lars P., and Thomas J. Sargent. 1980. Formulating and estimating dynamic linear rational expectations models. *Journal of Economic Dynamics and Control* 2(1):7–46.

——— 1981. Linear rational expectations models for dynamically interrelated variables. In *Rational Expectations and Econometric Practice,* ed. R. E. Lucas, Jr., and T. J. Sargent, pp. 127–156. Minneapolis: University of Minnesota Press.

——— 1982. Instrumental variables procedures for estimating linear rational expectations models. *Journal of Monetary Economics* 9(3):263–296.

Koopmans, T. C. 1963. On the concept of optimal economic growth. Cowles Foundation Discussion Paper. Yale University, New Haven.

Kwakernaak, Huibert, and Raphael Sivan. 1972. *Linear Optimal Control Systems.* New York: Wiley, 1972.

Kydland, Finn E., and Edward C. Prescott. 1977. Rules rather than discretion: the inconsistency of optimal plans. *Journal of Political Economy* 85(3):473–491.

——— 1982. Time to build and aggregate fluctuations. *Econometrica* 50(6):1345–1371.

Levhari, D., and T. N. Srinivasan. 1969. Optimal savings under uncertainty. *Review of Economic Studies* 36(2):153–163.

Lucas, Robert E., Jr. 1976. Econometric policy evaluation: a critique. In *The Phillips Curve and Labor Markets,* ed. K. Brunner and A. H. Meltzer, pp. 19–46. Amsterdam: North-Holland, 1976.

——— 1977. Class notes on dynamic programming. University of Chicago. Unpublished.

——— 1978. Asset prices in an exchange economy. *Econometrica* 46(6):1426–1445.

Lucas, Robert E., Jr., and Edward C. Prescott. 1971. Investment under uncertainty. *Econometrica* 39(5):659–681.

Lucas, Robert E., Jr., Edward C. Prescott, and Nancy L. Stokey. *Recursive Methods for Economic Dynamics.* Forthcoming.

Lucas, Robert E., Jr., and Nancy Stokey. 1983. Optimal monetary and fiscal policy in an economy without capital. *Journal of Monetary Economics* 12(1):55–94.

Sargent, Thomas J. 1981. Lecture notes on filtering, control, and rational expectations. University of Minnesota, Minneapolis. Unpublished.

——— 1979. *Macroeconomic Theory.* New York: Academic Press.

——— 1986. *Macroeconomic Theory.* 2nd ed. New York: Academic Press.

2 | Search

EXERCISE 2.1   Being Unemployed with Only a Chance of an Offer

An unemployed worker samples wage offers on the following terms. Each period, with probability ϕ, $1 > \phi > 0$, she receives no offer (we may regard this as a wage offer of zero forever). With probability $(1 - \phi)$ she receives an offer to work for w forever, where w is drawn from a cumulative distribution function $F(w)$. Successive drawings across periods are independently and identically distributed. The worker chooses a strategy to maximize

$$E \sum_{t=0}^{\infty} \beta^t y_t, \quad \text{where } 0 < \beta < 1,$$

$y_t = w$ if the worker is employed, and $y_t = c$ if the worker is unemployed. Here c is unemployment compensation, and w is the wage at which the worker is employed. Assume that, having once accepted a job offer at wage w, the worker stays in the job forever.

Let $v(w)$ be the expected value of $\sum_{t=0}^{\infty} \beta^t y_t$ for an unemployed worker who has offer w in hand and who behaves optimally. Write Bellman's functional equation for the worker's problem.

SOLUTION

$$v(w) = \max\left\{\frac{w}{1 - \beta}, c + \phi \beta v(0) + (1 - \phi)\beta \int v(w')F(dw')\right\}.$$

Here the maximization is over the two actions: accept the offer to work forever at wage w, or reject the current offer and take a chance on drawing a new offer next period.

EXERCISE 2.2 Two Offers per Period

Consider an unemployed worker who each period can draw *two* independently and identically distributed wage offers from the cumulative probability distribution function $F(w)$. The worker will work forever at the same wage after having once accepted an offer. In the event of unemployment during a period, the worker receives unemployment compensation c. The worker derives a decision rule to maximize $E \sum_{t=0}^{\infty} \beta^t y_t$, where $y_t = w$ or $y_t = c$, depending on whether she is employed or unemployed. Let $v(w)$ be the value of $E \sum_{t=0}^{\infty} \beta^t y_t$ for a currently unemployed worker who has best offer w in hand.

a. Formulate Bellman's equation for the worker's problem.

b. Prove that the worker's reservation wage is *higher* than it would be had the worker faced the same c and been drawing only *one* offer from the same distribution $F(w)$ each period.

SOLUTION

a. Note that the event $\max\{w_1, w_2\} < w$ is the event $(w_1 < w) \cap (w_2 < w)$. Therefore $\text{prob}\{\max(w_1, w_2) < w\} = F(w)^2$. The worker will evidently limit his choice to the larger of the two offers each period. Bellman's equation is therefore

$$v(w) = \max\left\{\frac{w}{1 - \beta}, c + \beta \int v(w')F^2(dw')\right\},$$

where w is the best offer in hand.

b. The reservation wage obeys the following version of Equation (2.16), *DMT:*

$$(\bar{w} - c) = \frac{\beta}{1 - \beta} \int_{\bar{w}}^{\infty} (w' - \bar{w})F^2(dw').$$

Let

$$h_1(w) = \frac{\beta}{1 - \beta} \int_{w}^{\infty} (w' - w)F(dw'),$$

$$h_2(w) = \frac{\beta}{1 - \beta} \int_{w}^{\infty} (w' - w)F^2(dw').$$

Because $0 < F(w) \leq 1$, we have $F^2(w) \leq F(w)$. It follows that $h_2(w) \geq h_1(w)$ for all $w \geq 0$. The reason is that $F^2(w')$ places more weight on high values of w' than does $F(w)$. Therefore, from versions of (2.16) and (2.17) or Figure 2.5 (*DMT*), $\bar{w}$ is higher for the worker confronting the distribution $F^2(w)$ than for the worker confronting $F(w)$.

The intuition underlying this result is as follows: the worker could choose always to ignore the second offer. This policy, possibly suboptimal, would leave the worker with a decision problem that is formally identical to the standard one-offer problem. The value of the objective function of the true problem is at least as high as the value of the objective function under the artificially restricted problem. Because the reservation wage has the property of equating the value of accepting a job, $w/(1 - \beta)$, with the value of rejecting, $c + \beta Ev(w')$, a higher value of $Ev(w')$, which results in the two-offer case, requires a higher reservation wage.

EXERCISE 2.3   A Random Number of Offers per Period

An unemployed worker is confronted with a random number, n, of job offers each period. With probability π_n, the worker receives n offers in a given period, where $\pi_n \geq 0$ for $n \geq 1$, and $\Sigma_{n=1}^{N} \pi_n = 1$ for $N < +\infty$. Each offer is drawn independently from the same distribution $F(w)$. Assume that the number of offers n is independently distributed across time. The worker works forever at wage w after having accepted a job and receives unemployment compensation of c during each period of unemployment. He chooses a strategy to maximize $E \Sigma_{t=0}^{\infty} \beta^t y_t$ where $y_t = c$ if he is unemployed, $y_t = w$ if he is employed.

Let $v(w)$ be the value of the objective function of an unemployed worker who has best offer w in hand and who proceeds optimally. Formulate Bellman's equation for this worker.

SOLUTION

$$v(w) = \max\left\{\frac{w}{1 - \beta}, c + \sum_{n=1}^{N} \pi_n \int v(w')F^n(dw')\right\}.$$

In effect, the worker is confronted with a lottery with probabilities π_n over distributions $F^n(w)$, from which he will sample next period. As in Exercise 2.1, w is the highest offer in hand.

EXERCISE 2.4 Cyclical Fluctuations in Number of Job Offers

Modify Exercise 2.3 as follows. Let the number of job offers n follow a Markov process, with

$$\text{prob\{number of offers next period} = m | \text{number of offers this}$$
$$\text{period} = n\} = \pi_{mn}, \qquad m = 1, \ldots, N, \qquad n = 1, \ldots, N$$
$$\sum_{m=1}^{N} \pi_{mn} = 1 \qquad \text{for } n = 1, \ldots, N.$$

Here $[\pi_{mn}]$ is a "stochastic matrix" generating a Markov chain. Keep all other features of the problem as in Exercise 2.3. The worker gets n offers per period, where n is now generated by a Markov chain so that the number of offers is possibly correlated over time.

  a. Let $v(w, n)$ be the value of $E \sum_{t=0}^{\infty} \beta^t y_t$ for an unemployed worker who has received n offers this period, the best of which is w. Formulate Bellman's equation for the worker's problem.

  b. Show that the optimal policy is to set a reservation wage $\bar{w}(n)$ that depends on the number of offers received this period.

SOLUTION

  a.

$$(1) \qquad v(w, n) = \max\left\{\frac{w}{1 - \beta}, c + \sum_{m=1}^{N} \pi_{m,n} \int v(w', m) F^m(dw')\right\}.$$

  b. From (1), we see that the right branch of the right side of the functional equation is evidently a function only of n. The argument in the text (see Figure 2.4, *DMT*) applies for each n and implies a reservation wage that is a function of n.

EXERCISE 2.5 Choosing the Number of Offers

An unemployed worker must choose the number of offers n to solicit. At a cost of $k(n)$ the worker receives n offers this period. Here $k(n + 1) > k(n)$ for $n \geq 1$. The number of offers n must be chosen in advance at the beginning of the period and cannot be revised during the period. The worker wants to maximize $E \sum_{t=0}^{\infty} \beta^t y_t$. Here y_t consists of w each period she is employed but not searching, $[w - k(n)]$ the first period she is employed but searches for n offers, and $[c - k(n)]$ each period she is unemployed but solicits and rejects n

offers. The offers are each independently drawn from $F(w)$. The worker who accepts an offer works forever at wage w.

Let Q be the value of the problem for an unemployed worker who has not yet chosen the number of offers to solicit. Formulate Bellman's equation for this worker.

SOLUTION

$$Q = \max_n \left\{ \int \max_{\substack{\text{accept} \\ \text{reject}}} \left\{ \frac{w}{1-b} - k(n),\ -k(n) + \beta Q \right\} F^n(dw) \right\}.$$

The worker proceeds sequentially each period, first choosing n, then deciding whether to accept or reject the best offer.

EXERCISE 2.6 Mortensen Externality

Two parties to a match (say, worker and firm) jointly draw a match parameter θ from a c.d.f. $F(\theta)$. Once matched, they stay matched forever, each one deriving a benefit of θ per period from the match. Each unmatched pair of agents can influence the number of offers received in a period in the following way. The worker receives n offers per period, with $n = f(c_1 + c_2)$, where c_1 is the resources the worker devotes to searching and c_2 is the resources the typical firm devotes to searching. Symmetrically, the representative firm receives n offers per period where $n = f(c_1 + c_2)$. (We shall define the situation so that firms and workers have the same reservation θ so that there is never unrequited love.) Both c_1 and c_2 must be chosen at the beginning of the period, prior to searching during the period. Firms and workers have the same preferences, given by the expected present value of the match parameter θ, net of search costs. The discount factor β is the same for worker and firm.

a. Consider a Nash equilibrium in which party i chooses c_i, taking c_j, $j \neq i$, as given. Let Q_i be the value for an unmatched agent of type i before the level of c_i has been chosen. Formulate Bellman's equation for agents of types 1 and 2.

b. Consider the social planning problem of choosing c_1 and c_2 sequentially so as to maximize the criterion of λ times the utility of agent 1 plus $(1 - \lambda)$ times the utility of agent 2, $0 < \lambda < 1$. Let $Q(\lambda)$ be the value for this problem for two unmatched agents before c_1 and c_2 have been chosen. Formulate Bellman's equation for this problem.

c. Comparing the results in (a) and (b), argue that, in the Nash equilibrium, the optimal amount of resources has not been devoted to search.

SOLUTION

a.

$$Q_1 = \max_{c_1} \left\{ \int \max_{\substack{\text{accept} \\ \text{reject}}} \left\{ \frac{\theta}{1-\beta} - c_1, -c_1 + \beta Q_1 \right\} F^n(d\theta) \right\},$$

subject to $n = f(c_1 + c_2)$, c_2 given

$$Q_2 = \max_{c_2} \left\{ \int \max_{\substack{\text{accept} \\ \text{reject}}} \left\{ \frac{\theta}{1-\beta} - c_2, -c_2 + \beta Q_2 \right\} F^n(d\theta) \right\},$$

subject to $n = f(c_1 + c_2)$, c_2 given.

b.

$$Q(\lambda) = \max_{c_1, c_2} \left\{ \int \max_{\substack{\text{accept} \\ \text{reject}}} \left[\lambda \frac{\theta}{1-\beta} - \lambda c_1 + (1-\lambda) \left(\frac{\theta}{1-\beta} - c_2 \right), \right. \right.$$

$$\left. \left. - \lambda c_1 - (1-\lambda)c_2 + \beta Q(\lambda) \right\} F^n(d\theta) \right\}$$

subject to $n = f(c_1 + c_2)$.

c. The Nash equilibrium is a (c_1, c_2) pair that solves the two functional equations in (a). In general, this (c_1, c_2) pair will not solve the functional equation in (b) because each agent in (a) neglects the effects of his choice of c_j on the welfare of the other agent. In general, there will be too little search in the Nash equilibrium if $f(c_1 + c_2)$ is increasing in $(c_1 + c_2)$.

EXERCISE 2.7   Variable Labor Supply

An unemployed worker receives each period a wage offer w drawn from the distribution $F(w)$. The worker has to choose whether to accept the job — and therefore to work forever — or to search for another offer and collect c in unemployment compensation. The worker who decides to accept the job must choose the number of hours to work in each period. The worker chooses a strategy to maximize

$$E \sum_{t=0}^{\infty} \beta^t u(y_t, l_t), \qquad \text{where } 0 < \beta < 1,$$

and $y_t = c$ if the worker is unemployed, and $y_t = w(1 - l_t)$ if the worker is employed and works $(1 - l_t)$ hours; l_t is leisure with $0 \le l_t \le 1$.

Analyze the worker's problem. Argue that the optimal strategy has the reservation wage property. Show that the number of hours worked is the same in every period.

SOLUTION

Let s be the state variable. We choose $s = (w, 0)$, where w is the wage offer and $0 = E$ if the worker is employed, and $0 = U$ if she is unemployed. Consider first the situation of an employed worker. Bellman's equation is

$$v(w, E) = \max_l \{ u[w(1 - l), l] + \beta v(w, E) \}.$$

Then it follows that

$$v(w, E) = \frac{u(w[1 - l(w)], l(w))}{1 - \beta},$$

where $l(w) \equiv \operatorname*{argmax}_l u(w(1 - l), l).$

Next consider an unemployed worker. Bellman's equation is

$$v(w, U) = \max \left\{ \max_l (u[w(1 - l), l] + \beta v(w, E), \right.$$

$$\left. u(c, 1) + \beta \int v(w', U) F(dw') \right\}.$$

The outside maximization is over two actions: accept the offer (in which case the worker chooses l optimally) or reject the offer, collect unemployment compensation, and wait for a new offer next period.

By our analysis of the behavior of the employed worker, the first term in brackets is $u(w[1 - l(w)], l(w))$, which is clearly increasing in w. On the other hand, the second term is independent of w. Therefore, by the argument used in analyzing Equation (2.14) in *DMT*, the optimal strategy is to accept offers that are at least equal to some w^*. On the other hand, once an offer has been accepted, hours worked are constant and equal to $l(w)$.

EXERCISE 2.8 Wage Growth Rate and the Reservation Wage

An unemployed worker receives each period an offer to work for wage w_t forever, where $w_t = w$ in the first period and $w_t = \phi^t w$ after t periods in the job. Assume $\phi > 1$, that is, wages increase with tenure. The initial wage offer is drawn from a distribution $F(w)$ that is constant over time (entry-level wages are stationary); successive drawings across periods are independently and identically distributed.

The worker's objective function is to maximize

$$E \sum_{t=0}^{\infty} \beta^t y_t, \qquad \text{where } 0 < \beta < 1,$$

and $y_t = w_t$ if the worker is employed and $y_t = c$ if the worker is unemployed, where c is unemployment compensation. Let $v(w)$ be the optimal value of the objective function for an unemployed worker who has offer w in hand. Write Bellman's equation for this problem. Argue that, if two economies differ only in the growth rate of wages of employed workers, say $\phi_1 > \phi_2$, the economy with the higher growth rate has the smaller reservation wage.

Note. Assume that $\phi_i \beta < 1$, $i = 1, 2$.

SOLUTION

If the worker accepts employment at wage w, the sequence $\{y_t\}$ is given by $y_t = w, y_{t+1} = \theta w \ldots , y_{t+j} = \theta^j w \ldots$. Therefore the value of the objective function if the worker accepts is $\sum_{j=0}^{\infty} \beta^j y_{t+j} = w/(1 - \beta\theta)$. Bellman's equation for the worker's problem is

$$v(w) = \max\left\{ \frac{w}{1 - \beta\theta}, c + \beta \int v(w')F(dw') \right\}.$$

If we follow the analysis of Section 2.6 in *DMT*, it is straightforward to establish that the optimal policy is to accept all offers to work with an initial wage higher than $\overline{w}$. Therefore Equation (2.15) in *DMT* shows that the value function is given by

$$v(w) = \begin{cases} \dfrac{\overline{w}}{1 - \theta\beta} & w \leq \overline{w} \\[2mm] \dfrac{w}{1 - \theta\beta} & w \geq \overline{w}. \end{cases}$$

Because, at $w = \bar{w}$, we have

$$\frac{\bar{w}}{1 - \theta\beta} = c + \beta \int_0^\infty v(w')F(dw'),$$

we get, after substituting for $v(w)$ its expression,

$$\frac{\bar{w}}{(1 - \theta\beta)} = \frac{c + \beta}{1 - \theta\beta} \bar{w} \int_0^{\bar{w}} F(dw') + \frac{\beta}{1 - \theta\beta} \int_{\bar{w}}^\infty w'F(dw').$$

This equation can be rearranged to give

$$(1 - \beta)\bar{w} - \beta \int_{\bar{w}}^\infty (w' - \bar{w})F(dw') = (1 - \beta\theta)c.$$

It is easy to see (using the Leibniz rule) that the left-hand side is increasing in $\bar{w}$. Therefore, if $\theta_1 > \theta_2$, that is, $(1 - \beta\theta_1)c < (1 - \beta\theta_2)c$, it must be that $\bar{w}_1 < \bar{w}_2$.

The intuition behind this result is simple: for any given offer w, the value of accepting the offer is higher, the higher the growth rate of wages θ. Therefore, the sooner an offer is accepted, the sooner the benefits of the growth in wages are realized. This pattern makes some job offers more attractive even though the initial wage is not very high.

EXERCISE 2.9   Search with a Finite Horizon

Consider a worker who lives two periods. In each period the worker, if unemployed, receives an offer of lifetime work at wage w, where w is drawn from a distribution F. Wage offers are identically and independently distributed over time. The worker's objective is to maximize $E\{y_1 + \beta y_2\}$, where $y_t = w$ if the worker is employed and is equal to c—unemployment compensation—if the worker is not employed.

Analyze the worker's optimal decision rule. In particular, establish that the optimal strategy is to choose a reservation wage in each period and to accept any offer with a wage at least as high as the reservation wage and to reject offers below that level. Show that the reservation wage decreases over time.

SOLUTION

We first analyze the worker's problem in the second period of life. We consider an unemployed worker; an employed worker does not have to solve any decision problem. Let $v_0(w)$ be the optimal value of the problem for an unemployed worker with offer w in hand. Then $v_0(w) \equiv \max\{w, c\}$. It follows that the optimal strategy is to accept offers that are at least c and to reject all others. The second-period reservation wage, $\bar{w}_0$, is equal to c. In the first period if the worker is faced with a wage w and accepts the offer, the value of the objective function is $w(1 + \beta)$. The worker who rejects gets c in the first period and $v_0(w')$, a random variable, in the following period. The expected value of rejecting the offer is thus $c + \beta \int_0^\infty v_0(w')F(dw')$. Therefore the optimal value of the objective function for a worker with offer w in hand is given by

$$v_1(w) = \max\left\{ w(1 + \beta),\ c + \beta \int_0^\infty v_0(w')F(dw') \right\}.$$

Notice that the second term in brackets is constant, whereas the first is increasing in w. Therefore, by an argument similar to that of Section 2.6, *DMT*, it follows that there exists a $\bar{w}_1$ such that, for $w \le \bar{w}_1$, the second term is higher, and therefore the optimal strategy is to reject the job offer and to remain unemployed. On the other hand, the first element dominates for offers w with $w > \bar{w}_1$, and in this case, the optimal strategy is to accept. Clearly at $w = \bar{w}_1$ we have $\bar{w}_1(1 + \beta) = c + \beta \int_0^\infty v_0(w')F(dw')$, but using the expression for $v_0(w')$, we have

$$\bar{w}_1(1 + \beta) = c + \beta c F(c) + \beta \int_c^\infty w' F(dw')$$

$$= c + \beta c F(c) + \beta c[1 - F(c)] + \beta \int (w' - c)F(dw')$$

$$= c + \beta c + \beta \int_c^\infty (w' - c)F(dw').$$

Therefore,

$$\bar{w}_1(1 + \beta) = c(1 + \beta) + \beta \int_c^\infty (w' - c)F(dw').$$

We have now seen that $\bar{w}_1 > c = \bar{w}_0$, that is, reservation wages decrease as the retirement date approaches. The intuition underlying this result is that, the shorter the horizon, the smaller the benefits of "waiting to see if next period the wage offer is really high," because those benefits cannot be enjoyed for a long period. The implication is hence that the alternative to waiting—that is, accepting a job—becomes more attractive. This aspect is reflected in the model by a decrease in the reservation wage, which in fact corresponds to an increase in the percentage of job offers that are accepted.

EXERCISE 2.10 Finite Horizon and Mean-Preserving Spread

Consider a worker who draws every period a job offer to work forever at wage w. Successive offers are independently and identically distributed drawings from a distribution $F_i(w)$, $i = 1, 2$. Assume that F_1 has been obtained from F_2 by a mean-preserving spread (see Section 2.4). The worker's objective is to maximize

$$E \sum_{t=0}^{T} \beta^t y_t, \qquad 0 < \beta < 1,$$

where $y_t = w$ if the worker has accepted employment at wage w and is zero otherwise. Assume that both distributions, F_1 and F_2, share a common upper bound, B.

a. Show that the reservation wages of workers drawing from F_1 and F_2 coincide at $t = T$ and $t = T - 1$.

b. Argue that for $t \le T - 2$ the reservation wage of the workers that sample wage offers from the distribution F_1 is higher than the reservation wage of the workers that sample from F_2.

c. Now introduce unemployment compensation: the worker who is unemployed collects c dollars. Prove that the result in (a) no longer holds, that is, the reservation wage of the workers that sample from F_1 is higher than the one corresponding to workers that sample from F_2 for $t = T - 1$.

SOLUTION

a. Let $v_t^i(w)$ be the optimal value of the objective function of an unemployed worker at time t who has offer w in hand and draws wage offers from the distribution F_i, $i = 1, 2$. Then it is clear that $v_T^i(w) = \max\{0, w\} = w$. Therefore $\int_0^B v_T^i(w) F_i(dw) = \int_0^B w F_i(dw) = Ew$, $i = 1, 2$. Clearly the reservation wage at time T is zero: the worker accepts every offer. At time $(T - 1)$, Bellman's equation for the worker's problem is

$$v_{T-1}^i(w) = \max\left\{ w(1 + \beta), \beta \int_0^B v_T^i(w') F_i(dw') \right\}$$

$$= \max\{w(1 + \beta), \beta Ew\}.$$

It is then clear that the worker will accept the offer if $w(1 + \beta) \ge \beta Ew$ and will reject it otherwise. Therefore the reservation wage $\bar{w}_{T-1}$ is $\beta Ew/(1 + \beta)$. Because the expectation of w is the same no matter whether w is drawn from F_1 or F_2, it follows that both types of workers have the same reservation wage.

b. To answer this point, we first show that, although $v_{T-1}^1 = v_{T-1}^2$, their expectations do not coincide. We showed in (a) that

$$v_{T-1}^1(w) = v_{T-1}^2(w) = \begin{cases} w(1 + \beta) & w \geq \dfrac{\beta E w}{1 + \beta} \\[2ex] \beta E w & w \leq \dfrac{\beta E w}{1 + \beta}, \end{cases}$$

but

$$\int_0^B v_{T-1}^i(w')F_i(dw') = \beta E w F_i\left(\frac{\beta E w}{1 + \beta}\right)$$
$$+ (1 + \beta) \int_{\beta E w/(1 + \beta)}^B w' F_i(dw').$$

Integrating the last term by parts we get

$$= \beta E w F_i\left(\frac{\beta E w}{1 + \beta}\right) + (1 + \beta)\left[B - \frac{\beta}{1 + \beta} E w F_i\left(\frac{\beta E w}{1 + \beta}\right)\right.$$
$$\left. - \int_{\beta E w/(1+\beta)}^B F_i(w')\, dw'\right]$$
$$= (1 + \beta)\left[B - \int_0^B F_i(w')\, dw' + \int_0^{\beta E w/(1+\beta)} F_i(w')\, dw'\right].$$

For a nonnegative random variable, however, $\int_0^B F_i(w)\, dw = Ew$. Therefore

$$E v_{T-1}^i(w) = (1 + \beta)(B - Ew) + (1 + \beta) \int_0^{\beta E w/(1+\beta)} F_i(w')\, dw'.$$

Because F_1 has been obtained from F_2 by a mean-preserving spread, condition (iii) of the definition of mean-preserving spread implies that, for any $0 \leq y \leq B$,

$$\int_0^y F_1(w')\, dw' \geq \int_0^y F_2(w')\, dw' \quad \text{and} \quad E v_{T-1}^1 \geq E v_{T-1}^2.$$

Then Bellman's equation at time $(T - 2)$ is simply

$$v_{T-2}^i(w) = \max\left\{ w(1 + \beta + \beta^2), \beta \int_0^B v_{T-1}^i(w')F_i(dw')\right\}.$$

By a standard argument the reservation wage leaves the worker indifferent between accepting and rejecting the wage offer, that is, $\overline{w}_{T-2}^i = \beta/(1 + \beta + \beta^2)E v_{T-1}^i$. Because $E v_{T-1}^1 \geq E v_{T-1}^2$, it follows that $\overline{w}_{T-2}^1 \geq$

$\overline{w}_{T-2}^2$. To establish that this result also holds for any $t = T - j$, $j = 3$, 4, . . . , T, it suffices to show that $Ev_t^1 \geq Ev_t^2 \; \forall \; t \leq T - 2$. To prove this point, let H^i be the mapping from the space of functions to itself given by

$$(H^i f)(w) \equiv \max\left\{x_t, \beta \int_0^B f(w')F_i(dw')\right\}.$$

Because F_1 has been obtained from F_2 by a mean-preserving spread, it follows that, for any convex function f, $(H^1 f)(w) \geq (H^2 f)(w)$. Similarly, if $f(w) \geq g(w)$, we have $(H^i f)(w) \geq (H^i g)(w)$, $i = 1, 2$. Finally, it is easy to see that H^i maps convex functions into convex functions. With these results we are now ready to show that, for any $t \leq T - 2$, $v_t^1(w) \geq v_t^2(w)$. First, because $Ev_{T-1}^1 \geq Ev_{T-1}^2$, we have that $v_{T-2}^1(w) \geq v_{T-2}^2(w)$. Then

$$v_{T-3}^1(w) \equiv H^1 v_{T-2}^1(w) \geq H^1 v_{T-2}^2(w) \geq H^2 v_{T-2}^2(w) \equiv v_{T-3}^2(w),$$

where the first inequality follows from the monotonicity of the mapping and the second from the fact that $v_{T-2}^2(w)$ is convex. Then we have shown that $v_{T-2}^1(w) \geq v_{T-2}^2(w)$ implies that $v_{T-3}^1(w) \geq v_{T-3}^2(w)$. Using the same argument we can proceed sequentially to establish that $v_t^1 \geq v_t^2$ implies that $v_{t-1}^1 \geq v_{t-1}^2$, for $t = T - 1, \ldots, 1$. This procedure suffices to show that $\overline{w}_t^1 \geq \overline{w}_t^2$, as desired.

c. The value of the problem at $t = T$ is $v_T^i(w) = \max\{w, c\}$, $i = 1, 2$. Then $\overline{w}_T^1 = \overline{w}_T^2 = c$. If we use the same argument as in (b), however, it follows directly that $\int_0^B \max\{w, c\}F_1(dw) \geq \int_0^B \max\{w, c\}F_2(dw)$, or $Ev_T^1 \geq Ev_T^2$. On the other hand, the reservation wage at $(T - 1)$ satisfies $\overline{w}_{T-1}^i = \beta/(1 + \beta)Ev_T^i$. Therefore $\overline{w}_{T-1}^1 \geq \overline{w}_{T-1}^2$.

EXERCISE 2.11   Pissarides' Analysis of Taxation and Variable Search Intensity

An unemployed worker receives each period a zero offer (or no offer) with probability $[1 - \pi(e)]$. With probability $\pi(e)$ the worker draws an offer w from the distribution F. Here e stands for effort—a measure of search intensity—and $\pi(e)$ is increasing in e. A worker who accepts a job offer can be fired with probability α, $0 < \alpha < 1$. The worker chooses a strategy, that is, whether to accept an offer or not and how much effort to put into search when unemployed, to maximize

$$E \sum_{t=0}^{\infty} \beta^t y_t, \qquad 0 < \beta < 1,$$

where $y_t = w$ if the worker is employed with wage w and $y_t = 1 - e + z$ if the worker spends e units of leisure searching and does not accept a job. Here z is unemployment compensation. For the worker who searched and accepted a job, $y_t = w - e - T(w)$; that is, in the first period the wage is net of search costs. Throughout, $T(w)$ is the amount paid in taxes when the worker is employed. We assume that $w - T(w)$ is increasing in w. Assume that $w - T(w) = 0$ for $w = 0$, that, if $e = 0$, $\pi(e) = 0$—that is, the worker gets no offers—and that $\pi'(e) > 0$, $\pi''(e) < 0$.

a. Analyze the worker's problem. Establish that the optimal strategy is to choose a reservation wage. Display the condition that describes the optimal choice of e, and show that the reservation wage is independent of e.

b. Assume that $T(w) = t(w - a)$ where $0 < t < 1$ and $a > 0$. Show that an increase in a decreases the reservation wage and increases the level of effort, increasing the probability of accepting employment.

c. Show under what conditions a change in t has the opposite effect.

SOLUTION

a. Let the state variable that completely summarizes current and future opportunities be $x = (w, e, s)$, where w is the wage, e is effort, and $s = E$ if the worker is employed and $s = U$ if he is unemployed. Recall that, if the worker is employed, then $e = 0$. Let Q be the expected value of the objective function for an unemployed worker who behaves optimally before getting an offer. Then if the worker is employed, the value of the objective function is given by

$$v(w, 0, E) = w - T(w) + \beta(1 - \alpha)v(w, 0, E) + \beta\alpha Q,$$

or $\quad v(w, 0, E) = \dfrac{w - T(w)}{1 - \beta(1 - \alpha)} + \dfrac{\beta\alpha Q}{1 - \beta(1 - \alpha)}.$

If the worker is unemployed, has an offer w in hand, and spent $e > 0$ units of leisure searching this period, the value of the objective function is

$$v(w, e, U) = \max\{w - T(w) - e + \beta(1 - \alpha)v(w, 0, E) \\ + \beta\alpha Q, 1 - e + z + \beta Q\},$$

where the first term reflects the value of accepting employment and the second the value of rejecting the offer. Using the expression we found for $v(w, 0, E)$, we get

$$v(w, e, U) = \max\left\{\dfrac{w - T(w)}{1 - \beta(1 - \alpha)} - e \right. \\ \left. + \dfrac{\beta\alpha Q}{1 - \beta(1 - \alpha)}, 1 - e + z + \beta Q\right\}.$$

Then, using a standard argument, we see from the above equation that the optimal strategy is to accept offers greater than or equal to $\bar{w}$ and to reject all others; $\bar{w}$ is such that it makes the worker indifferent between accepting or rejecting the job offer; that is, $\bar{w}$ solves

$$\frac{\bar{w} - T(\bar{w})}{1 - \beta(1 - \alpha)} - e + \frac{\beta\alpha Q}{1 - \beta(1 - \alpha)} = 1 - e + z + \beta Q,$$

or

(1) $$\bar{w} - T(\bar{w}) = [1 - \beta(1 - \alpha)](1 + z + \beta Q) - \beta\alpha Q.$$

Notice that we cannot use this expression for $\bar{w}$ to compute the reservation wage, because Q must be determined endogenously. It is clear, however, that, if Q is independent of e (as we will show that it is), then $\bar{w}$ does not depend on e.

Because we established that the optimal policy is of the reservation wage variety, we can compute $v(w, e, U)$. This function is given by

$$v(w, e, U) = \begin{cases} \dfrac{w - T(w)}{1 - \beta(1 - \alpha)} - e + \dfrac{\beta\alpha Q}{1 - \beta(1 - \alpha)} & w \geq \bar{w} \\ 1 - e + z + \beta Q & w \leq \bar{w}. \end{cases}$$

Let $\Phi(e) = Ev(w, e, U) = \int_0^\infty v(w, e, U)F(dw)$,

$$\Phi(e) = (1 + z + \beta Q)F(\bar{w})$$

$$+ \frac{1}{1 - \beta(1 - \alpha)} \int_{\bar{w}}^\infty [w - T(w)]F(dw) - e$$

$$+ [1 - F(\bar{w})] \frac{\beta\alpha Q}{1 - \beta(1 - \alpha)}.$$

Because we have shown that

$$\frac{\beta\alpha Q}{1 - \beta(1 - \alpha)} = (1 + z + \beta Q) - \frac{\bar{w} - T(\bar{w})}{1 - \beta(1' - \alpha)},$$

we have, after some substitution, that

$$\Phi(e) = \frac{1}{1 - \beta(1 - \alpha)}$$

$$\cdot \int_{\bar{w}}^\infty ([w - T(w)] - [\bar{w} - T(\bar{w})])F(dw) + 1 + z + \beta Q - e.$$

Now consider $\Phi(0)$. Recall that, if $e = 0$, the worker gets no offers, and hence

$v(w, 0, U) = 1 + z + \beta Q$. This expression is independent of w, and so $\Phi(0) = 1 + z + \beta Q$. Therefore

$$\Phi(e) = \frac{1}{1 - \beta(1 - \alpha)}$$
$$\cdot \int_{\underline{w}}^{\infty} ([w - T(w)] - [\overline{w} - T(\overline{w})])F(dw) + \Phi(0) - e.$$

To simplify notation let $(w - T(w)) - (\overline{w} - T(\overline{w})) \equiv \Delta Y(w)$. Then the above expression becomes

$$\Phi(e) = \frac{1}{1 - \beta(1 - \alpha)} \int_{\underline{w}}^{\infty} \Delta Y(w)F(dw) + \Phi(0) - e.$$

If the worker chooses to spend e units of effort, he gets an offer with probability $\pi(e)$ and expected value $\Phi(e)$. With probability $[1 - \pi(e)]$ he gets no offers. This alternative has value $\Phi(0) - e$.

Then the value of the problem for an unemployed worker who behaves optimally is given by Q, where Q satisfies

$$Q \equiv \max_{0 \le e \le 1} \{\pi(e)\Phi(e) + [1 - \pi(e)][\Phi(0) - e]\}$$

or $\quad Q \equiv \max_{0 \le e \le 1} \{\pi(e)[\Phi(e) - \Phi(0) + e] + \Phi(0) - e\}$

(2) $\quad Q = \max_{0 \le e \le 1} \left\{ \frac{\pi(e)}{1 - \beta(1 - \alpha)} \int_{\underline{w}}^{\infty} \Delta Y(w)F(dw) + 1 - e + z + \beta Q \right\}.$

The right-hand side defines a mapping from Q into the reals. To guarantee that the problem is well behaved, we want to show that one such Q exists. This is not a trivial problem: Q affects $\overline{w}$ and $\Delta Y(w)$, so that the mapping is highly nonlinear. In any case, it is clear that Q, and therefore $\overline{w}$, are independent of e.

Let H be the mapping defined by the right-hand side of (2). Because $\pi(e)$ is increasing in e, we have that

$$HQ \le \frac{1}{1 - \beta(1 - \alpha)} \int_{\underline{w}}^{\infty} \Delta Y(w)F(dw) + 1 + z + \beta Q$$

$$\le \overline{H}Q \equiv \frac{1}{1 - \beta(1 - \alpha)} \int_{0}^{\infty} [w - T(w)]F(dw) + 1 + z + \beta Q.$$

Therefore, if Q_1 is such that $Q_1 = \overline{H}Q_1$ (such a Q_1 is easy to compute directly), it follows that, for all $Q \ge Q_1, Q \ge \overline{H}Q$. Thus $\forall Q \ge Q_1, HQ \le Q$. On the other hand,

$$HQ \geq \left\{ \frac{\pi(0)}{1 - \beta(1 - \alpha)} \int_{\underline{w}}^{\infty} \Delta Y(w)F(dw) + 1 + z + \beta Q \right\}$$
$$= 1 + z + \beta Q \equiv \underline{H}Q.$$

Then we have that, for all $Q \geq 0$, $\underline{H}Q \leq HQ \leq \overline{H}Q$ and $\underline{H}0 > 0$. Hence we have established that $H0 > 0$ and that there exists $Q_1 < \infty$ such that $HQ \leq Q$ for $Q \geq Q_1$.

Inasmuch as H is a continuous function of Q [this follows because $\overline{w}$ is continuous in Q, as is $\Delta Y(w)$], we establish that there exists a $\overline{Q}$ such that $H\overline{Q} = \overline{Q}$.

We next prove that $\overline{Q}$ is unique. To do so it suffices to show that the mapping H is monotone in Q. A sufficient condition is that

$$0 \leq \frac{\partial}{\partial \overline{w}} \left[\int_{\underline{w}}^{\infty} \Delta Y(w)F(dw) \right] \frac{\partial \overline{w}}{\partial Q} + \beta < 1.$$

Still, $(\partial/\partial \overline{w}) \int_{\underline{w}}^{\infty} \Delta Y(w)F(dw)$ is (using the Leibniz rule) equal to $-[1 - (\partial T/\partial w)(\overline{w})][1 - F(\overline{w})]$. From the equation determining $\overline{w}$, we get that $[1 - (\partial T/\partial w)(\overline{w})](\partial \overline{w}/\partial Q) = \beta(1 - \beta)(1 - \alpha)$. Because $-[1 - F(\overline{w})]\beta(1 - \beta)(1 - \alpha) + \beta \in (0, 1)$, however, H is increasing. Next we use (2) to characterize the optimal choice of e. It is clear that it satisfies

(3) $$\pi'(e) \frac{1}{1 - \beta(1 - \alpha)} \int_{\underline{w}}^{\infty} \Delta Y(w)F(dw) = 1$$

if the solution is interior. We assume that the distribution of w has sufficient mass in the tail to make search attractive—that is, we assume that the solution is interior. It is being claimed that it is possible to make assumptions about the deep parameters of the model, $F(w)$, α, β, z, $\pi(e)$, that will guarantee that the optimal choice of e is $e > 0$. We focus on this case only because the other is trivial.

From (2) it is clear that the optimal Q satisfies

$$\overline{Q} = (1 - \beta)^{-1} \left[\frac{\pi(\overline{e})}{1 - \beta(1 - \alpha)} \int_{\underline{w}}^{\infty} \Delta Y(w)F(dw) + 1 - \overline{e} + z \right].$$

Using this equation in 1, we obtain another, more familiar characterization of the optimal reservation wage,

(4) $$\overline{w} - T(\overline{w}) = (1 + z) - \beta(1 - \alpha)\overline{e} + \frac{\beta(1 - \alpha)\pi(\overline{e})}{1 - \beta(1 - \alpha)} \int_{\underline{w}}^{\infty} \{[w - T(w)] - [\overline{w} - T(\overline{w})]\}F(dw).$$

Then (4) and (3) summarize the determination of the endogenous variables, e and $\bar{w}$.

b. Assume that $T(w) = t(w - a)$. To explore the effect of a change in a, we differentiate completely (4) and (3) with respect to a. We start with (4).

$$
(1-t)\frac{\partial \bar{w}}{\partial a} + t = -\beta(1-\gamma)\frac{\partial \bar{e}}{\partial a} + \frac{\beta(1-\alpha)}{1-\beta(1-\alpha)}
$$

$$
\cdot \int_{\bar{w}}^{\infty} \Delta Y(w)F(dw)\pi'(\bar{e})\frac{\partial e}{\partial a}
$$

$$
- \frac{\beta(1-\alpha)\pi(\bar{e})}{1-\beta(1-\alpha)}(1-t)[1-F(\bar{w})]\frac{\partial \bar{w}}{\partial a}.
$$

Using (3) to eliminate $1/[1-\beta(1-\alpha)]\int_{\bar{w}}^{\infty}\Delta Y(w)F(dw)\pi'(\bar{e}) = 1$, we get

$$
(1-t)\left[1 + \frac{\beta(1-\alpha)\pi(\bar{e})[1-F(\bar{w})]}{1-\beta(1-\alpha)}\right]\frac{\partial \bar{w}}{\partial a} = -t.
$$

Then $(\partial \bar{w}/\partial a) < 0$.

The intuition underling this result is that an increase in a makes the income tax more progressive, as it increases the subsidy to low-income workers. Because taxes are paid (and the subsidy is received) only if the worker is employed, the increased attractiveness of low-income jobs is reflected by a reduction in the minimum wage at which an unemployed worker is willing to accept an offer. Notice that the term $(\partial e/\partial a)$ disappears in the above equation. This is just another consequence of the property that e does not affect the choice of the reservation wage.

We next explore the effect on e. From (3) we get

$$
\frac{\pi''(\bar{e})}{1-\beta(1-\alpha)}\int_{\bar{w}}^{\infty}\Delta Y(w)F(dw)\frac{\partial e}{\partial a}
$$

$$
= \frac{\pi'(\bar{e})}{1-\beta(1-\alpha)}(1-t)\frac{\partial \bar{w}}{\partial a}[1-F(\bar{w})]
$$

or $$\frac{\pi''(\bar{e})}{\pi'(\bar{e})^2}\frac{\partial e}{\partial a} = \frac{(1-t)(1-F(\bar{w}))}{1-\beta(1-\alpha)}\frac{\partial \bar{w}}{\partial a}.$$

Because $\pi''(e) < 0$, we have that $(\partial e/\partial a) > 0$, that is, effort is increased. Notice that the increase in e increases $\pi(\bar{e})$, and hence the probability of getting an acceptable offer $\pi(\bar{e})[1-F(\bar{w})]$ rises. To fix the notation, let

$p = \pi(e)[1 - F(\overline{w})]$. Then

$$\frac{\partial p}{\partial a} = [1 - F(\overline{w})]\pi'(\overline{e})\frac{\partial e}{\partial a} - F'(\overline{w})\pi(e)\frac{\partial \overline{w}}{\partial a},$$

and our results show that $(\partial p/\partial a) > 0$.

c. Next we analyze the effects of changing the marginal tax rate t. We follow exactly the same method of totally differentiating (4) and (3) to get, from (4),

$$(1 - t)\frac{\partial \overline{w}}{\partial t}\left\{1 + \frac{\beta(1 - \alpha)\pi(\overline{e})[1 - F(\overline{w})]}{1 - \beta(1 - \alpha)}\right\}$$

$$= \overline{w} - a - \frac{\beta(1 - \alpha)\pi(\overline{e})}{1 - \beta(1 - \alpha)}\int_{\overline{w}}^{\infty} (w - \overline{w})F(dw).$$

From (4), however, we got that

$$\overline{w} - \frac{\beta(1 - \alpha)\pi(\overline{e})}{1 - \beta(1 - \alpha)}\int_{\overline{w}}^{\infty} (w - \overline{w})F(dw)$$

$$= (1 - t)^{-1}[(1 + z) - a - \beta(1 - \alpha)\overline{e}].$$

Then

$$\text{sign}\,\frac{\partial \overline{w}}{\partial t} = \text{sign}[(1 + z) - a - \beta(1 - \alpha)\overline{e}].$$

From (3), after we substitute into the expression for $(\partial \overline{w}/\partial t)$, we get

$$\frac{\pi''(\overline{e})}{\pi'(\overline{e})}\frac{\partial e}{\partial t} = \frac{\pi'(\overline{e})}{[1 - \beta(1 - \alpha) + \beta(1 - \alpha)\pi(\overline{e})[1 - F(\overline{w})]}$$

$$\cdot \left\{\overline{w} + \int_{\overline{w}}^{\infty} (w - \overline{w})F(dw)\right\}.$$

Therefore $(\partial e/\partial t) < 0$ unambiguously.

Notice that, in this case, an increase in t reduces the returns of being employed and therefore makes working less attractive. Consequently, it is optimal for the unemployed worker to reduce the level of effort, decreasing the probability of finding a job. On the other hand, it is possible for the reservation wage to decrease, that is, for some wage offers to be acceptable to the worker after the increase in the tax rate. Such a decrease becomes more likely as a grows larger. In this case, the increase in the marginal rate can actually increase payments to the worker when $w - a < 0$. This higher subsidy makes working more attractive, consequently reducing the reservation wage.

EXERCISE 2.12   Search and Nonhuman Wealth

An unemployed worker receives every period an offer to work forever at wage w, where w is drawn from the distribution $F(w)$. Offers are independently and identically distributed. Every agent has another source of income, which we denote ϵ_t, and that may be regarded as nonhuman wealth. In every period all agents get a realization of ϵ_t, which is independently and identically distributed over time, with distribution function $G(\epsilon)$. We also assume that w_t and ϵ_t are independent. The objective of a worker is to maximize

$$E \sum_{t=0}^{\infty} \beta^t y_t, \qquad 0 < \beta < 1,$$

where $y_t = w + \phi \epsilon_t$ if the worker has accepted a job that pays w, and $y_t = c + \epsilon_t$ if the worker remains unemployed. We assume that $0 < \phi < 1$ to reflect the fact that an employed worker has less time to engage in the collection of nonhuman wealth. Assume $1 > \text{prob}\{w \geq c + (1 - \phi)\epsilon\} > 0$.

Analyze the worker's problem. Write down Bellman's equation and show that the reservation wage increases with the level of nonhuman wealth.

SOLUTION

If the worker accepts a job that pays w, her total utility is given by

$$w + \theta \epsilon_t + E \sum_{j=1}^{\infty} \beta^j (w + \theta \epsilon_{t+j}) = w + \theta \epsilon + \frac{\beta}{1 - \beta}(w + \theta E \epsilon).$$

Then let $v(w, \epsilon)$ be the optimal value of the objective function for an unemployed worker who has an offer w in hand and nonhuman wealth equal to ϵ. Then

$$v(w, \epsilon) = \max \left\{ w + \theta \epsilon + \frac{\beta}{1 - \beta}(w + E\epsilon), \right.$$

$$\left. c + \epsilon + \beta \iint v(w', \epsilon')F(dw')G(d\epsilon') \right\}.$$

Because the second term in the bracketed expression does not depend on w, it is easy to see that, for each ϵ, the optimal strategy is to choose a reservation wage.

Consider now an agent with a level of nonhuman wealth equal to $(\epsilon + \Delta)$, $\Delta > 0$. Then we want to show that her reservation wage $\bar{w}(\epsilon + \Delta)$ is higher than $\bar{w}(\epsilon)$. To establish this point, it suffices to check that the second term in brackets (which corresponds to remaining unemployed) exceeds the first when evaluated at $\bar{w}(\epsilon)$. To see that it does so, recall that

$$c + \epsilon + \beta \iint v(w', \epsilon') F(dw') G(d\epsilon')$$

$$= \bar{w}(\epsilon) + \theta\epsilon + \frac{\beta}{1-\beta} [\bar{w}(\epsilon) + \theta E\epsilon].$$

Then the second term evaluated at $\bar{w}(\epsilon + \Delta) = \bar{w}(\epsilon)$ is

$$c + \epsilon + \Delta + \beta \iint v(w', \epsilon') F(dw') G(d\epsilon')$$

$$= \bar{w}(\epsilon) + \theta(\epsilon + \Delta) + \frac{\beta}{1-\beta} (w + \theta E\epsilon) + (1 - \theta) \Delta.$$

Because $(1 - \theta) \Delta > 0$, it follows that the reservation wage increases. In this model, wealthier workers are less willing to accept low-paying jobs. Notice that it is crucial for the result that accepting a job result in some sacrifice of income from the alternative source. If θ equaled 1, the reservation wage would be independent of nonhuman wealth.

EXERCISE 2.13   Search and Asset Accumulation

A worker receives, when unemployed, an offer to work forever at wage w, where w is drawn from the distribution $F(w)$. Wage offers are identically and independently distributed over time. The worker maximizes

$$E \sum_{t=0}^{\infty} \beta^t u(c_t, l_t), \qquad 0 < \beta < 1,$$

where c_t is consumption and l_t is leisure. Assume R_t is i.i.d. with distribution $H(R)$. The budget constraint is given by

$$a_{t+1} \leq R_t(a_t + w_t n_t - c_t)$$

and $l_t + n_t \leq 1$ if the worker has a job that pays w_t. If the worker is unemployed, the budget constraint is $a_{t+1} \leq R_t(a_t + z - c_t)$ and $l_t = 1$. Here z is unemployment compensation. It is assumed that $u(\cdot)$ is bounded and that a_t, the worker's asset position, cannot be negative. This corresponds to a no borrowing assumption. Write down Bellman's equation for this problem.

SOLUTION

A natural choice for the state variable in this problem is the vector (w, a, R, s), where $s = E$ if the worker is employed and $s = U$ if the worker is unemployed. We first analyze the problem faced by an employed worker. This problem is

$$v(w, a, R, E) = \max_{c,l,n,a'} u(c, l) + \beta \int v(w, a', R', E) H(dR'),$$

subject to $\quad a' \le R(a + wn - c), \quad l + n \le 1.$

If the worker is unemployed, the value function is given by

$$v(w, a, R, U) = \max\Big\{ v(w, a, R, E), \max[u(c, 1)$$
$$+ \beta \iint v(w', a', R', U) F(dw') H(dR')] \Big\},$$

subject to $\quad a' \le R(a + z - c),$

where the first term in brackets reflects the value of accepting the job, whereas the second represents the value of remaining unemployed. In each case the asset position is chosen optimally. It is possible to argue that the optimal strategy is to set a reservation wage $\overline{w}(a, R)$ that depends on both the asset position and the rate of interest R.

References and Suggested Readings

Albrecht, James, and Bo Axell. 1984. An equilibrium model of search unemployment. *Journal of Political Economy* 92(5):824–840.

Bertsekas, Dimitri. 1976. *Dynamic Programming and Stochastic Control.* New York: Academic Press.

Blackwell, David. 1965. Discounted dynamic programming. *Annals of Mathematical Statistics* 36(1):226–235.

Diamond, Peter A. 1981. Mobility costs, frictional unemployment, and efficiency. *Journal of Political Economy* 89(4):798–812.

Diamond, Peter A., and Joseph Stiglitz. 1974. Increases in risk and in risk aversion. *Journal of Economic Theory* 8(3):337–360.

Gabel, R. A., and R. A. Roberts. 1973. *Signals and Linear Systems.* New York: Wiley.

Johnson, Norman, and Samuel Kotz. 1971. *Continuous Univariate Distributions.* New York: Wiley.

Jovanovic, Boyan. 1979. Job matching and the theory of turnover. *Journal of Political Economy* 87(5):972–990.

Lippman, Steven A., and John J. McCall. 1976. The economics of job search: a survey. *Economic Inquiry* 14(3):347–368.

Lucas, Robert E., Jr., and Edward C. Prescott. 1974. Equilibrium search and unemployment. *Journal of Economic Theory* 7(2):188–209.

McCall, John J. 1970. Economics of information and job search. *Quarterly Journal of Economics* 84(1):113–126.

Mortensen, Dale T. 1982. The matching process as a noncooperative bargaining game. In *The Economics of Information and Uncertainty,* ed. John J. McCall, pp. 233–258. Chicago: University of Chicago Press for the National Bureau of Economic Research.

Phelps, Edmund S. 1970. Introduction to *Microeconomic Foundations of Employment and Inflation Theory.* New York: Norton.

Pissarides, Christopher A. 1983. Efficiency aspects of the financing of unemployment insurance and other government expenditures. *Review of Economic Studies* 50(1):57–69.

Prescott, Edward C., and Robert M. Townsend. 1980. Equilibrium under uncertainty: multiagent statistical decision theory. In *Bayesian Analysis in Econometrics and Statistics,* ed. Arnold Zellner, pp. 169–194. Amsterdam: North-Holland.

Reinganum, Jennifer F. 1979. A simple equilibrium model of price dispersion. *Journal of Political Economy* 87(4):851–858.

Rothschild, Michael, and Joseph Stiglitz. 1970. Increasing risk I: a definition. *Journal of Economic Theory* 2(3):225–243.

———— 1971. Increasing risk II: its economic consequences. *Journal of Economic Theory* 3(1):66–84.

Sargent, Thomas J. 1979. *Macroeconomic Theory.* New York: Academic Press.

Stigler, George. 1961. The economics of information. *Journal of Political Economy* 69(3):213–225.

Watanabe, Shinichi. 1984. Search unemployment, the business cycle, and stochastic growth. Ph.D. diss., University of Minnesota.

Wright, Randall. Job search and cyclical unemployment. *Journal of Political Economy.* Forthcoming.

3 | Asset Prices and Consumption

EXERCISE 3.1 Taxation and Stock Prices

Consider a version of Lucas's one-tree model along the lines of the discussion in Section 3.3, with $u(c) = \ln c$. Let d_t follow a Markov process with $\text{prob}\{d_{t+j} \le d' | d_t = d\} = \int_0^{d'} f(s, d)\, ds$. Let a government spend or "throw away" g_t per capita in period t, where $0 \le g_t < d_t$. Let g_t be given by $g_t = d_t \epsilon_t$, where ϵ_t is a Markov process with $\text{prob}\{\epsilon_{t+1} \le \epsilon' | \epsilon_t = \epsilon\} = \int_0^{\epsilon'} k(s, \epsilon)\, ds$. Assume that the only assets traded are titles to trees or shares.

a. Assume that all government expenditures are financed by a lump-sum head tax of τ_t per worker at time t. This tax is independent of the property owned by the representative consumer. Calculate the equilibrium price function for shares (that is, titles to trees).

b. Now assume that there is an income tax on dividends. In particular, at time t, dividends are taxed at the rate of τ_t/d_t, so that τ_t units of time t good are collected on dividends.

1. Assume the balanced budget rule $g_t = \tau_t$. Calculate the equilibrium price function for titles to trees.
2. Assume the taxing rule $\tau_t = g_t + b(1 - 1/R_{1t})$, where $b > 0$ is a permanent level of borrowing. Now calculate the equilibrium price function of titles to trees.

In what sense are your results consistent with the claim that (state-contingent) prices are independent of the tax strategy, given a stochastic process for per capita government expenditures?

SOLUTION

We first note that, regardless of the tax regime, equilibrium in the market for consumption goods requires that $c_t = d_t - g_t = d_t(1 - \epsilon_t)$. We define the state at time t by $x_t = (d_t, \epsilon_t)$. The standard pricing formulas [for example, Equations (3.11), (3.12), and (3.13), *DMT*] still apply to our economy with taxes, provided that we are careful to identify dividends with "after-tax dividends."

a. We apply the pricing formula

(1)
$$p(d_t, \epsilon_t) = \sum_{j=1}^{\infty} \beta^j E_t \left\{ \frac{u'(c_{t+j})}{u'(c_t)} d_{t+j} \right\}.$$

Substituting $u'(c) = c^{-1}$ and $c_t = d_t(1 - \epsilon_t)$, we get

$$p^a(d_t, \epsilon_t) = \left[\sum_{j=1}^{\infty} \beta^j E_t \left(\frac{1}{1 - \epsilon_{t+j}} \right) \right] d_t (1 - \epsilon_t).$$

b. In this section we identify dividends, d_t in (1), with after-tax dividends, $d_t - \tau_t$. Therefore our version of (1) is

$$p^b(d_t, \epsilon_t) = \sum_{j=1}^{\infty} \beta^j E_t \left\{ \frac{u'(c_{t+j})}{u'(c_t)} (d_{t+j} - \tau_{t+j}) \right\}.$$

In case (i) we have that $d_t - \tau_t = d_t - g_t = d_t(1 - \epsilon_t)$. Substituting the specific form of the utility function, we get

$$p_1^b(d_t, \epsilon_t) = \sum_{j=1}^{\infty} \beta^j E_t \left\{ \frac{d_t(1 - \epsilon_t)}{d_{t+j}(1 - \epsilon_{t+j})} d_{t+j}(1 - \epsilon_{t+j}) \right\}$$

$$= \frac{\beta}{1 - \beta} d_t(1 - \epsilon_t).$$

In subcase (ii), we have that $d_t - \tau_t = d_t - g_t - b(1 - R_{1t}^{-1}) = d_t(1 - \epsilon_t) - b(1 - R_{1t}^{-1})$, where R_{1t}^{-1} is given by

$$R_{1t}^{-1} = \beta E_t \left\{ \frac{d_t(1 - \epsilon_t)}{d_{t+1}(1 - \epsilon_{t+1})} \right\}.$$

Making the corresponding substitutions we get

$$p_2^b(d_t, \epsilon_t) = \left[\sum_{j=1}^{\infty} \beta^j \left\{ 1 - E_t \frac{b(1 - R_{1t+j}^{-1})}{d_{t+j}(1 - \epsilon_{t+j})} \right\} \right] d_t(1 - \epsilon_t).$$

If we are willing to assume that $R_{1t}^{-1} \leq 1$ for every realization of (d_t, ϵ_t), so that the second term in brackets is nonnegative, we can compare the effects of different tax structures on the state-contingent price of shares.

Notice that all three prices can be written as

$$p_t = \left[\sum_{j=1}^{\infty} \beta^j E_t x_{t+j} \right] d_t(1 - \epsilon_t)$$

and that different tax structures correspond to different x_{t+j}. In case (a), $x_{t+j} = 1/(1 - \epsilon_{t+j})$. In case (b)(i), $x_{t+j} = 1$, and in case (b)(ii), $x_{t+j} = 1 - [b(1 - R_{1t+j}^{-1})/d_{t+j}(1 - \epsilon_{t+j})]$.

Therefore we have that $x_{t+j}^a \geq x_{t+j}^{b(i)} \geq x_{t+j}^{b(ii)}$ and consequently that $p^a(d_t, \epsilon_t) \geq p_1^b(d_t, \epsilon_t) \geq p_2^b(d_t, \epsilon_t)$. This last inequality depends heavily on the assumption that $b > 0$ and that $R_{1t}^{-1} < 1$. The latter can be justified when β is small.

To sum up, these results show that a given stochastic process for per capita government expenditure is consistent with different stochastic processes for stock prices; that is, that asset prices depend not only on government expenditures but also on how they are financed. This statement is true even though state-contingent prices are independent of the way in which the government finances its expenditures. A tree is a claim to a bundle of state-contingent securities, the nature of the bundle being affected by the taxing rule. The nature of the scheme for taxing dividends affects the state-contingent stream of returns to which owners of trees are entitled and therefore also affects their price.

EXERCISE 3.2   Contingent Claims Prices in a Brock-Mirman Economy

Consider the stochastic growth model: maximize $E_0 \sum_{t=0}^{\infty} \beta^t \ln c_t$, subject to $c_t + k_{t+1} \leq A k_t^{\alpha} \theta_t$, $A > 0$, $0 < \alpha < 1$, k_0 given, where θ is an independently and identically distributed positive random variable with density $f(\theta_t)$. At time t the planner knows $\{\theta_{t-j}, k_{t-j}, j = 0, 1, \ldots \}$.

a. Show that the optimizing consumption and capital accumulation plans are

$$c_t = (1 - \alpha\beta) k_t^{\alpha} \theta_t$$
$$k_{t+1} = \alpha\beta A k_t^{\alpha} \theta_t.$$

b. Show that, for a competitive economy with these preferences and technology, the contingent claims prices can be expressed as

$$q[(\theta_{t+1}, k_{t+1}), (\theta_t, k_t)] = \frac{\beta}{(\alpha\beta A)^{\alpha}} k_t^{\alpha(1-\alpha)} \theta_t^{1-\alpha} \theta_{t+1}^{-1} f(\theta_{t+1}),$$

where the state of the economy is defined as $(\theta_t, k_t) \equiv x_t$. Show that

$$q^{(2)}[(\theta_{t+2}, k_{t+2}), (\theta_t, k_t)]$$

$$= \beta^2 \frac{1}{(\beta\alpha A)^{(\alpha+\alpha^2)}} k_t^{\alpha(1-\alpha^2)} \theta_t^{(1-\alpha^2)} \frac{f(\theta_{t+2})}{\theta_{t+2}} E\left(\frac{1}{\theta_{t+1}^\alpha}\right).$$

c. Show that, in a competitive economy with these preferences and technology, the interest rates on sure one-period and two-period loans are given by

$$1/R_{1t} = \frac{\beta}{(\alpha\beta A)^\alpha} k_t^{\alpha(1-\alpha)} \theta_t^{1-\alpha} E(\theta_{t+1}^{-1})$$

$$1/R_{2t} = \frac{\beta^2}{(\beta\alpha A)^{(\alpha+\alpha^2)}} k_t^{\alpha(1-\alpha^2)} \theta_t^{1-\alpha^2} E\left(\frac{1}{\theta_{t+1}^\alpha}\right) E\left(\frac{1}{\theta_{t+2}}\right).$$

SOLUTION

To solve this exercise, we will use the techniques introduced in Chapter 1, *DMT*. In particular, we will use Bellman's equation to verify a conjecture about the form of the value function. In Exercise 1.1 it is shown how to generate the conjecture.

a. Recall from Chapter 1, *DMT*, that Bellman's equation is

(1) $$v(k, \theta) = \max_{c, k'}\{u(c) + \beta \int v(k', \theta') f(\theta') \, d\theta'\}$$

subject $c + k' \le AK^\alpha\theta,$

where a prime denotes next period's variables. First, we have to find a function $v(k, \theta)$ that satisfies the functional equation. *Given this function,* the right-hand side of (1) is a standard maximization problem whose maximizers are the optimal consumption and capital accumulation plans.

To find the function $v(k, \theta)$, we start with the conjecture that $v(k, \theta) = v_0 + v_1 \ln k + v_2 \ln \theta$; that is, we search over the class of functions of that form parameterized by (v_0, v_1, v_2). To find out whether our conjecture is correct, we solve the right-hand side of (1)

$$\max_{c_t, k_{t+1}} \ln c_t + \beta \left[v_0 + v_1 \ln k_{t+1} + v_2 \int \ln \theta_{t+1} f(\theta_{t+1}) \, d\theta_{t+1}\right],$$

subject to $c_t + k_{t+1} \le Ak_t^\alpha\theta_t.$

The maximizers are

(2) $$c_t = \frac{1}{1 + \beta v_1} Ak_t^\alpha\theta_t, \qquad k_{t+1} = \frac{\beta v_1}{1 + \beta v_1} Ak_t^\alpha\theta_t.$$

Then, substituting these values back into the objective function, we get that the maximized right-hand side of (1) is, under our conjecture,

$$\ln \frac{A}{1 + \beta v_1} + \beta v_1 \ln \frac{\beta v_1}{1 + \beta v_1} + \beta v_0$$

$$+ \beta v_2 \int \ln \theta_{t+1} f(\theta_{t+1}) \, d\theta_{t+1} + \alpha(1 + \beta v_1) \ln k_t + (1 + \beta v_1) \ln \theta_t.$$

Hence, to "recover" the $v(\cdot)$ function as required by (1), we must have that

$$v_1 = \alpha(1 + \beta v_1), \qquad v_2 = (1 + \beta v_1)$$

$$v_0 = \ln \frac{A}{a + \beta v_1} + \beta v_1 \ln \frac{\beta v_1}{1 + \beta v_1} + \beta v_0$$

$$+ \beta v_2 \int \ln \theta_{t+1} f(\theta_{t+1}) \, d\theta_{t+1}.$$

This requirement is satisfied by $v_1 = \alpha/(1 - \alpha\beta)$ and $v_2 = 1/(1 - \alpha\beta)$ and a value for v_0 that depends on the precise form of the density f. For our problem, though, it suffices to convince ourselves that some such value exists. This statement completes our first step, that is, we have "discovered" the value function that satisfies (1).

Now we must find the optimal decision rules, but we have already done so for any value function of the form $v_0 + v_1 \ln k + v_2 \ln \theta$, and the result is the pair of functions (2). The "optimal" consumption and investment plans correspond to those functions evaluated using the "right" v_1; that is, $v_1 = \alpha/(1 - \beta\alpha)$. If we substitute this value of v_1, we get

(3) $$c_t = (1 - \alpha\beta)Ak_t^\alpha \theta_t, \qquad k_{t+1} = \alpha\beta Ak_t^\alpha \theta_t.$$

b. In step (a), we found the "optimal" decision rules. We know that, in a competitive equilibrium of the sort we study, optimal and equilibrium decisions rules coincide. Therefore we can use our "pricing" formulas and (3) in place of c_t.

To find the one-period-ahead contingent price $q(x_{t+1}, x_t)$ where $x_t = (k_t, \theta_t)$, we use the pricing formula

$$q(x', x) = \beta \frac{u'[c(x')]}{u'[c(x)]} f(x', x).$$

In this example

$$c(x') = (1 - \alpha\beta)Ak_{t+1}^\alpha \theta_{t+1}$$
$$c(x) = (1 - \alpha\beta)Ak_t^\alpha \theta_t, \qquad u'(c) = c^{-1},$$

and finally, $f(x_{t+1}, x_t)$—the distribution of next period's state conditional on information available in the current period — is given by

$$f(x_{t+1}, x_t) = \begin{cases} f(\theta_{t+1}) & \text{if } k_{t+1} = \alpha\beta k_t^\alpha\theta_t \\ 0 & \text{otherwise.} \end{cases}$$

This particular form of the transition density simply reflects the fact that part of the state sector, k_{t+1}, is a fixed function of the state at t.

Substituting, we get

$$q[(\theta_{t+1}, k_{t+1}), (\theta_t, k_t)] = \beta \frac{(1-\alpha\beta)Ak_t^\alpha\theta_t}{(1-\alpha\beta)A(\alpha\beta Ak_t^\alpha\theta_t)^\alpha\theta_{t+1}} f(\theta_{t+1})$$

$$= \frac{\beta}{(\alpha\beta A)^\alpha} k_t^{\alpha(1-\alpha)}\theta_t^{1-\alpha}\theta_{t+1}^{-1} f(\theta_{t+1}).$$

Now, to compute $q^{(2)}(x_{t+2}, x_t)$, we use the result that $q^{(2)}(x_{t+2}, x_t) = \int q(x_{t+2}, x)q(x, x_t)\, dx$, which follows from an arbitrage argument. Then

$$q(x, x_t) = \frac{\beta}{(\alpha\beta A)^\alpha} k_t^{\alpha(1-\alpha)}\theta_t^{1-\alpha}\theta^{-1}f(\theta)$$

and

$$q(x_{t+2}, x) = \frac{\beta k^{\alpha(1-\alpha)}}{(\alpha\beta A)^\alpha} \theta^{1-\alpha}\theta_{t+2}^{-1} f(\theta_{t+2}),$$

but $k = \beta\alpha Ak_t^\alpha\theta_t$ if $q(x_{t+2}, x)$ is nonzero. Hence

$$q(x_{t+2}, x) = \frac{\beta(\beta\alpha A)^{\alpha(1-\alpha)}}{(\alpha\beta A)^\alpha} k_t^{\alpha^2(1-\alpha)}\theta^{1-\alpha}\theta_t^{\alpha(1-\alpha)}\theta_{t+2}^{-1} f(\theta_{t+2}),$$

$$q^{(2)}(x_{t+2}, x_t) = \int \frac{\beta}{(\alpha\beta A)^{\alpha^2}} k_t^{\alpha^2(1-\alpha)}\theta_t^{\alpha(1-\alpha)}\theta_{t+2}^{-1} f(\theta_{t+2})\theta^{1-\alpha}$$

$$\cdot \frac{\beta k_t^{\alpha(1-\alpha)}}{(\alpha\beta A)^\alpha} \theta_t^{1-\alpha}\theta^{-1}f(\theta)\, d\theta$$

$$= \frac{\beta^2}{(\alpha\beta A)^{\alpha+\alpha^2}} k_t^{\alpha(1-\alpha^2)}\theta_t^{(1-\alpha^2)}\theta_{t+2}^{-1} f(\theta_{t+2})E(\theta_{t+1}^{-\alpha}).$$

c. To compute the risk-free rate of interest, we can use the prices for consumption contingent on the state of the economy. In particular in Section 3.5, *DMT*, it was proved that $R_{1t}^{-1} = \int q(x', x)\, dx'$. Then

$$R_{1t}^{-1} = \int \frac{\beta}{(\alpha\beta A)^\alpha} k_t^{\alpha(1-\alpha)}\theta_t^{1-\alpha}\theta_{t+1}^{-1} f(\theta_{t+1})\, d\theta_{t+1}$$

$$= \frac{\beta}{(\alpha\beta A)^\alpha} k_t^{\alpha(1-\alpha)}\theta_t^{1-\alpha}E[\theta_{t+1}^{-1}].$$

Similarly it can be shown that $R_{2t}^{-1} = \int q^{(2)}(x', x)\, dx'$. Therefore it follows

that

$$R_{2t}^{-1} = \frac{\beta^2}{(\alpha\beta A)^{(\alpha+\alpha_2)}} k_t^{\alpha(1-\alpha^2)}\theta_t^{(1-\alpha^2)}E(\theta_{t+2}^{-1})E(\theta_{t+1}^{-\alpha}).$$

EXERCISE 3.3   Trees (Stocks) in the Utility Function

Consider the following version of Lucas's tree economy. There are two kinds of trees. The first kind is ugly and gives no direct utility in itself but yields a stream of fruit $\{d_{1t}\}$, where d_{1t} is a positive random process obeying a first-order Markov process. The fruit is nonstorable and gives utility. The second kind of tree is beautiful and so yields utility in itself. This tree also yields a stream of the same kind of fruit $\{d_{2t}\}$, where it happens that $d_{2t} \equiv d_{1t} \equiv (1/2)d_t$ for all t, so that the physical yields of the two kinds of trees are equal. There is one of each kind of tree for each of the N individuals in the economy. Trees last forever, but the fruit is not storable. Trees are the only source of fruit.

Each of the N individuals in the economy has preferences described by

$$E_0 \sum_{t=0}^{\infty} \beta^t u(c_t, s_{2t}),$$

where $u(c_t, s_{2t}) = \ln c_t + \gamma \ln s_{2t}$, $\gamma \geq 0$, where c_t is consumption of fruit in period t and s_{2t} is the stock of beautiful trees owned at the beginning of period t. The owner of a tree of either kind i at the beginning of a period receives the fruit d_{it} produced by the tree during that period.

Let p_{it} be the price of a tree of type i ($i = 1, 2$) during period t. Let R_{it} be the gross rate of return on trees of type i held from t to $(t + 1)$. Consider a rational expectations competitive equilibrium of this economy with markets in stocks of each kind of tree.

a. Find pricing functions mapping the state of the economy at t into p_{1t} and p_{2t} (give precise formulas).

b. Prove that, if $\gamma > 0$, then $R_{1t} > R_{2t}$ for all t (that is, beautiful trees are dominated in rate of return).

SOLUTION

We start by noting that the "optimal"—and competitive—allocation in this economy is trivially given by $c_t = d_{1t} + d_{2t} = d_t$, and the whole "stock" of type 2 trees is "consumed." Given that we know the competitive allocation, we can proceed to the second stage of the three-step procedure outlined in Chapter 3, *DMT,* and concentrate on computing prices.

a. We want to find asset prices as a function of the state. Recall that the problem faced by an agent is to maximize

$$E \sum_{t=0}^{\infty} \beta^t (\ln c_t + \gamma \ln s_{2t})$$

subject to $p_{1t}s_{1t+1} + p_{2t}s_{2t+1} + c_t \leq (p_{1t} + d_{1t})s_{1t} + (p_{2t} + d_{2t})s_{2t}.$

Denote $R_{it} = (p_{it+1} + d_{it+1})/p_{it}.$

This problem is a version of the stochastic control problems in Chapter 1, *DMT*, where the controls at t are $(c_t, s_{2t+1}, s_{1t+1})$ and the state $(s_{1t}, s_{2t}, d_{1t}, d_{2t}, p_{1t}, p_{2t})$. The Euler equations for this problem are

$$c_t^{-1} = \beta E_t \{ c_{t+1}^{-1} R_{1t} \}, \qquad c_t^{-1} = \beta E_t \left\{ c_{t+1}^{-1} R_{2t} + \frac{\gamma}{p_{2t}s_{2t+1}} \right\}.$$

We already know, however, that, in equilibrium, $c_t = d_t$ and $s_{2t} = s_2 = 1$, as there is *one* tree per individual. Hence the two Euler equations are

$$p_{1t}d_t^{-1} = \beta E_t \{ d_{t+1}^{-1} (p_{1t+1} + d_{1t+1}) \},$$
$$p_{2t}d_t^{-1} = \beta E_t \{ d_{t+1}^{-1} (p_{2t+1} + d_{2t+1}) + \gamma \}.$$

Using the equation for pricing a sequence of dividends, that is,

$$p_t = E_t \left\{ \sum_{j=1}^{\infty} \beta^j \frac{u'(d_{t+j})}{u'(d_t)} d_{1t+j} \right\},$$

we get

$$p_1(d_t) = \frac{\beta}{1-\beta} \frac{1}{2} d_t.$$

To find $p_2(d_t)$, we can use the second Euler equation recursively to find an expression for p_{2t} as was done in Chapter 3, *DMT*. Here we use the alternative method of conjecturing that p_{2t} is a linear function of d_t; that is, we conjecture that $p_2(d_t) = kd_t$, some k. We substitute this conjecture into the Euler equation to get

$$k = \beta E_t \left\{ d_{t+1}^{-1} \left(kd_{t+1} + \frac{1}{2} d_{t+1} \right) + \gamma \right\}, \qquad k = \beta k + \frac{\beta}{2} + \beta\gamma.$$

Therefore our guess is verified if and only if $k = (\beta\gamma + \beta/2)/(1-\beta)$. Then we have

$$p_2(d_t) = \left(\beta\gamma + \frac{\beta}{2} \right) \frac{1}{1-\beta} d_t$$

Notice that we showed that

$$p_2(d_t) = p_1(d_t) + \frac{\beta\gamma}{1-\beta} d_t.$$

In other words, beautiful trees are more expensive $p_{2t} > p_{1t}$ for every t.

b. Now, using our definition of R_{it}, we have

$$R_{2t} = \frac{p_{1t+1} + \frac{1}{2} d_{t+1} + \frac{\beta\gamma}{1-\beta} d_{t+1}}{p_{1t} + \frac{\beta\gamma}{1-\beta} d_t}, \qquad R_{1t} = \frac{p_{1t+1} + \frac{1}{2} d_{t+1}}{p_{1t}}.$$

Then it follows that

$$R_{2t} = \frac{p_{1t+1} + \frac{1}{2} d_{t+1}}{p_{1t}} \frac{p_{1t}}{p_{1t} + \frac{\beta\gamma}{1-\beta} d_t} + \frac{\frac{\beta\gamma}{1-\beta} d_t}{p_{1t} + \frac{\beta\gamma}{1-\beta} d_t} \frac{\frac{\beta\gamma}{1-\beta} d_{t+1}}{\frac{\beta\gamma}{1-\beta} d_t}.$$

Denote $p_{1t}/\{p_{1t} + [\beta\gamma/(1-\beta)]\, d_t\} \equiv \theta_t, 0 < \theta_t < 1$. Then

$$R_{2t} = R_{1t}\theta_t + (1-\theta_t)\frac{d_{t+1}}{d_t},$$

$$R_{2t} - R_{1t} = (1-\theta_t)\left[\frac{d_{t+1}}{d_t} - R_{1t}\right],$$

but

$$R_{1t} = \frac{\frac{\beta}{1-\beta}\frac{1}{2} d_{t+1} + \frac{1}{2} d_{t+1}}{\frac{\beta}{1-\beta}\frac{1}{2} d_t} = \frac{\beta^{-1} d_{t+1}}{d_t}.$$

Therefore

$$R_{2t} - R_{1t} = (1-\theta_t)\frac{d_{t+1}}{d_t}(1 - \beta^{-1}) < 0$$

whenever $\gamma > 0$.

Notice that $\gamma = 0$ implies that $\theta_t = 1$ and hence that there is no rate-of-return dominance.

EXERCISE 3.4   Government Debt in the Utility Function

Take the model of Section 3.7, but replace preferences with the alternative

$$E_0 \sum_{t=0}^{\infty} \beta^t u(c_t, b_{gt+1}/R_{gt}),$$

where $u_{12} \neq 0$. Is the rate of return in private securities independent of the government financing decision?

SOLUTION

The representative agent solves

$$\max E_0 \sum_{t=0}^{\infty} \beta^t u\left(c_t, \frac{b_{gt+1}}{R_{gt}}\right)$$

subject to $c_t + \dfrac{b_{gt+1}}{R_{gt}} + p_t s_{t+1} + \tau_t \leq (p_t + d_t)s_t + b_{gt}.$

We know that the equilibrium consumption satisfies $c_t = d_t - g_t$. We also know that in equilibrium $s_t = 1$ and $g_t = \tau_t + (b_{gt+1})/(R_{gt}) - b_{gt}$.

The Euler equations for this problem are

$$u_1\left(c_t, \frac{b_{gt+1}}{R_{gt}}\right) p_t = \beta E_t \left\{ u_1\left(c_{t+1}, \frac{b_{gt+2}}{R_{gt+1}}\right)(p_{t+1} + d_{t+1}) \right\}$$

$$\left[u_1\left(c_t, \frac{b_{gt+1}}{R_{gt}}\right) + u_2\left(c_t, \frac{b_{gt+1}}{R_{gt}}\right) \right] R_{gt}^{-1} = \beta E_t \left\{ u_1\left(c_{t+1}, \frac{b_{gt+2}}{R_{gt+1}}\right) \right\}.$$

Now consider a change in b_{gt+1} that leaves (c_t, g_t) unchanged and hence requires an adjustment in taxes. Moreover, assume that c_{t+1}, g_{t+1}, b_{gt+2}, R_{gt+1} also remain unchanged so that we can analyze the effect of b_{gt+1} upon R_{gt} and p_t. (This can always be done by suitable choice of τ_t and τ_{t+1}.) Differentiating the Euler equations we get

$$p_t u_{12}(\,\cdot\,)\left(R_{gt}^{-1} - b_{gt+1} R_{gt}^{-2}\frac{dR_{gt}}{db_{gt+1}} \right) + u_1(\,\cdot\,)\frac{dp_t}{db_{gt+1}} = 0$$

$$(u_{12} + u_{22})\left(R_{gt}^{-1} - b_{gt+1} R_{gt}^{-2}\frac{dR_{gt}}{db_{gt+1}} \right) = \frac{dR_{gt}}{db_{gt+1}} R_{gt}^{-2}(u_1 + u_2).$$

This equation can be rearranged to read

$$\frac{b_{gt+1}}{R_{gt}}\frac{dR_{gt}}{db_{gt+1}} = \frac{b_{gt+1}(u_{12} + u_{22})}{b_{gt+1}(u_{12} + u_{22}) + (u_1 + u_2)}.$$

For fixed c, define $f(b/R) \equiv u_1(c, b/R) + u_2(c, b/R)$. The previous formula for the elasticity of the return on government bonds can be written as

$$\frac{b}{R}\frac{dR}{db} = \frac{bf'\left(\dfrac{b}{R}\right)}{bf'\left(\dfrac{b}{R}\right) + f\left(\dfrac{b}{R}\right)}.$$

If we assume that $f'(b/R) = u_{12} + u_{22} < 0$, it follows that, if $(dR/db) \cdot b/R \geq 0$, then $(dR/db) \cdot b/R \geq 1$.

Now, the first equation of the system can be written (neglecting subindexes) as

$$\frac{dp}{db} = -u_1^{-1}\left\{pu_{12}R^{-1}\left(1 - \frac{b}{R}\frac{dR}{db}\right)\right\}.$$

If $(dR/db) \cdot b/R \geq 1$ and $u_{12} > 0$, $dp/db \geq 0$. If $(dR/db) \cdot b/R < 0$ and $u_{12} > 0$, then $dp/db < 0$.

Now as $(p_{t+1} + d_{t+1})$ is unaffected by the experiment being conducted, we have that $\text{sign}(dR_{pt}/dR_{gt}) = -\text{sign}[(dp/db) \cdot (dR/db)]$. For the two cases described above, we have that $dR_{pt}/dR_{gt} < 0$. Notice that, if $u_{12} = 0$, changes in b_{gt+1} do not affect the rate of return on private securities.

To sum up, when government debt enters the utility function, different tax-debt combinations that finance a given stochastic process for government expenditures g_t affect not only the rate of return of assets issued by the government but also the rate of return on private assets. The direction of the effect depends on the form of the utility function. A necessary condition for dependence of the two rates of return is that the utility function not be separable in private consumption and the value of government debt.

EXERCISE 3.5   Tobin's q

Consider a version of Lucas's one-kind-of-tree model in which "fruit" is storable with no physical depreciation. Letting k_t be the amount of fruit stored per representative agent from time $(t - 1)$ to time t, the social planning problem is: maximize $E_0 \sum_{t=0}^{\infty} \beta^t u(c_t)$, subject to $c_t + k_{t+1} \leq (d_t + k_t)$ and $k_{t+1} \geq 0$ for all $(t + 1)$. Notice that only nonnegative amounts of fruit can be stored. Assume that dividends follow a Markov process with transition $f(d', d)$. The social planner chooses sequences $\{c_t, k_{t+1}\}$.

a. Let $v(k + d, d)$ be the value function for the social planning problem. Show that the marginal conditions for the social planning problem imply

that

$$\beta \int v_1(k' + d', d')f(d', d)\, dd' \leq u'(c),$$

with equality if $k' > 0$.

b. Now imagine a competitive equilibrium with markets in trees and stocks of capital (stores of fruit). The representative consumer faces the problem of maximizing $E_0\sum_{t=0}^{\infty}\beta^t u(c_t)$, subject to

$$c_t + p_{kt}k_{t+1} + p_t s_{t+1} \leq s_t(p_t + d_t) + k_t$$
$$k_{t+1} \geq 0,$$

where p_{kt} is the price of capital, p_t the price of trees, s_t number of trees held at the beginning of time t, and k_t the number of units of fruit held over from time $(t-1)$. Show that in equilibrium the prices of trees and capital obey the conditions

$$p_t = \beta E_t\left[\frac{u'(c_{t+1})}{u'(c_t)}(p_{t+1} + d_{t+1})\right]$$

$$p_{kt} > \beta E_t\left[\frac{u'(c_{t+1})}{u'(c_t)}\right], \quad = \quad \text{if } k_{t+1} > 0.$$

c. Show that, in this model, given the pair (d_t, k_t), investment $(k_{t+1} - k_t)$ is positively correlated with Tobin's q, that is, p_k, which is the price of the existing stock of capital relative to the cost of newly produced goods (fruit).

SOLUTION

In this exercise we will need to differentiate the value function at a "corner." In principle the results of Benveniste and Scheinkman (1979) are not directly applicable. Sargent (1980) has analyzed this case, however, and has shown that the expression derived in Chapter 1, *DMT*, remains valid.

a. We know that the optimal value for this problem is a function $v(\,\cdot\,)$ that satisfies the following functional equation

$$v(k + d, d) = \max_{c, k'}\left\{u(c) + \beta \int v(k' + d', d')f(d', d)\, dd'\right\}$$

subject to $c + k' \leq k + d, \quad c, k' \geq 0$.

We assume that $v(\,\cdot\,)$ is known and concentrate on the decision rules that achieve the maximum on the right-hand side.

Let λ be a nonnegative Lagrange multiplier associated with the feasibility constraint. The first-order conditions (that are necessary and sufficient, given concavity) are

$$c: \quad u'(c) - \lambda \leq 0, \qquad = 0 \quad \text{if } c > 0$$

$$k': \quad \beta \int v_1(k' + d', d') f(d', d) \, dd' - \lambda \leq 0, \qquad = 0 \quad \text{if } k' > 0.$$

If $k + d > 0$ and the utility function has enough curvature, we will always get an interior solution for c. In this case, the second condition becomes $\beta \int v_1(k' + d', d') f(d', d) \, dd' \leq u'(c)$, with equality if $k' > 0$.

b. Let the value function for this competitive problem be $w(\cdot)$. We know from Chapter 1, *DMT,* that $w(\cdot)$ has to satisfy the relevant version of Bellman's equation. At the individual level, the state variable (the variable of minimal dimension that is sufficient to describe the current and future choices open to the individual), is simply the vector containing wealth, $s(p + d) + k$ and the value of d. As in (a), we concentrate on the optimal decision rules, that is, on the maximizers of

$$\max \left\{ u(c) + \beta \int w[s'(p' + d') + k', d'] f(d', d) \, dd' \right\}$$

subject to $\quad c + p_k k' + p s' \leq s(p + d) + k, \qquad (c, k', s') \geq 0.$

The first-order conditions are

$$c: \quad u'(c) - \lambda \leq 0, \qquad = 0 \quad \text{if } c > 0$$

$$k': \quad \beta \int w_1[s'(p' + d') + k', d'] f(d', d) \, dd' - \lambda p_k \leq 0,$$

$$= 0 \quad \text{if } k' > 0$$

$$s': \quad \beta \int w_1[s'(p' + d') + k', d'](p' + d') f(d', d) \, dd' - \lambda p \leq 0,$$

$$= 0 \quad \text{if } s' > 0.$$

Because we can assume that $c > 0$, and in equilibrium monotonicity of preferences guarantees that trees will be held by some agent (otherwise some "fruit" would not be consumed), we have

$$u'(c)p = \beta \int w_1[s'(p' + d') + k', d'](p' + d') f(d, d') \, dd'$$

$$u'(c)p_k \leq \beta \int w_1[s'(p' + d') + k', d'] f(d, d') \, dd'.$$

Still, the formula for the derivative of the value function indicates that

$w_1[s(p+d)+k, d] = u'(c)$. Therefore the previous two equations can be written (explicitly taking into account the subindexes) as

$$p_t = \beta E_t \left\{ \frac{u'(c_{t+1})}{u'(c_t)} (p_{t+1} + d_{t+1}) \right\}, \qquad p_{kt} \le \beta E_t \left\{ \frac{u'(c_{t+1})}{u'(c_t)} \right\},$$

with equality if $k_{t+1} > 0$.

c. Notice that in this economy, the price of existing capital—k_t at time t—is one. This is so because existing capital and the consumption good are in fact the same good. On the other hand, k_{t+1} is different from c_t and at $(t+1)$ will be equivalent to c_{t+1}. One way to understand the difference is to regard k_{t+1} as "seeds" of corn that are planted and will yield exactly the same number of seeds, or kernels, of corn. Before the agents decide to plant them, they are equivalent to c_t (this is a consequence of the linearity of the technology). Once they have been planted, they cannot be dug out of the ground until next period, when they are again "corn." Then k_t—which was planted at $(t-1)$—is the same good as c_t, and k_{t+1}, which is also seed but is already in the ground, is a different good at t.

In this interpretation the price of newly produced capital, k_{t+1}, can be thought of as

$$p_{kt} \equiv \alpha_t \beta E_t \left\{ \frac{u'(c_{t+1})}{u'(c_t)} \right\},$$

where $\alpha_t = 1$ if $\bar{k}_{t+1} > 0$, and $\alpha_t < 1$ if $\bar{k}_{t+1} = 0$ and $\bar{k}_{t+1}$ is interpreted as the solution to the planner's problem which—in equilibrium—coincides with the choices of the representative agent, k_{t+1}.

Let (d_t, k_t) be given. Then conditional on this variable, k_{t+1} is higher (either positive or zero), the higher p_{kt}. To establish the stronger result that this also holds unconditionally, we would need to describe how the planner's choice of k_{t+1} depends on $(k_t + d_t)$, and this lies outside the scope of the present exercise.

EXERCISE 3.6   A Generalization of Logarithmic Preferences

Consider an economy with a single representative consumer who maximizes

$$E \sum_{t=0}^{\infty} \beta^t u(c_t), \qquad 0 < \beta < 1, \qquad \text{where}$$

$$u(c_t) = \ln(c_t + \alpha), \qquad \alpha \neq 0.$$

The sole source of the single good is an everlasting tree that produces d_t units of the consumption good in period t. At the beginning of time 0, each consumer owns one such tree. The dividend process d_t is Markov, with

$$\text{prob}\{d_{t+1} \le d' | d_t = d\} = F(d', d).$$

Assume that the conditional density $f(d', d)$ of F exists. There are competitive markets in titles to trees and in state-contingent claims. Let p_t be the price at t of a title to all *future* dividends from the tree.

a. Prove that equilibrium price p_t satisfies

$$p_t = (d_t + \alpha) \sum_{j=1}^{\infty} \beta^j E_t \left(\frac{d_{t+j}}{d_{t+j} + \alpha} \right).$$

b. Find a formula for the risk-free one-period interest rate R_{1t}. Prove that, in the special case in which $\{d_t\}$ is independently and identically distributed, R_{1t} is given by $R_{1t}^{-1} = \beta k(d_t + \alpha)$, where k is a constant. Give a formula for k.

c. Find a formula for the risk-free two-period interest rate R_{2t}. Prove that, in the special case in which d_t is independently and identically distributed, R_{2t} is given by $R_{2t}^{-1} = \beta^2 k(d_t + \alpha)$, where k is the same constant that you found in part b.

SOLUTION

a. The problem faced by the representative consumer is

$$\max E_0 \sum_{t=0}^{\infty} \beta^t u(c_t)$$

$$\text{subject to} \quad c_t + p_t s_{t+1} + \int q(x_{t+1}, x_t) y(x_{t+1}) \, dx_{t+1}$$

$$\le (p_t + d_t) s_t + y(x_t),$$

where $y(x_{t+1})$ is the net amount of date $(t+1)$ good contingent on the state of the economy at $(t+1)$, being x_{t+1}, $q(x_{t+1}, x_t)$ is the price of such a contingent commodity and s_{t+1} is the number of titles to trees bought by the consumer at time t. On the other hand, wealth is given by the value of the trees the agent owns plus dividends, $(p_t + d_t) s_t$, and $y(x_t)$ units of c_t bought (or issued if negative) yesterday.

In this economy the state x_t is simply dividends, d_t. Because we know that in equilibrium $c_t = d_t$, all t, we will use the Euler equations of the representative agent maximization problem to find the corresponding prices. The optimization problem is

$$\max_{c,s',y(x')} \left\{ u(c) + \beta \int v[(p' + d')s' + y(x'), x']f(x', x)\, dx' \right\}$$

subject to $c + ps' + \int q(x', x)y(x')\, dx' \le (p + d)s + y(x),$

where a prime denotes next-period values and $v(\,\cdot\,)$ is the unique solution to Bellman's equation (for details, see Chapter 1, *DMT*).

Forming the Lagrangian (or Hamiltonian) for this problem and differentiating with respect to the controls, we obtain the following first-order conditions:

$$u'(c) \le \lambda, \quad = 0 \;\; \text{if } c > 0$$

$$\beta \int v_1[(p' + d')s' + y(x'), x'](p' + d')f(x', x)\, dx' - \lambda p \le 0,$$

$$= 0 \;\; \text{if } s' > 0$$

$$\beta v_1[(p' + d')s' + y(x'), x']f(x', x) = \lambda q(x', x),$$

where in the last equation equality holds, because there are no constraints on the sign of $y(x')$. Using the formula given by Benveniste and Scheinkman (1979) for the derivative of the value function, we have $v_1[(p' + d')s' + y(x'), x'] = u(c').$

Substituting this equation in the first-order condition gives, if $s' > 0$,

$$q(x', x) = \beta \frac{u'[c(x')]}{u'[c(x)]} f(x', x),$$

$$u'[c(x)]p(x) = \beta \int u'[c(x')][p(x') + d(x')]f(x', x)\, dx'.$$

For the problem at hand, with $u(c) = \ln(c + \alpha)$, the last equation can be written as

$$p_t = \beta E_t \left\{ \frac{\alpha + c_t}{\alpha + c_{t+1}} (p_{t+1} + d_{t+1}) \right\}.$$

Still equilibrium (which we are free to impose now but could not do before this step) implies that $c_t = d_t$ and $s_t = 1$, all t.

$$p_t = (d_t + \alpha)\left[\beta E_t\left(\frac{p_{t+1}}{\alpha + d_{t+1}}\right) + \beta E_t\left(\frac{d_{t+1}}{\alpha + d_{t+1}}\right)\right]$$

$$p_t = (d_t + \alpha)\left[\beta^2 E_t\left(\frac{p_{t+2}}{\alpha + d_{t+2}}\right) + \beta^2 E_t\left(\frac{d_{t+2}}{\alpha + d_{t+2}}\right)\right.$$
$$\left. + \beta E_t\left(\frac{d_{t+1}}{\alpha + d_{t+1}}\right)\right],$$

where we use the fact that $E_t[E_{t+1}(z)] = E_t z$, because the information set available at $(t + 1)$ is assumed to be strictly "larger" than that at t. If we iterate N times, we have

$$p_t = (d_t + \alpha)\left[\beta^N E_t\left(\frac{p_{t+N}}{\alpha + d_{t+N}}\right) + \sum_{j=1}^{N} \beta^j E_t\left(\frac{d_{t+j}}{\alpha + d_{t+j}}\right)\right].$$

Notice that, if $p_{t+N}/(\alpha + d_{t+N})$ is such that its rate of growth in expectation is less than $1/\beta$, when we take limits $N \to \infty$, the first term on the right side should disappear. We make such a conjecture, and we later verify it. Therefore, taking limits as $N \to \infty$ on both sides, we have

$$p_t = (d_t + \alpha) \sum_{j=1}^{\infty} \beta^j E_t\left[\frac{d_{t+j}}{d_{t+j} + \alpha}\right].$$

It is easy to see that $\beta^t p_t/(d_t + \alpha)$ goes to zero in expectation if the process $\{d_t\}$ has a finite expectation, which verifies our conjecture.

b. Recall that a risk-free bond is defined as a security that pays one unit of consumption in every state of nature. It is equivalent to buying a contingent claim to consumption tomorrow for every possible state of nature. Simple arbitrage arguments show that the cost of those two "forms" of securing consumption sould be the same. (For an argument, see Chapter 3, *DMT.*) Then if $R_1(x)$ is the risk-free one-period interest rate, we have

$$R_1(x)^{-1} = \int q(x', x)\, dx', \quad \text{all } x,$$

where the right side is the price that must be paid in the contingent market for all the contracts necessary to obtain one unit of $c(x')$ for every x'.

Still, we found in (a) a formula for $q(x', x)$. When we use the particular utility function of this example, we get

$$q(x', x) = \beta \frac{c(x) + \alpha}{c(x') + \alpha} f(x', x),$$

$$R_{1t}^{-1} = \beta \int \frac{\alpha + d_t}{\alpha + d_{t+1}} f(d_{t+1}, d_t) \, dd_{t+1}.$$

If $\{d_t\}$ is an identically and independently distributed process, the density function $f(d_{t+1}, d_t)$, if it exists, does not depend on d_t. In that case, the formula is

$$R_{1t}^{-1} = \beta \left[\int \frac{1}{z + \alpha} f(z) \, dz \right] (d_t + \alpha) \equiv \beta k (\alpha + d_t)$$

and
$$k = \int \frac{1}{z + \alpha} f(z) \, dz = E \frac{1}{d_{t+1} + \alpha}.$$

c. A two-period, risk-free bond at t promises to pay one unit of consumption two periods in the future no matter what the state of nature is (i.e., for all states of nature) at $(t + 1)$ and $(t + 2)$. In order to get the same pattern of return buying (or selling) contracts in the market for contingent claims, we can do the following.

i. Consider the price of a contract (when the state of nature at t is x_t) that pays one unit of consumption if the state at $(t + 2)$ is x_{t+2} and the state at $(t + 1)$ is x_{t+1} and zero otherwise. If we work "backwards," it is clear that, at $(t + 1)$ if the state is x_{t+1}, such a contract will sell for $q(x_{t+2}, x_{t+1})$ and zero otherwise. The reason is that under these circumstances the contract we analyze and a standard state-contingent contract are indistinguishable. Therefore we have to price at t a contract that "tomorrow" (at $t + 1$) will be worth $q(x_{t+2}, x_{t+1})$ if the state is x_{t+1} and zero otherwise. Notice that the "value" of the contract at $(t + 1)$ is given in units of consumption at that date. Still we know how to price such one-period-ahead contingent contracts. The market value is simply $q(x_{t+1}, x_t) q(x_{t+2}, x_{t+1})$ [i.e., a contract that pays N units at $(t + 1)$ is worth $q(x_{t+1}, x_t)N$]. Denote this price $q^*(x_{t+2}, x_{t+1}, x_t)$.

ii. To achieve the desired pattern of consumption, we have to buy as many contracts as there are combinations of (x_{t+2}, x_{t+1}) that can occur. The price of those contracts is simply given by

$$\int_{x_{t+2}} \int_{x_{t+1}} q^*(x_{t+2}, x_{t+1}, x_t) \, dx_{t+1} \, dx_{t+2}.$$

Then the price of a two-period, risk-free bond and of such a combination of contracts should be the same, because otherwise buying one and selling the other can result in an instantaneous profit that is inconsistent with equilibrium. Consequently we must have

$$R_{2t}^{-1} = \int_{x_{t+2}} \int_{x_{t+1}} q(x_{t+2}, x_{t+1}) q(x_{t+1}, x_t) \, dx_{t+1} \, dx_{t+2}$$

$$= \beta^2 \int_{x_{t+2}} \int_{x_{t+1}} \frac{c(x_t) + \alpha}{c(x_{t+2}) + \alpha}$$

$$\cdot f(x_{t+2}, x_{t+1}) f(x_{t+1}, x_t) \, dx_{t+1} \, dx_{t+2}$$

$$= \beta^2 (d_t + \alpha) \int \frac{1}{\alpha + d_{t+2}} f^{(2)}(d_{t+2}, d_t) \, dd_t$$

where $f^{(2)}(x_{t+2}, x_t) = \int_{x_{t+1}} f(x_{t+2}, x_{t+1}) f(x_{t+1}, x_t) \, dx_{t+1}$

is the two-period-ahead transition density. In the i.i.d. case, we have, as before, that $f(x_{t+1}, x_t) = f(x_{t+1})$ all (x_{t+1}, x_t). Then the formula is

$$R_{2t}^{-1} = \beta^2 (d_t + \alpha) \int \frac{1}{\alpha + d_{t+2}} f(d_{t+2})$$

$$\cdot \left[\int f(d_{t+1}) \, dd_{t+1} \right] dd_{t+2}.$$

If $f(\cdot)$ is a density, however, it follows that $\int f(x) \, dx = 1$ when integrated over the whole space, as we are doing. Therefore we get

$$R_{2t}^{-1} = \beta^2 (d_t + \alpha) \, E \frac{1}{d_{t+2} + \alpha}.$$

EXERCISE 3.7 Arbitrage Pricing

At t when $x_t = x$, an asset A promises to pay off $w(x')$ when $x_{t+1} = x'$. The price of this asset at t, p_{At}, is given by the function $p_{At} = g(x_t)$. Construct an argument to show that, unless $g(x) = \int w(x') q(x', x) \, dx'$, there exist arbitrage opportunities.

SOLUTION

The basic insight needed to solve this problem comes from the interpretation of the pricing kernel $q(x', x)$. It basically says that the price today of a contract that offers to deliver one unit of the consumption good in state B

and zero otherwise is given by $\int_B q(x', x)\, dx'$. Consider, then, the value of a contract that is a promise to deliver $w(x')$ units of the consumption good in state x'. The value of such a contract is simply $V_w(x) = \int w(x')q(x', x)\, dx'$. Now suppose $g(x) < \int w(x')q(x', x)\, dx'$, that is, the asset is "undervalued." A trader can sell a contract and raise $V_w(x)$ units of consumption. Part of this amount is used to purchase the asset of $g(x)$. The difference $[V_w(x) - g(x)]$ is pure profits, because the liabilities that the trader will have next period [the payment of $w(x')$ units of the good in state x'] are perfectly matched with his assets [the trader also gets $w(x')$ units in state x' from the asset he buys]. Because there are constant returns to scale in this activity—that is, if the trader sells N contracts and buys N assets to back the contracts, profits are $N[V_w(x) - g(x)]$—the optimal scale is infinite, which cannot possibly be the case in equilibrium. Therefore the *equilibrium* price of the asset $g(x)$ must be greater than or equal to $\int w(x')q(x', x)\, dx'$. Using a symmetric argument that involves selling instead of buying the asset, one can show that $g(x) \leq V_w(x)$. In other words, we have shown that $g(x) \geq V_w(x)$ and $g(x) \leq V_w(x)$. Thus $g(x) = V_w(x)$.

EXERCISE 3.8   Modigliani-Miller

An agent L lives in a Lucas tree economy with a very large number of other agents. The one-step-ahead equilibrium pricing kernel in this economy is $q(x', x)$. At time t, the agent L is given a gift of a lottery ticket that has a nonnegative function $w(x')$ written on it. The lottery ticket entitles its owner to receive $w(x')$ units of consumption good at time $(t + 1)$ contingent on $(x_{t+1} = x')$.

Agent L decides to sell claims to parts of her lottery ticket in order to increase her consumption of time t goods. She proceeds as follows. She plans to sell B units of bonds bearing coupon rate R, a fixed number. Each bond will pay off at $(t + 1)$ as follows:

> payoff per bond if $w(x') \geq RB$: R
> payoff per bond if $w(x') \leq RB$: $w(x')/B$.

In addition to selling bonds, agent L sells equities in the amount of S shares. Each unit of equities promises to pay off as follows:

> payoff per share if $w(x') \geq RB$: $[w(x') - RB]/S$
> payoff per share if $w(x') \leq RB$: 0.

The agent chooses the coupon rate R and numbers of bonds and shares, B and S, to maximize the value of the lottery ticket. If we let $p_B(t)$ be the price of the bonds and $p_s(t)$ the price of the shares, the value of the lottery ticket in time t goods is $p_B(t)B + p_s(t)S$.

a. Use an arbitrage argument to find formulas for $p_B(t)$ and $p_s(t)$ in terms of $q(x', x)$.

b. Find the value of the lottery ticket $p_B(t)B + p_s(t)S$ as a function of B, S, R, $w(x')$, and $q(x', x)$.

c. What values of R, B, and S does agent L choose?

SOLUTION

In this exercise, as in the previous one, we use a basic result derived in the text, namely that, if we are given the pricing kernel, that is, the price of a contract that delivers one unit of the consumption good if a given state is realized in the following period and zero otherwise, we can price *any* bundle of goods. Because we can identify assets with the bundles to which they are claims, we have a straightforward procedure to price assets: first identify precisely the bundle of goods associated with the asset, then price that bundle.

We first derive the value of the lottery, or the amount that the individual can raise from the sale of equity alone. The lottery is a claim to $w(x')$ units of the consumption good in state x'. Therefore the value of this bundle is given by

$$V(x) = \int w(x')q(x', x)\, dx'.$$

Clearly if N shares are issued, the price per share is just $V(x)/N$.

a. We first identify the bundle associated with a bond. A bond is a claim to R units of the good if $w(x') \ge RB$, and to $w(x')/B$ otherwise, where B is the total number of bonds. Then the "bundle" is R for x' such that $w(x') \ge RB$ and $w(x')/B$ otherwise. The price of such a bundle is

$$p_B(x) = \int_{w(x') \ge RB} Rq(x', x)\, dx' + \int_{w(x') < RB} \frac{w(x')}{B} q(x', x)\, dx'$$

$$= R \int_{w(x') \ge RB} q(x', x)\, dx' + \int_{w(x') < RB} \frac{w(x')}{B} q(x', x)\, dx'.$$

A "share," on the other hand, is a claim to the following bundle:

$$\begin{cases} \dfrac{w(x') - RB}{S} & \text{on the set where } w(x') \ge RB \\ 0 & \text{otherwise} \end{cases}$$

Then a price of a share is

$$p_s(x) = \int_{w(x') \geq RB} \frac{w(x') - RB}{S} q(x', x) \, dx'.$$

b. The value of the lottery ticket is the amount that the agent gets by selling "bonds" and "shares" and is given by $p_B(x)B + p_s(x)S$. If we use the formulas we derived in (a), we get

$$p_B(x)B = \int_{w(x') \geq RB} RBq(x', x) \, dx'$$

$$+ \int_{w(x') < RB} w(x')q(x', x) \, dx',$$

$$p_s(x)S = \int_{w(x') \geq RB} (w(x') - RB)q(x', x) \, dx'.$$

Therefore

$$p_B(x)B + p_s(x)S = \int w(x')q(x', x) \, dx' = V(x).$$

c. It is clear that the total value of the lottery ticket is independent of R, S, and B. The intuition is that the nature of the financial instruments does not change the total returns to the lottery. This example illustrates the Modigliani-Miller theorem. The result says that the total value of the firm is independent of its financial structure. In this case, the firm is represented by an exogenous stream of dividends $w(x)$, and its value is independent on its financial structure, that is, on the way its liabilities are divided between bonds and shares. Note that this theory predicts that the capital structure is indeterminate.

EXERCISE 3.9   Arbitrage Pricing and the Term Structure of Interest Rates

Let R_{2t} be the two-period sure rate of interest. Construct an arbitrage argument to show that

$$R_{2t}^{-1} = \int q^{(2)}(x_{t+2}, x_t) \, dx_{t+2}.$$

SOLUTION

We proceed, as in Exercise 3.7, by showing that unless $R_{2t}^{-1} = \int q^{(2)}(x', x) \, dx' = V(x)$, there exist profit opportunities that are inconsistent with an equilibrium.

Suppose $R_{2t}^{-1} < V(x)$. Because $V(x)$ is the value of a contract that promises to deliver one unit of the consumption good two periods ahead, it is possible to fund that contract fully by buying a risk-free bond. The price of such a bond is R_{2t}^{-1}, however, and therefore this activity yields positive profits $[V(x) - R_{2t}^{-1}]$. This cannot be an equilibrium, because we would operate this intermediation activity at an infinite level (we would sell infinitely many contracts and buy infinitely many bonds to fund those contracts). It must therefore be that $R_{2t}^{-1} \geq V(x)$. To show that the expression holds with equality, suppose $R_{2t}^{-1} > V(x)$. In this case, we can sell risk-free bonds and "buy" contracts of price $V(x)$. As before, this activity yields positive profits, which is inconsistent with an equilibrium. We conclude that $V(x) = R_{2t}^{-1}$.

EXERCISE 3.10 Pricing One-Period Options

Consider a one-tree, one-good Lucas tree model. Preferences of the representative agent are

$$E_0 \sum_{t=0}^{\infty} \beta^t u(c_t), \qquad 0 < \beta < 1,$$

where $u(c_t) = \ln c_t$. Each tree gives off a nonstorable "fruit" or dividend x_t where x_t is a nonnegative random variable governed by a Markov process with stationary one-step transition density $f(x', x)$. We assume that, for any x', $\partial F(x', x)/\partial x < 0$. The sign is implied by positive serial correlation of x_t. The economy starts off with each household owning one tree.

a. Derive the equilibrium pricing function, mapping x_t into the price of trees p_t.

b. Derive a formula for the equilibrium kernel $q(x', x)$ for pricing one-step-ahead contingent claims.

c. Consider an "option" that entitles the current owner to exercise the right to buy, but only if the owner chooses to do so, one tree one period into the future at the fixed price $\bar{p}$. The price $\bar{p}$ is known at t, whereas the option to buy is exercised at $(t + 1)$. Let $\sigma(x_t)$ be the function that prices this option at time t. Find a formula for the pricing function $\sigma(x_t)$ in terms of the parameters describing preferences and endowments.

d. Show that, if there are two options at prices $\bar{p}_1$ and $\bar{p}_2$, and $\bar{p}_1 > \bar{p}_2$, then $\sigma(x_t, \bar{p}_1) < \sigma(x_t, \bar{p}_2)$. Prove that the covariance between share prices and option prices is positive.

e. Consider two economies that are identical except for the discount factor β. Show that, in the economy with a higher degree of patience (that is, higher β), the price of trees is higher, and the one-period-ahead risk-free interest rate is lower for each x.

SOLUTION

a. The maximization problem solved by the representative agent in this economy is

$$\max E \left\{ \sum_{t=0}^{\infty} \beta^t u(c_t) \right\}$$

subject to $\quad c_t + p(x_t)s_{t+1} + \int y(x_{t+1})q(x_{t+1}x_t)\, dx_{t+1}$
$$\leq (p(x_t) + x_t)s_t + y(x_t).$$

Where c_t is consumption, s_t is the number of shares or claims to the stream of dividends produced by the tree held at the beginning of period t, and $y(x_{t+1})$ is the number of units of consumption good to be delivered to this agent if x_{t+1} is observed the following period. Finally, $q(x_{t+1}, x_t)$ is the price of one such contract if the current state of the economy is x_t. The first-order conditions for a maximum are

(1) $\qquad u'(c_t)p(x_t) = \beta \int u'(c_{t+1})[p(x_{t+1}) + x_{t+1}]f(x_{t+1}, x_t)\, dx_{t+1}$

(2) $\qquad u'(c_t)q(x_{t+1}x_t) = \beta u'(c_{t+1})f(x_{t+1}, x_t),$

where (1) is obtained by differentiating the Lagrangian associated with the maximization problem with respect to s_{t+1}. The second condition corresponds to the optimal choice of the function $y(x)$.

In this pure exchange one-consumer economy, it is easy to compute the equilibrium choice of c_t, namely $c_t = x_t$. Given that the consumption allocation is known, we can use the first-order conditions to find prices that will support that allocation as the solution to the representative agent maximization problem. Therefore we want a pricing function $p(x)$ that satisfies the functional equation

$$p(x) = \beta \int \frac{u'(x')}{u'(x)} [p(x') + x'] f(x', x)\, dx'.$$

Because $u(c) = \ln c$, we can rewrite the expression as

(3) $\qquad p(x) = \beta \int \dfrac{x}{x'}\, [p(x') + x']f(x', x)\, dx'.$

We know from Chapter 1, *DMT*, that this equation has a unique solution. Consequently if we "guess" a form for the function $p(x)$ and it turns out to satisfy (3), we are done. The guess we use is $p(x) = kx$ for some constant k. Substituting the guess in (3) gives $kx = \beta(k + 1)x$. In order for our guess to be a solution, it must therefore be that $k = \beta/1 - \beta$. The pricing function is $p(x) = \beta x/(1 - \beta)$. An alternative route to find the pricing function is to use the formula (3.11) derived in Chapter 3, *DMT*. It was shown there that

(4) $\qquad p(x_t) = E_t \displaystyle\sum_{j=1}^{\infty} \beta^j \dfrac{u'(c_{t+j})}{u'(c_t)}\, d_{t+j}.$

Substituting into this formula the expressions for $u'(\,\cdot\,)$, we get the same pricing function.

b. To derive this formula consider the second first-order condition we derived in part (a), namely (2). It follows that the pricing kernel is given by

$$q(x', x) = \beta \dfrac{u'[c(x')]}{u'[c(x)]}\, f(x', x)$$

or, for this example,

$$q(x', x) = \beta \dfrac{x}{x'}\, f(x', x).$$

c. One way of approaching the problem of pricing functions in general is to think of an option as a bundle of state-contingent commodities. We know how to price these bundles, because we derived the pricing kernel in part (b). Consider, for example, the bundle that pays one unit of the consumption good if tomorrow's state is in the set A and zero otherwise, then the value of such a bundle is given by

$$\int_A 1 \cdot q(x', x)\, dx' + \int_{X-A} 0 \cdot q(x', x)\, dx' = \int_A q(x', x)\, dx'.$$

Now, an option to buy shares at the fixed price $\bar{p}$ is a bundle that pays nothing if the price tomorrow is less than $\bar{p}$, because it is cheaper to buy the tree in the spot market at the price $p(x')$ than to exercise the option and pay the (higher) price $\bar{p}$. On the other hand, if the price tomorrow is higher than $\bar{p}$, there is an instantaneous profit equal to $[p(x) - \bar{p}]$ that is realized by buying the tree at

$\bar{p}$ (and thus exercising the option) and selling it immediately at its market price $p(x')$. Therefore the value of the option bundle is given by

$$\sigma(x, \bar{p}) = \int_{p(x') \geq \bar{p}} [p(x') - \bar{p}]q(x', x)\, dx'$$

$$+ \int_{p(x) < \bar{p}} 0 \cdot q(x', x)\, dx'$$

or, equivalently,

$$\sigma(x, \bar{p}) = \int_{X} \max\{p(x') - \bar{p}, 0\}q(x', x)\, dx'.$$

For the particular utility function of this exercise, we have that the set $p(x') \geq \bar{p}$ is the set $\{x : x \geq \bar{p}(1 - \beta)\beta^{-1}\}$. Then we have that

(5) $$\sigma(x, \bar{p}) = \beta \int_{x' \geq \bar{p}(1-\beta)\beta^{-1}} \left(\frac{\beta}{1 - \beta} x' - \bar{p}\right) \frac{x}{x'} f(x', x)\, dx'$$

$$\sigma(x, \bar{p}) = \beta \left\{ \frac{x\beta}{1 - \beta} \int_{x' \geq \bar{p}(1-\beta)\beta^{-1}} f(x', x)\, dx' - \bar{p} \right.$$

$$\left. \cdot \int_{x' \geq \bar{p}(1-\beta)\beta^{-1}} \frac{x}{x'} f(x', x)\, dx' \right\}$$

Recall, however, that

$$\int_{x' \geq \bar{p}(1-\beta)/\beta} f(x', x)\, dx' = P\left[x_{t+1} \geq \frac{\bar{p}(1 - \beta)}{\beta} \middle| x_t = x \right]$$

$$= P\left[\frac{\beta}{1 - \beta} x_{t+1} \geq \bar{p} \middle| x_t = x \right]$$

$$= P[p(x_{t+1}) \geq \bar{p} | x_t = x].$$

On the other hand,

$$\bar{p} \int_{x' \geq \bar{p}(1-\beta)\beta^{-1}} \frac{x}{x'} f(x', x)\, dx' = \bar{p} \int_{x' \geq \bar{p}(1-\beta)\beta^{-1}} \frac{(\beta/1 - \beta)x}{(\beta/1 - \beta)x'}$$

$$\cdot f(x', x)\, dx'$$

$$= \bar{p} \int_{x' \geq \bar{p}(1-\beta)\beta^{-1}} \frac{p(x)}{p(x')} f(x', x)\, dx'$$

$$= \bar{p}P[p(x_{t+1}) \geq \bar{p} | x_t = x] \int \frac{p(x)}{p(x')}$$

$$\cdot \hat{f}[x', x, p(x') \geq \bar{p}]\, dx',$$

where $\hat{f}[x', x, p(x') \geq \bar{p}]$ is the density associated with the random variable x_{t+1} conditional on $x_t = x$ and $p(x_{t+1}) \geq \bar{p}$ and is given by

$$\hat{f}[x', x, p(x_{t+1}) \geq \bar{p}] = \frac{f(x', x)}{\int_{x' \geq \bar{p}(1-\beta)\beta^{-1}} f(x', x) \, dx'}.$$

Thus we have that

$$\bar{p} \int_{x' \geq \bar{p}(1-\beta)\beta^{-1}} \frac{x}{x'} f(x', x) \, dx'$$

$$= \bar{p} P[p(x_{t+1}) \geq \bar{p}|x_t = x] E\left[\frac{p(x_t)}{p(x_{t+1})} \middle| x_t = x, p(x_{t+1}) \geq \bar{p}\right].$$

Therefore we can write $\sigma(x_t, \bar{p})$ as

$$\sigma(x_t, \bar{p}) = \beta P[p(x_{t+1}) \geq \bar{p}|x_t = x]p(x_t)$$

$$\cdot E\left[\frac{p(x_{t+1}) - \bar{p}}{p(x_{t+1})} \middle| x_t = x, p(x_{t+1}) \geq \bar{p}\right].$$

The value of the option is proportional to its current price multiplied by the conditional probability that tomorrow's price exceeds the strike price, that is, the price at which the option is exercised. This quantity is discounted and adjusted for the expected relative gains $[p(x_{t+1}) - \bar{p}]/p(x_{t+1})$, conditional on the current information and on the option being exercised. It is important to notice that our pricing formula does not include terms that contain products of marginal utility and prices because, given the particular utility function with which we work, the price of a tree is proportional to the inverse of the marginal utility. In general we expect to find that pricing formulas depend on the covariance between the marginal utility and the asset price.

d. We first show that, if $\bar{p}$ increases, then the value of the option decreases. To do so, we differentiate the right-hand side of (5) with respect to $\bar{p}$ to get, using Leibniz's rule (see Sargent 1979),

$$\frac{\partial \sigma(x, \bar{p})}{\partial \bar{p}} = -\beta \int_{x' \geq \bar{p}(1-\beta)\beta^{-1}} \frac{x}{x'} f(x', x) \, dx' < 0.$$

It is clear that an increase in the strike price $\bar{p}$ makes the option less attractive and must therefore reduce its price. To determine the sign of $\text{cov}[\sigma(x, \bar{p}), p(x)]$, we use a very well known inequality (see, for example, Kihlstrom and Mirman 1974).

INEQUALITY. *If $f(x)$ and $g(x)$ are both increasing in x, then*

$$\text{cov}[f(x), g(x)] = \int f(x)g(x)\mu(dx) - \int f(x)\mu(dx)$$
$$\cdot \int g(x)\mu(dx) \geq 0.$$

The strategy is to show that $\partial\sigma/\partial x > 0$, because $p(x)$ is increasing in x the inequality guarantees that $\text{cov}[\sigma(x, \bar{p}), p(x)]$ is positive. Equation (5) can be rearranged as

$$\sigma(x, \bar{p}) = \beta x \left\{ \int_{\bar{p}(1-\beta)\beta^{-1}}^{\bar{x}} \left(\frac{\beta}{1-\beta} - \frac{\bar{p}}{x'} \right) f(x', x) \, dx' \right\}.$$

Next integrate by parts and use the fact that $F(\bar{x}, x) = 1$ for all x to get

$$\sigma(x, \bar{p}) = \beta x \left\{ \left(\frac{\beta}{1-\beta} - \frac{\bar{p}}{\bar{x}} \right) - \int_{\bar{p}(1-\beta)\beta^{-1}}^{\bar{x}} \frac{\bar{p}}{(x')^2} F(x', x) \, dx' \right\}.$$

Then

$$\frac{\partial\sigma}{\partial x}(x, \bar{p}) = \beta \left\{ \left(\frac{\beta}{1-\beta} - \frac{\bar{p}}{\bar{x}} \right) - \int_{\bar{p}(1-\beta)\beta^{-1}}^{\bar{x}} \frac{\bar{p}}{(x')^2} F(x', x) \, dx' \right\}$$
$$- \beta x \int_{\bar{p}(1-\beta)\beta^{-1}}^{\bar{x}} \frac{\bar{p}}{(x')^2} \frac{\partial F}{\partial x}(x', x) \, dx'.$$

The assumption $\partial F/\partial x < 0$, however, implies $\partial\sigma/\partial x > 0$.

e. The price of an asset that pays one unit of consumption at $(t + 1)$ in every state of nature is given by

$$R^{-1}(x) = \int q(x', x) \, dx' = \beta \int \frac{x}{x'} f(x', x) \, dx'.$$

Therefore $\beta_1 \geq \beta_2$ implies $R^{-1}(x, \beta_1) \geq R^{-1}(x, \beta_2)$. Thus $R(x, \beta_2) \geq R(x, \beta_1)$.

Consequently the "more patient" the representative agent (i.e., the higher β), the lower the interest rate. The intuition underlying this result is the following. Consider an economy with a given β. The interest rate in equilibrium is such that desired savings are zero, because there is only one agent and no technology to shift consumption across periods. Suppose now that the same interest rate is announced in the market for risk-free loans in another economy that has a higher β. At zero savings the marginal unity of postponing consumption $[\beta \int u'(x')f(x', x) \, dx']$ is higher than the loss of utility due to saving $[u'(x)R(x)^{-1}]$. Therefore the representative agent will choose to save more to reduce the expected marginal utility of future consumption and, at the same time, to increase the marginal utility of saving. For these two magnitudes to be equal, as required by any interior solution, the amount of saving must be positive. Positive savings, however, are not compatible with an equilibrium. It is therefore necessary to decrease the interest rate so that desired savings are reduced to zero. Notice that this result is quite general, because it does not depend on the form of the utility function.

Finally, we want to look at the price of a tree. For this example we have computed the pricing function explicitly. Then it is clear that for all x

$$p(x, \beta_1) = \frac{\beta_1}{1 - \beta_1} x \geq \frac{\beta_2}{1 - \beta_2} x = p(x, \beta_2), \qquad \text{if } \beta_1 \geq \beta_2.$$

This result is also quite general. To see this point, notice that the pricing formula (2) that we used in (a) is increasing in β. The intuition behind this result is also straightforward: the price of a tree is the price of a claim to an infinite future stream of dividends. In the economy with the higher β, future utility (and therefore higher future consumption) is more valuable. As a result, the price of a stream of future utility (or consumption) should be higher.

EXERCISE 3.11 Pricing *n*-Period Options

Consider a pure exchange economy where the representative agent has preferences over stochastic processes for consumption given by

$$E\left[\sum_{t=0}^{\infty} \beta^t u(c_t)\right], \qquad 0 < \beta < 1,$$

where we assume that u is continuously differentiable and strictly concave. Let the state of the economy be given by the stochastic process $\{x_t\}$. We assume that x_t is a Markov process with density $f(x', x)$ and is such that for every continuous function $h(x)$ the function $y(x) = \int h(x')f(x', x) \, dx'$ is a continuous function of x. We also assume that x_t has compact support (that is, the state space is compact) and that the equilibrium level of consumption, $c(x)$, is a continuous function of the state. Let the price of a stock be given by $p_t = p(x_t)$, where $p(\cdot)$ is assumed continuous. Let $w^n(x, \bar{p})$ be the value of an option to buy, ex-dividend, one share at price $\bar{p}$ either in the current period or in one of the following n periods. The holder of this option is free not to exercise it.

a. Show how to compute $w^n(\cdot)$ as a function of $w^{n-1}(\cdot)$. In particular, show explicitly how to compute $w^1(\cdot)$. Argue that, for any pair $(x, \bar{p})$, $w^n(x, \bar{p}) \geq w^{n-1}(x, \bar{p}) \geq \ldots \geq w^1(x, \bar{p})$.

Hint. It may be helpful to price options as "bundles" of commodities and to use the prices of contingent claims $q(x', x)$.

b. Display the functional equation whose solution is $w^\infty(x, \bar{p})$: the price of an option that can be exercised at any time.

c. (Optional.) Establish that there is only one solution $w^\infty(\cdot)$ and also show that

$$w^\infty(x, \bar{p}) = \lim_{n \to \infty} w^n(x, \bar{p}).$$

d. Suppose we know that, in the next n periods, the stock will not pay dividends. Let $z^n(x, \bar{p})$ be the value of an option to buy one share at price $\bar{p}$, n periods ahead. Notice that, although $w^n(\cdot)$ is the price of a contract that allows the owner to exercise the option in any of the following n periods, $z^n(\cdot)$ does so only in the nth period; that is, $z^n(\cdot)$ is a more constrained contract. Show, however, that, for such a dividendless stock, $z^n(x, \bar{p}) = w^n(x, \bar{p})$, provided that the risk-free interest rate, $R(x)$, is greater than one for almost all x—in other words, show that the option will never be exercised until the last period.

SOLUTION

a. Recall that the price of a contract to deliver one unit of the consumption good next period if the state is x', given that the current state is x, satisfies

$$q(x', x) = \frac{\beta u'[c(x')]}{u'[c(x)]} f(x', x).$$

Consider then the price of a contract that offers the option to buy a share next period at price $\bar{p}$. This asset is a claim to the following bundle of goods:

$$\begin{cases} p(x') - \bar{p} & \text{whenever } p(x') \geq \bar{p} \\ 0 & \text{otherwise.} \end{cases}$$

In the event that the option is exercised, the holder has a claim to $p(x') - \bar{p}$ goods: the profit in the operation. If the price of the stock is less than $\bar{p}$, the option to buy at a price higher than the market price is worthless and therefore corresponds to a bundle that pays nothing.

The current price of such a bundle is given by

$$e(x, \bar{p}) = \int_{p(x')-\bar{p}\geq 0} [p(x') - \bar{p}]q(x', x)\, dx'$$

$$+ \int_{p(x')-\bar{p}<0} 0 \cdot q(x', x)\, dx'$$

$$= \int \max[0, p(x') - \bar{p}]q(x', x)\, dx'.$$

Then if the option can be exercised today, its price will be given by

(1) $$w^1(x, \bar{p}) = \max\{e(x, \bar{p}), p(x) - \bar{p}\}.$$

Consider now an n-period option. If it is not exercised, it is claim to an $(n-1)$-period option next period:

$$\int w^{n-1}(x', \bar{p})q(x', x)\, dx'.$$

If it is exercised it has value to $p(x) - \bar{p}$; the profits that can be made instantaneously. Then its market price will be the higher of the two values. In other words,

(2) $$w^n(x, \bar{p}) = \max\left\{\int w^{n-1}(x', \bar{p})q(x', x)\, dx', p(x) - \bar{p}\right\}.$$

This formula holds for $n = 2, 3, \ldots\ldots$ The corresponding expression for $w^1(\,\cdot\,)$ is give by (1).

Note that we can think of the sequence $\{w^n\}$ as being generated by an operator that maps functions defined on the state space (the range of x_t). Define T, an operator on the space of continuous and bounded functions, by

$$(Tf)(x) = \max\left\{\int f(s)q(s, x)\, ds, p(x) - \bar{p}\right\}.$$

Then if $w^0(x, \bar{p})$ is the price of an option that can be exercised *only* today, it follows that

$$w^0(x, \bar{p}) = (T0)(x),$$

where 0 stands for the zero function. In other words $w^0(x, p) = \max\{0, p(x) - \bar{p}\}$. It also follows that $w^1(x, \bar{p}) = (Tw^0)(x)$. In general, $w^n(x, \bar{p}) = (Tw^{n-1})(x)$.

By definition of T, it follows that if f and g are two functions such that: $\forall\, x$ $f(x) \geq g(x)$, then $(Tf)(x) \geq (Tg)(x)$, that is, the operator T is monotone.

Notice that

$$w^0(x, \bar{p}) \geq 0.$$

Applying the operator T to both sides of the above inequality, we have that: $w^1(x, \bar{p}) = (Tw^0)(x) \geq (T0)(x) = w^0(x, \bar{p})$. Proceeding in this way, we get $w^n(x, \bar{p}) \geq w^{n-1}(x, \bar{p}) \geq \ldots \geq w^0(x, \bar{p})$. The intuition is fairly simple: an n-period option can be "made into" an $(n-1)$-period option if the holder commits himself to either exercise in the following $(n-1)$ periods or not at all. Because this situation is equivalent to placing additional constraints on the bundle to which the option is a claim to, however, we cannot possibly increase its value. Therefore the more constrained asset cannot have a higher price.

b. We follow the same argument as in (a). If the option is not exercised in the current period, it is still an infinite option next period. In this case, its value is given by

$$\int w^\infty(x', \bar{p})q(x', x)\, dx'.$$

If it is exercised its value is simply $[p(x) - \bar{p}]$. Thus the price of such an option is

(3) $$w^\infty(x, \bar{p}) = \max\left\{\int w^\infty(x', \bar{p})q(x', x)\, dx', p(x) - \bar{p}\right\}.$$

We want to show that there is a unique solution to (3). First multiply both sides by $u'[c(x)]$ to get

$$w^\infty(x, \bar{p})u'[c(x)] = \max\left\{u'[c(x)]\int w^\infty(x', \bar{p})\right.$$
$$\left. \cdot \frac{\beta u'[c(x')]}{u'[c(x)]} f(x', x)\, dx', u'[c(x)](p(x) - \bar{p})\right\}.$$

Denote by $\phi^\infty(x, \bar{p}) \equiv u'[c(x)]w^\infty(x, \bar{p})$, and $h(x, \bar{p}) = u'[c(x)][p(x) - \bar{p}]$. Then the above equation can be written as

$$\phi^\infty(x, \bar{p}) = \max\left\{\beta\int \phi^\infty(x', \bar{p})f(x', x)\, dx', h(x, \bar{p})\right\}.$$

Note that, if we find a function ϕ^∞ that satisfies this functional equation, we can get the desired solution w^∞ simply by setting $w^\infty = \phi^\infty/u'(\cdot)$ The basic strategy is to show that the operator F defined by

$$(Fg)(x, \bar{p}) = \max\left\{\beta \int g(x', \bar{p})f(x', x) \, dx', h(x, \bar{p})\right\}.$$

is a contraction mapping (see the appendix, *DMT*, for a definition).

First we show that F maps the space of real valued, bounded continuous functions defined on the state space into itself. This space with the supremum norm is a Banach space, as required by the contraction mapping theorem. First we check boundedness.

$$|(Fg)(x, \bar{p})| \le \max\left\{\beta \int |g(x', \bar{p})||fx', x) \, dx', |h(x, \bar{p})|\right\},$$

$$\le \max\{\beta\|g\|_\infty, \|h\|_\infty\} < \infty,$$

$$\text{where} \quad \|g\|_\infty = \sup_x |g(x, \bar{p})|, \quad \|h\|_\infty = \sup_x |h(x, \bar{p})|.$$

Because consumption is a continuous function of x, so is the marginal utility of consumption. Therefore, $u'[c(x)]$ is a continuous function of x. Since x lies in a compact set, this function is bounded. Similarly, $p(x)$ is also bounded. Consequently, $\|h\|_\infty < \infty$. Because $\|g\|_\infty < \infty$ by assumption, it follows that $\sup_x|(Fg)(x, \bar{p})| < B$. To verify continuity with respect to x, notice that the max of two continuous functions is also continuous. Continuity of $h(x)$ follows from continuity of $u'[c(x)]$ and $p(x)$. Similarly, because $g(\,\cdot\,)$ is assumed continuous in its first argument, we get that the first term in the right-hand side of F is continuous.

To verify that F is, indeed, a contraction mapping, we can check to see whether Blackwell's sufficient conditions are satisfied (see the appendix, *DMT*). These are

(1)   If $\forall x, g_1(x) \ge g_2(x) \rightarrow (Fg_1)(x) \ge Fg_2)(x)$

(2) $\forall a \in R_+, (Fg + a) \le Fg + \delta a, \quad \text{where} \quad 0 \le \delta < 1.$

The first condition can be verified directly. To check the second, notice that

$$(Fg + a)(x, \bar{p}) = \max\left\{\beta \int [g(x', \bar{p}) + a]f(x', x) \, dx', h(x, \bar{p})\right\}$$

$$= \max\left\{\beta \int g(x', \bar{p})f(x', x) \, dx' + \beta a, h(x, \bar{p})\right\}$$

$$\le \max\left\{\beta \int g(x', \bar{p})f(x', x) \, dx', h(x, \bar{p})\right\} + \beta a$$

$$= (Fg)(x, \bar{p}) + \beta a.$$

Then, because $0 < \beta < 1$, (2) is verified. Therefore, by the contraction mapping theorem, there is a unique solution to the equation $\phi^\infty = F\phi^\infty$. Moreover, this solution is approached as the limit of the sequence $\{F^n\phi_0\}$ as $n \to \infty$. If we pick $\phi_0 = 0$, each element of the sequence $\phi^n = F^n\phi_0$ has the property that

$$\frac{\phi^n(x, \bar{p})}{u'[c(x)]} = w^n(x, \bar{p}).$$

Therefore we proved that $w^n(x, \bar{p}) \to w^\infty(x, \bar{p})$ as $n \to \infty$. From a practical point of view, this result not only allows us to compute the finite-period values of the option recursively but also shows that, for n large, we can approximate the value of an infinite option as precisely as desired.

d. We first price $z^n(\,\cdot\,)$. Notice that, in the last period, $w^0(x, \bar{p}) = z^0(x, \bar{p})$, because both have to be exercised in that period. The difference between $z^1(\,\cdot\,)$ and $w^1(\,\cdot\,)$ is that $z^1(\,\cdot\,)$ cannot be exercised. Therefore we have

$$z^1(x, \bar{p}) = \int z^0(s, \bar{p})q(s, x)\, ds$$

and in general

$$z^k(x, \bar{p}) = \int z^{k-1}(s, \bar{p})q(s, x)\, ds, \qquad k = 1, \ldots, n.$$

To show that $z^k(x, \bar{p}) = w^k(x, \bar{p})$, it suffices to show that the first of the two terms that define the operator T in section (a) always dominates. Consider $k = 1$.

$$w^1(x, \bar{p}) = \max\left\{\int \max[0, p(s) - \bar{p}]q(s, x)\, ds,\ p(x) - \bar{p}\right\}$$

$$= \max\left\{\int_{p(s)-\bar{p}\geq 0} [p(s) - \bar{p}]q(s, x)\, ds,\ p(x) - \bar{p}\right\}$$

$$= \max\left\{\int_S [p(s) - \bar{p}]q(s, x)\, ds\right.$$

$$\left. - \int_{p(s)-\bar{p}<0} [p(s) - \bar{p}]q(s, x)\, ds,\ p(x) - \bar{p}\right\}$$

$$= \max\left\{\int_S p(s)q(s, x)\, ds - R(x)\overset{-1}{}\bar{p}\right.$$

$$\left. - \int_{p(s)-\bar{p}<0} [p(s) - \bar{p}]q(s, x)\, ds,\ p(x) - \bar{p}\right\}$$

Because the stock does not pay dividends, however, the standard stock-pricing formula gives

$$p(x) = \int_S p(s)q(s, x)\, ds.$$

Therefore

$$w^1(x, \bar{p}) = \max\left\{ p(x) - \bar{p} + \left[1 - R(x) \right]^{-1} \bar{p} \right.$$
$$\left. - \int_{p(s) - \bar{p} < 0} [p(s) - \bar{p}]q(sx)\, ds, \, p(x) - \bar{p} \right\}.$$

Still, clearly

$$\left[1 - R(x) \right]^{-1} \bar{p} - \int_{p(s) - \bar{p} < 0} [p(s) - \bar{p}]q(s, x)\, ds > 0$$

Therefore the first term dominates, and the option will never be exercised. Consequently

$$z^1(x, \bar{p}) = w^1(x, \bar{p}).$$

Next we can proceed recursively to get the desired result.

References and Suggested Readings

Altug, Sumru. 1985. Time to build and equilibrium pricing. University of Minnesota, Minneapolis.

Barro, Robert J. 1974. Are government bonds net wealth? *Journal of Political Economy* 82(6):1095–1117.

Benveniste, Lawrence, and José Scheinkman. 1979. On the differentiability of the value function in dynamic models of economics. *Econometrica* 47(3):727–732.

Breeden, Douglas T. 1979. An intertemporal asset pricing model with stochastic consumption and investment opportunities. *Journal of Financial Economics* 7(3):265–296.

Brock, William A. 1982. Asset prices in a production economy. In *The Economics of Information and Uncertainty,* ed. J. J. McCall, pp. 1–43. Chicago: University of Chicago Press.

Brock, William A., and Leonard Mirman. 1972. Optimal economic growth and uncertainty: the discounted case. *Journal of Economic Theory* 4(3):479–513.

Cox, John C., Jonathan E. Ingersoll, Jr., and Stephen A. Ross. 1985a. An intertemporal general equilibrium model of asset prices. *Econometrica* 53(2):363–384.

——— 1985b. A theory of the term structure of interest rates. *Econometrica* 53(2):385–408.

Eichenbaum, Martin, and Lars P. Hansen. 1985. Estimating models with intertemporal substitution using aggregate time series data. Carnegie-Mellon University, Pittsburgh, Pa.

Eichenbaum, Martin, Lars P. Hansen, and S. F. Richard. 1984. The dynamic equilibrium pricing of durable consumption goods. Carnegie Mellon University, Pittsburgh, Pa.

Fama, Eugene F. 1976a. *Foundations of Finance: Portfolio Decisions and Securities Prices.* New York: Basic Books.

———— 1976b. Inflation uncertainty and expected returns on treasury bills. *Journal of Political Economy* 84(3):427–448.

Granger, C. W. J. 1969. Investigating causal relations by econometric models and cross-spectral methods. *Econometrica* 37(3):424–438.

Grossman, Sanford J., and Robert J. Shiller. 1981. The determinants of the variability of stock market prices. *American Economic Review* 71(2):222–227.

Hall, Robert E. 1978. Stochastic implications of the life cycle-permanent income hypothesis: theory and evidence. *Journal of Political Economy* 86(6):971–988. (Reprinted in *Rational Expectations and Econometric Practice,* ed. Thomas J. Sargent and Robert E. Lucas, Jr., pp. 501–520. Minneapolis: University of Minnesota Press, 1981.)

Hansen, Lars P., and Kenneth J. Singleton. 1982. Generalized instrumental variables estimation of nonlinear rational expectations models. *Econometrica* 50(5):1269–1286.

———— 1983. Stochastic consumption, risk aversion, and the temporal behavior of asset returns. *Journal of Political Economy* 91(2):249–265.

Hirshleifer, Jack. 1966. Investment decision under uncertainty: applications of the state preference approach. *Quarterly Journal of Economics* 80(2):252–277.

Huffman, Gregory. 1984. The representative agent, overlapping generations, and asset pricing. Working Paper 8405. University of Western Ontario, Department of Economics. London.

Kihlstrom, Richard E., and Leonard J. Mirman. 1974. Risk aversion with many commodities. *Journal of Economic Theory* 8:361–388.

Labadie, Pamela. 1986. Comparative dynamics and risk premia in an overlapping generations model. *Review of Economic Studies* 53(1):139–152.

LeRoy, Stephen F. 1973. Risk aversion and the Martingale property of stock prices. *International Economic Review* 14(2):436–446.

———— 1982. Risk-aversion and the term structure of interest rates. *Economics Letters* 10(3–4):355–361. (Correction in *Economics Letters* [1983] 12(3–4):339–340.)

LeRoy, Stephen F., and Richard D. Porter. 1981. The present-value relation: tests based on implied variance bounds. *Econometrica* 49(3):555–574.

Lucas, Robert E., Jr. 1978. Asset prices in an exchange economy. *Econometrica* 46(6):1426–1445.

———— 1982. Interest rates and currency prices in a two-country world. *Journal of Monetary Economics* 10(3):335–359.

Mehra, Rajnish, and Edward C. Prescott. 1985. The equity premium: a puzzle. *Journal of Monetary Economics* 15(2):145–162.

Modigliani, F., and M. H. Miller. 1958. The cost of capital, corporation finance, and the theory of investment. *American Economic Review* 48(3):261–297.

Roll, Richard. 1970. *The Behavior of Interest Rates: An Application of the Efficient Market Model to U.S. Treasury Bills.* New York: Basic Books.

Ross, Stephen A. 1976. The arbitrage theory of capital asset pricing. *Journal of Economic Theory* 13(3): 341–360.

Samuelson, Paul A. 1965. Proof that properly anticipated prices fluctuate randomly. *Industrial Management Review* 6(1):41–49.

Sargent, Thomas J. 1979. *Macroeconomic Theory.* New York: Academic Press.

Sargent, Thomas J. 1980. Tobin's *q* and the rate of investment in general equilibrium. In *On the State of Macroeconomics,* Carnegie-Rochester Conference Series 12, ed. K. Brunner and A. Meltzer, pp. 107–154. Amsterdam: North-Holland.

Shiller, Robert J. 1981. Do stock prices move too much to be justified by subsequent changes in dividends? *American Economic Review* 71(3): 421–436.

Sims, Christopher A. 1972. Money, income, and causality. *American Economic Review* 62(4):540–552.

Stiglitz, Joseph E. 1969. A reexamination of the Modigliani-Miller theorem. *American Economic Review* 59(5):784–793.

5 | Cash-in-Advance Models

EXERCISE 5.1   Private Wealth

Prove that in equilibrium the wealth $\theta_t(x_t)$ that appears in Equation (5.6) satisfies

$$\theta_t(x_t) = (\tau_t + \xi_t - g_t) + \sum_{j=1}^{\infty} \int q^{(j)}(x_{t+j}, x_t)(\tau_{t+j} + \xi_{t+j} - g_{t+j})\, dx_{t+j}.$$

SOLUTION

Equation (5.6), *DMT,* says that

$$\tau_t + c_t + \int \theta_{t+1}(x_{t+1})q(x_{t+1}, x_t)\, dx_{t+1} = \theta_t(x_t).$$

Operating recursively with this equation, we get

$$\tau_t + c_t + \int (\tau_{t+1} + c_{t+1})q(x_{t+1}, x_t)\, dx_{t+1} + \cdot \quad \cdot \quad \cdot$$

$$+ \int (\tau_{t+j} + c_{t+j})q^{(j)}(x_{t+j}, x_t)\, dx_{t+j}$$

$$+ \int \theta_{t+j+1}(x_{t+j+1})q^{(j+1)}(x_{t+j+1}, x_t)\, dx_{t+j+1} = \theta_t(x_t).$$

Because $\theta_t(x_t)$ must be bounded and $\int q^{(j)}(s, x_t)\, ds$ goes to zero as j goes to infinity, taking limits on both sides we get

$$\sum_{j=0}^{\infty} \int (\tau_{t+j} + c_{t+j}) q^{(j)}(x_{t+j}, x_t) \, dx_{t+j} = \theta_t(x_t),$$

where we use the convention that $q^{(0)}(s, x_t) = 1$ if $s = x_t$ and equals zero otherwise.

To simplify notation let $p_v(x_t)$ be the present value of the stream of consumption goods represented by $\{v(x_t)\}$ contingent on the state's being x_t. Then

$$p_v(x_t) = \sum_{j=0}^{\infty} \int v(x_{t+j}) q^{(j)}(x_{t+j}, x_t) \, dx_{t+j}.$$

We have that wealth at time t is given by

$$\theta_t(x_t) = p_c(x_t) + p_\tau(x_t).$$

We can derive the same result by looking at the composition of wealth at time t. Wealth at time t (for $t \geq 1$) is given by the real value of dividends collected in the previous period, $\xi_{t-1} p_{t-1}/p_t$, plus the value of the tree at t, $r(x_t)$, and the amount of government bonds held, $b_t(x_t)$. Notice that $r(x_t)$ obeys [see Equation (5.11), *DMT*].

$$r(x_t) = \int r(x_{t+1}) q(x_{t+1}, x_t) \, dx_{t+1} + \int \frac{\xi_t p_t}{p_{t+1}} q(x_{t+1}, x_t) \, dx_{t+1}$$

$$= \int r(x_{t+1}) q(x_{t+1}, x_t) \, dx_{t+1} + \int \xi_{t+1} q(x_{t+1}, x_t) \, dx_{t+1}$$

$$- \int \left(\xi_{t+1} - \frac{\xi_t p_t}{p_{t+1}} \right) q(x_{t+1}, x_t) \, dx_{t+1}.$$

Let $S_{t+1} \equiv \xi_{t+1} - (\xi_t p_t/p_{t+1})$. Then because the case-in-advance constraint is binding, S_{t+1} is the amount of seignorage collected at $(t + 1)$. To see this point, notice that

$$S_{t+1} = \frac{M_{t+2} - M_{t+1}}{p_{t+1}} = \frac{M_{t+2}}{p_{t+1}} - \frac{M_{t+1}}{p_t} \frac{p_t}{p_{t+1}}.$$

But $M_{t+j}/p_{t+j-1} = \xi_{t+j-1}$, for all j. Therefore

$$S_{t+1} = \xi_{t+1} - \xi_t \frac{p_t}{p_{t+1}}.$$

Consequently $r(x_t)$ satisfies

$$r(x_t) = \int r(x_{t+1})q(x_{t+1}, x_t) + \int (\xi_{t+1} - S_{t+1})q(x_{t+1}, x_t)\, dx_{t+1}.$$

The same type of recursive argument that we used to obtain the integrated version of the flow equation for wealth establishes that the above expression is equivalent to

$$r(x_t) = p_\xi(x_t) - \xi_t - p_S(x_t) + S_t$$
$$r(x_t) = p_\xi(x_t) - p_S(x_t) - (\xi_t - S_t).$$

If we ignore the second term $(\xi_t - S_t)$, this equation says that the value of the capital asset in this model decreases with the amount of seignorage collected. The reason is that dividends are paid out in currency and are subject to the inflation tax. Consequently the smaller the revenue from this source of taxation, the higher the real value of dividends and of the tree.

Therefore, wealth at t is given by

$$\theta_t(x_t) = \frac{\xi_{t-1}p_{t-1}}{p_t} + p_\xi(x_t) - p_S(x_t) - \xi_t + S_t + b_t(x_t)$$

$$= p_\xi(x_t) - p_S(x_t) + b_t(x_t).$$

Because the government's budget constraint Equation (5.17), *DMT*, shows that

$$p_g(x_t) + b_t(x_t) = p_\tau(x_t) + p_S(x_t),$$

it follows that—for a given stochastic process for $\{g_t\}$—the higher $b_t(x_t) - p_S(x_t)$ is, the higher $p_\tau(x_t)$ must be. Therefore wealth increases with $p_\tau(x_t)$ or $b_t(x_t) - p_S(x_t)$. Notice that in this setup, if we compared two economies with different amounts of bonds outstanding, say $b_t^1(x_t)$ and $b_t^2(x_t)$, with $b_t^1(x_t) > b_t^2(x_t)$, and if we assume that a higher value of bonds in economy 1 corresponds to a higher present value of taxes (with seignorage being the same in both economies), then there is a sense in which government bonds that are fully backed by future taxes increase wealth. As Proposition 5.1 (*DMT*) shows, however, these changes in wealth are not enough to violate the neutrality of the government's financing decisions. In other words, even if bonds affect wealth (as they can in this model), this is not sufficient to establish that irrelevance propositions fail to hold.

Finally notice that if we again compare two economies with $b_t^1(x_t) > b_t^2(x_t)$ and we were able to measure the market value of private wealth $\theta_t^1(x_t)$ and $\theta_t^2(x_t)$, this model tells us that in the absence of additional information about government policy we have no restrictions between the magnitudes $b_t^1(x_t) - b_t^2(x_t)$ and $\theta_t^1(x_t) - \theta_t^2(x_t)$. To see this point, consider that in the polar case where $p_{S^1}(x_t) = p_{S^2}(x_t)$, we have

$$b_t^1(x_t) - b_t^2(x_t) = \theta_t^1(x_t) - \theta_t^2(x_t).$$

If $p_{r^i}(x_t)$, $p_{S^i}(x_t)$ are free to vary, however, we can find values (within some limits) that are consistent with

$$b_t^1(x_t) > b_t^2(x_t) \quad \text{and} \quad \theta_t^1(x_t) < \theta_t^2(x_t),$$

provided that $p_{S^1}(x_t)$ is sufficiently higher than $p_{S^2}(x_t)$.

EXERCISE 5.2   Unpleasant Monetarist Arithmetic

Describe what is happening to the quantity of one-period government bonds in the example in Proposition 5.5.

SOLUTION

The key to solving this exercise is to use repeatedly the "flow" version of the government budget constraint that for this particular setup is

$$(1) \qquad g = \tau_t + R^{-1}b_{t+1} - b_t + \frac{M_{t+1} - M_t}{p_t}.$$

The problem assumes that: (a) $\forall\, 1 \le t \le T - 1$, $M_{t+1} - M_t = 0$; (b) $M_{T+1} - M_T = M_{T+1} - M_1$; (c) $\forall\, t \ge T + 1$, $M_{t+1} - M_t = 0$. Moreover the "stock" version of the government budget constraint can be written

$$\sum_{j=0}^{\infty} \int q^{(j)}(x_{t+j}, x_t)[g_{t+j} - \tau_{t+j}]\, dx_{t+j} + b_t(x_t)$$

$$= \sum_{j=0}^{\infty} \int q^{(j)}(x_{t+j}, x_t) \frac{M_{t+1+j} - M_{t+j}}{p_{t+j}}\, dx_{t+j},$$

where, as before, $q^{(0)}(x_t, x_t) \equiv 1$. For the special case of this exercise, we can rewrite the last equation at $t = 0$ as

$$\sum_{j=0}^{\infty} R^{-j}(g - \tau_j) + b_0 = \frac{M_1 - M_0}{p_0} + R^{-T}\frac{M_{T+1} - M_1}{p_T}$$

and

$$\frac{M_1 - M_0}{p_0} = \xi\left(1 - \frac{M_0}{M_1}\right).$$

Because (g, τ_j) and b_0 are taken as given, the present value of seignorage must be constant and is given by

$$b_0 + \sum_{j=0}^{\infty} R^{-j}(g - \tau_j) = K.$$

Now we "solve" equation (1) recursively.

$$b_1 = R\left[g - \tau_0 + b_0 - \xi\left(1 - \frac{M_0}{M_1}\right)\right]$$

$$b_2 = R[g - \tau_1 + b_1]$$

$$= R\left\{g - \tau_1 + R\left[g - \tau_0 + b_0 - \xi\left(1 - \frac{M_0}{M_1}\right)\right]\right\}$$

$$b_2 = R^2\left[b_0 - \xi\left(1 - \frac{M_0}{M_1}\right) + \sum_{j=0}^{1}(g - \tau_j)R^{-j}\right].$$

Proceeding in this way, we have that, for $1 \le t \le T$,

(2) $$b_t = R^t\left[b_0 - \xi\left(1 - \frac{M_0}{M_1}\right) + \sum_{j=0}^{t-1} R^{-j}(g - \tau_j)\right], \qquad t = 1, \ldots, T$$

Still,

$$b_{T+1} = R\left[b_T + g - \tau_T - \frac{M_{T+1} - M_1}{p_T}\right]$$

and $$\frac{M_{T+1} - M_1}{p_T} = \frac{M_{T+1} - M_1}{M_{T+1}}\frac{M_1}{p_0} = \left(1 - \frac{M_1}{M_{T+1}}\right)\frac{M_1}{p_0}.$$

Substituting the expression for K and taking into account that $M_1/P_0 = \xi$, we get

$$\frac{M_{T+1} - M_1}{P_T} = R^T K - R^T \xi\left(1 - \frac{M_0}{M_1}\right).$$

Hence

$$b_{T+1} = R\left\{b_T + R^T\left[R^{-T}(g - \tau_T) - K + \xi\left(1 - \frac{M_0}{M_1}\right)\right]\right\}.$$

Using the formula for b_T given by (2), we get

$$b_{T+1} = R^{T+1}\left[b_0 - K + \sum_{j=0}^{T} R^{-j}(g - \tau_j)\right].$$

Now, for all $s > 0$ we have

$$b_{T+1+s} = R[b_{T+s} + (g - \tau_{T+s})]$$

(3) $\qquad b_{T+s} = R^{T+s} \left[b_0 - K + \sum_{j=0}^{T+s-1} R^{-j}(g - \tau_j) \right], \qquad s \geq 1.$

So the solution for the path of $\{b_t\}$ is given by (2) and (3). Without further restrictions on the path of $\{\tau_j\}$, not much can be said about the behavior of $\{b_t\}$. Assume that, for every t, $\sum_{j=0}^{t}(g - \tau_j)R^{-j} > 0$ and that $b_0 = 0$ and $K > 0$. Then (2) shows that, if the government wants to lower the price level at time zero, that is, to choose $M_1 < M_0$, then $b_t > 0$ for $t = 0, \ldots, T$. Moreover, if $g - \tau_t > 0$ for each t between 0 and T, the sequence b_t is increasing, that is, a government that runs permanent deficits without collecting seignorage must resort to more borrowing. Finally notice that for $t \geq T + 1$, $b_t < 0$, that is, the amount of seignorage collected at T must be big enough to pay off the outstanding debt and to provide resources to pay for future deficits. For this case the government becomes a lender.

To get a more precise picture of the time path of b_t, we specialize the example even more and assume $b_0 = 0$, $\tau_t = \tau$. Hence $\sum_{j=0}^{\infty} R^{-j}(g - \tau) = K$ implies $(g - \tau) = [(R - 1)/R]K$. In this case we get

$$b_t = R^t \left[-\frac{M_1 - M_0}{p_0} + (1 - R^{-t})K \right],$$

$$t = 0, \ldots, T, \qquad b_t = -K \qquad t \geq T + 1,$$

which shows an increasing stock of debt from time zero to time T and then a decrease to a constant level $-K$. This level is enough to use the interest of these loans to the private sector to finance current deficits.

Finally, to illustrate the sense in which the structure of the exercise is not sufficient to restrict the behavior of b_t as t grows, consider the case $b_0, K > 0$, $(g - \tau_t) = \delta^t(g - \tau_0)$ with $|\delta/R| < 1$, we have that

$$b_{T+s} = \delta^{T+s}(-K).$$

Hence the behavior of b_{T+s} depends on δ. If deficits are increasing over time, that is, $\delta > 1$, then b_{T+s} goes to $-\infty$, whereas if deficits get smaller, the stock of bonds goes to zero.

EXERCISE 5.3   A Permanent (McCallum) Government Deficit

Consider McCallum's definition of the government deficit, $d_m(t) = [b_t(x_t) - \int b_t(x_t)q(x_t, x_{t-1}) \, dx_t] + g_t - \tau_t$. Let $\{g_t, \xi_t\}_{t=0}^{\infty}$ be a given stochastic process. Given g_t, let the government run a constant "deficit" $d_m(t) = \bar{d}_m$ for all $t \geq 0$.

a. Show that the equilibrium values of c_t, p_t, and $q(x_{t+1}, x_t)$ are independent of the deficit $\bar{d}_m$.

b. Calculate the present value of the constant sequence $\{\bar{d}_m\}$.

c. Show that, taking the stochastic process $\{M_t\}$ as given, the present value of taxes at time zero is independent of d_m. Argue that this is no longer true for $t > 0$.

SOLUTION

a. The equilibrium condition in the market of the single consumption good is that total consumption — public and private — equal availability, in other words, $c_t + g_t = \xi_t$.

Consequently, in any equilibrium, $c_t = \xi_t - g_t$, and so the financial strategy adopted by the government does not affect private consumption. Given the equilibrium allocation, we can price any asset using the pricing kernel

$$q(x', x) = \beta \frac{u'(c')}{u'(c)} f(x', x).$$

As $c = \xi - g$, however, the one-period-ahead pricing kernel is given by

$$q(x', x) = \beta \frac{u'(\xi' - g')}{u'(\xi - g)} f(x', x),$$

where, as before, we denote the pair (ξ, g) as x, and a prime indicates both a derivative and next period's value. From the expression for $q(x', x)$ it follows that although government purchases affect $q(x', x)$, the form in which they are financed does not. Notice that, because c_t does not depend on $\bar{d}_m$, neither does p_t.

b. Let $v(x_t)$ denote a stream of consumption good at t contingent on the state of the economy's being x_t. The present value of a stream $\{v(x_t)\}_{t=0}^{\infty}$ is

$$p_v(x_t) = \sum_{j=0}^{\infty} \int q^{(j)}(x_{t+j}, x_t) v(x_{t+j}) \, dx_{t+j}.$$

The infinite stream of government deficits $d_m(t) = \bar{d}_m$ is a special case of such a $\{v(x_t)\}_{t=0}^{\infty}$ stream, namely, $v(x_t) = \bar{d}_m$ for all t and all possible realizations of x_t. Define

$$r^{(j)}(x_t) \equiv \int q^{(j)}(x_{t+j}, x_t) \, dx_{t+j}, \quad r^{(0)}(x_t) = 1.$$

The interpretation of $r^{(j)}(x_t)$ is that of the price—at time t and in state x_t—of a risk-free asset that pays one unit of consumption at time $(t+j)$, regardless of the state of the world. That price does depend on the current state x_t. It is easy to see that it is just the inverse of the risk-free interest rate for an asset that matures j periods ahead. Then

$$p_d(x_t) = d_m \sum_{j=0}^{\infty} r^{(j)}(x_t),$$

which is a standard present-value formula.

c. As we know, the government budget constraint requires that

$$g_t - \tau_t + b_t(x_t) - \frac{M_{t+1} - M_t}{p_t}$$
$$= \sum_{j=1}^{\infty} \int q^{(j)}(x_{t+j}, x_t) \left[\tau_{t+j} - g_{t+j} + \frac{M_{t+1+j} - M_{t+j}}{p_{t+j}} \right] dx_{t+j}.$$

If we denote revenue raised through money creation at t as $S_t(x_t)$, that is,

$$S_t(x_t) = \frac{M_{t+1} - M_t}{p_t},$$

then we can rewrite the government budget constraint as

(1) $$p_g(x_t) + b_t(x_t) = p_\tau(x_t) + p_S(x_t).$$

We want to claim that for all admissible d_m the right-hand side of (1) does not change. To prove this point, notice that because the pricing kernel $q(x', x)$ is not affected by d_m and the process $\{g_t\}$ is taken as given, $p_g(x_t)$ does not depend on d_m. Furthermore, because the process $\{M_{t+1}\}$ remains unchanged and $\{p_t\}$ does not depend on d_m, $S_t(x_t)$ is not a function of d_m. As before, the result that $q(x', x)$ does not change implies that $p_S(x_t)$ remains the same. Hence

$$p_g(x_t) - p_S(x_t) = p_\tau(x_t) - b_t(x_t).$$

Let $\bar{b}_t(x_t)$ be the sequence of contingent bonds associated with $d_m = \bar{d}_m$, and $\bar{\tau}_t(x_t)$ the sequence of taxes corresponding to that level of deficit. The corresponding processes for $d_m = \hat{d}_m$ are $\hat{b}_t(x_t)$ and $\bar{\tau}_t(x_t)$.

Consider now the situation at $t = 0$. The givens are $b_0(x_0)$, $\int q(s, x_{-1})b_0(s)\, ds$, and g_0. Then we have

$$p_g(x_0) - p_S(x_0) = p_{\hat{\tau}}(x_0) - b_0(x_0) = p_{\bar{\tau}}(x_0) - b_0(x_0).$$

Hence

$$p_{\hat{\tau}}(x_0) = p_{\bar{\tau}}(x_0).$$

Notice that, at $t > 0$, we have that

$$\hat{b}_t(x_t) - \bar{b}_t(x_t) = p_{\hat{\tau}}(x_t) - p_{\bar{\tau}}(x_t).$$

In other words, if we compute the present value of taxes sometime in the future, they are *not* the same. The reason is that, although the present value at $t = 0$ is the same, the stochastic processes for taxes are not the same. This point is easy to see from

$$\bar{d}_m = b_0(x_0) - \int b_0(s)q(s, x_{-1}) \, ds - \bar{\tau}_0 + g_0$$

$$\hat{d}_m = b_0(x_0) - \int b_0(s)q(s, x_{-1}) \, ds - \hat{\tau}_0 + g_0.$$

Then if $\hat{d}_m \neq \bar{d}_m$, $\hat{\tau}_0 \neq \bar{\tau}_0$. Consequently $p_{\bar{\tau}}(x_0) = p_{\hat{\tau}}(x_0)$ implies $p_{\bar{\tau}}(x_1) \neq p_{\hat{\tau}}(x_1)$.

McCallum (1984) and Liviatan (1984) have recently noted that it is feasible to run a permanent gross-of-interest government deficit. Define the gross-of-interest government deficit as

(2) $$d_m(t) = b_t(x_t) - \int b_t(x_t)q(x_t, x_{t-1}) \, dx_t + g_t - \tau_t.$$

The term $b_t(x_t) - \int b_t(x_t)q(x_t, x_{t-1}) \, dx_t$ is the interest payment at t made on debt issued at $(t - 1)$. Using (2), the government budget constraint with $M_{t+1} - M_t = 0$ for all t can be written

(3) $$\int b_{t+1}(x_{t+1})q(x_{t+1}, x_t) \, dx_{t+1} = \int b_t(x_t)q(x_t, x_{t-1}) \, dx_t + d_m(t).$$

Now suppose, given a process for g_t, that $d_m(t)$ is set equal to a positive constant:

(4) $$d_m(t) = \bar{d}_m > 0.$$

Under the policy (4), (3) implies that the stock of bonds $\int b_{t+1}(x_{t+1})$ $\cdot q(x_{t+1}, x_t) \, dx_{t+1}$ will be diverging to $+\infty$ as $t \to \infty$. Equations (2) and (4) imply that

(5) $$\int \tau_t(x_t)q(x_t, x_{t-1}) \, dx_t$$

$$= \int g_t q(x_t, x_{t-1}) \, dx_t + \left[\int b_t(x_t)q(x_t, x_{t-1}) \, dx_t \right]$$

$$\cdot [1 - 1/R_{t-1}] - \bar{d}_m/R_{t-1},$$

where $R_{t-1}^{-1} = \int q(x_t, x_{t-1}) \, dx_t$. The facts that $\bar{d}_m$ is a constant, that $R_t > 1$, and that $\int b_t(x_t)q(x_t, x_{t-1}) \, dx_t$ is diverging to $+\infty$ as $t \to \infty$ imply that $\int \tau_t(x_t)q(x_t, x_{t-1}) \, dx_t$ is diverging to $+\infty$ as $t \to \infty$. Thus, with the gross-of-interest deficit constant and positive, the stock of bonds is growing without bound, and so are the taxes that are being levied to service the interest payments on the bonds. Households have the income to pay these lump-sum taxes because the interest payments on their holdings of government bonds are rising without bound. More precisely, substituting (2) with $d_m(t) = \bar{d}_m$ into the household's budget constraint gives, after cancellation,

$$\frac{m_t^p}{p_t} + g_t + r(x_t)s_t + \int y_{t+1}(x_{t+1})q(x_{t+1}, x_t) \, dx_{t+1}$$

$$\leq \frac{p_{t-1}\xi_t s_{t-1}}{p_t} + r(x_t)s_{t-1} + y_t(x_t) + \frac{m_{t-1}^p - c_{t-1}p_{t-1}}{p_t}.$$

Thus private agents' opportunity sets are left unaltered by alternative choices of the parameter $\bar{d}_m = d_m(t)$. By construction any feasible choice of $\bar{d}_m$ leaves the government budget constraints satisfied with $M_{t+1} - M_t = 0$. It follows that for all choices of $\bar{d}_m$, the present value of taxes obeys (5.17), *DMT*, and so equals the present value of government expenditures plus $b_t(x_t)$ at each date. Consequently, given a process for $\{g_t\}$, different choices for $\bar{d}_m$ amount to reallocations of taxes over time in a way that preserves their present value.

We summarize these results informally as

PROPOSITION. *It is possible to run a permanent gross-of-interest deficit while keeping the currency stock constant forever.*

Consider an economy with given processes for (ξ_t, g_t). Consider a class of policies that set the gross-of-interest deficit

$$d_m(t) = b_t(x_t) - \int b_t(x_t)q(x_t, x_{t-1}) \, dx_t + g_t - \tau_t$$

equal to a constant $\bar{d}_m$ for all time. For any choice of $\bar{d}_m$, the government budget constraint remains satisfied with $M_{t+1} - M_t = 0$ for all t. The present value of taxes at $t = 0$ is independent of the choice of $\bar{d}_m$.

EXERCISE 5.4 A Useful Identity under Interest on Reserves

Prove that for the model of Section 5.5

$$\sum_{j=1}^{\infty} \int (R_{j-1} - 1)q(x_j, x_{j-1})q(x_{j-1}, x_{j-2}) \cdots$$

$$q(x_1, x_0) \, dx_j \, dx_{j-1} \cdots dx_1 = 1.$$

SOLUTION

Recall that $R_{j-1} = (\int q(x_j, x_{j-1})\, dx_j)^{-1}$. Therefore

$$\int \cdots \iint R_{j-1} q(x_j, x_{j-1}) q(x_{j-1}, x_{j-2})$$

$$\cdots q(x_1, x_0)\, dx_j dx_{j-1} \cdots dx_1$$

$$= \int \cdots \int \left[\left(\int q(s, x_{j-1})\, ds \right)^{-1} q(x_j, x_{j-1})\, dx_j \right]$$

$$\cdot q(x_{j-1}, x_{j-2}) \cdots q(x_1, x_0)\, dx_{j-1} \cdots dx_1$$

$$= \int \cdots \int q(x_{j-1}, x_{j-2}) \cdots q(x_1, x_0)\, dx_{j-1} \cdots dx_1.$$

Consequently, the term multiplying R_{j-1} cancels out, with the previous term multiplying minus one, for all $j \geq 2$. The first term is

$$\int R_0 q(x_1, x_0)\, dx_1 = \int \left(\int q(x_1, x_0)\, dx_1 \right)^{-1} q(x_1, x_0)\, dx_1 = 1.$$

Therefore, the finite sum (up to period T) is given by

$$1 - \int \cdots \int q(x_T, x_{T-1}) \cdots q(x_1, x_0)\, dx_T \cdots dx_1$$

$$= 1 - \int q^{(T)}(x, x_0)\, dx.$$

Because the second term goes to zero as T goes to infinity, this establishes the result.

EXERCISE 5.5   Defining the State Vector (Optional)

Assume that the state vector contains (M_{t+1}, τ_t) in addition to (ξ_t, g_t). Denote $(\xi_t, g_t) = X_t$; $(M_{t+1}, \tau_t) = V_t$ and $Z_t = (V_t, X_t)$. Assume that Z_t is Markov, with transition density $h(z'; z)$. Furthermore assume that the x-component of z is itself an independent Markov process with the same transition function as in the text, $f(x', x)$. We assume that $P[X_{t+1} \leq x'|V_t = v, X_t = x] = P[X_{t+1} \leq x'|V_t = v', X_t = x]$ for every (v, v').[1] Then we can decompose the

---

1. As the purpose of this exercise is to show that the neutrality Proposition 5.1 still holds, we must assume that the "real" aspects of the economy, as represented by X_t, are independent of the financial decisions represented by V_t. If that were not the case, then we would be *assuming* the noneutrality of the government financial decision, as we would be asserting that the distribution of today's X_t depends on yesterday's financial mix, V_{t-1}.

transition density $h(\cdot)$ as follows:

$$h(z'; z) = h(v', x'; v, x) = f(x', x)g(v'; x', v, x),$$

where $g(v'; x', v, x)$ is interpreted as the density of V_{t+1}, given $(X_{t+1} = x', V_t = v, X_t = x)$, and therefore has the property that[2]

$$\int g(v'; x', v, x)\, dv' = 1.$$

For this new setup, show that the following version of Proposition 5.1 holds. Given a stochastic process for $X_t = (\xi_t, g_t)$, the equilibrium values of $(c_t, M_{t+1}/p_t, t \geq 0)$ are independent of the government's financing method. That is, all choices of $[\tau_t, M_{t+1}, b_{t+1}(z_{t+1}), t \geq 0]$ that satisfy the government budget constraint—the relevant version of (5.16) in the text—give rise to the same equilibrium processes for $(c_t, M_{t+1}/p_t, t \geq 0)$. Moreover, the pricing kernel $\eta(z', z)$ can be decomposed as $q(x', x)$ times $g(v'; x', v, x)$. Among other things the implication is that

(1) $$\int \eta(v', x'; v, x)\, dv' = q(x', x).$$

The intertemporal prices given by the right side of (1) are independent of the government's method of financing expenditures.

SOLUTION

It is clear that market equilibrium and the assumption of a positive nominal interest rate imply that $c_t = \xi_t - g_t$ and $M_{t+1}/p_t = \xi_t$, and consequently are both independent of the government's financing decisions. For this economy the pricing kernel satisfies the obvious equivalent of (5.12) in Chapter 5, *DMT*, that is,

$$\eta(z'; z) = \beta \frac{u'(\xi' - g')}{u'(\xi - g)} h(z'; z).$$

Now using the decomposition of $h(z'; z)$ we have

$$\eta(v', x'; v, x) = \beta \frac{u'(\xi' - g')}{u'(\xi - g)} f(x', x)g(v'; x', v, x).$$

Yet contingent prices when the state contains only x were found to be given

---

2. Here and below we assume that every finite dimensional distribution of the stochastic process $\{Z_t\}$ possesses a density.

by

$$q(x', x) = \beta \frac{u'(\xi' - g')}{u'(\xi - g)} f(x', x).$$

Therefore

$$\eta(v', x'; v, x) = q(x', x)g(v'; x', v, x).$$

Notice that a "new" financial policy corresponds to a "new" $g(\cdot)$ function. Denote the contingent prices under two different financial policies by $\bar{\eta}(v', x'; v, x)$ and $\hat{\eta}(v', x'; v, x)$. Then in general, $\bar{\eta}(\cdot) \neq \hat{\eta}(\cdot)$. Nevertheless we showed that $\bar{c}(v', x') = \hat{c}(v', x')$. (Actually we have shown something stronger than that, namely, that c does not depend on the v component at all.) This finding is not paradoxical, as the change in the pricing kernel is matched by a similar change in the density of the stochastic process with respect to which the expectation of the objective function is taken; that is, if we denote the transition densities by $\bar{h}(\cdot)$ and $\hat{h}(\cdot)$, then it follows that $\bar{\eta}(\cdot)/\hat{\eta}(\cdot) = \bar{h}(\cdot)/\hat{h}(\cdot)$.

We can also verify that the relevant version of the agent's budget constraint is not affected by the financing decision. We first want to show that the present value of wealth remains unchanged. To do so we need an explicit formula for $\eta^{(j)}(z_{t+j}, z_t)$. The natural conjecture, given our previous result, is that

(1) $$\eta^{(j)}(z_{t+j}, z_t) = q^{(j)}(x_{t+j}, x_t)g^{(j)}(v_{t+j}; x_{t+j}, v_t, x_t),$$

where $g^{(j)}(v_{t+j}; x_{t+j}, v_t, x_t)$ is the density of V_{t+j}, given $(X_{t+j} = x_{t+j}, V_t = v_t, X_t = x_t)$, which under our assumption does not depend on t. We proceed by induction. First we establish that (1) holds for $j = 2$. A basic arbitrage argument establishes (see also Chapter 3, *DMT*) that

$$\eta^{(2)}(z_{t+2}, z_t) = \int \eta(z_{t+2}, z)\eta(z, z_t)\, dz$$

$$= \int_x \int_v q(x_{t+2}, x)q(x, x_t)$$

$$\cdot\ g(v_{t+2}; x_{t+2}, v, x)g(v; x, v_t, x_t)\, dv dx.$$

If we assume that $q^{(2)}(x_{t+2}, x_t) \neq 0$, inasmuch as otherwise $\eta^{(2)}(z_{t+2}, z_t) = 0$,[3]

---

3. Recall that $q^{(2)}(x_{t+2}, x_t) = \int q(x_{t+2}, x)q(x, x_t)\, dx$. Hence because $q(x', x) \geq 0$, $q^{(2)}(x_{t+2}, x_t) = 0$ implies that $q(x_{t+2}, x)\, q(x, x_t) = 0$, which in turn implies $\eta^{(2)}(z_{t+2}, z_t) = 0$.

we have

$$\frac{\eta^{(2)}(z_{t+2}, z_t)}{q^{(2)}(x_{t+2}, x_t)} = \int \frac{q(x_{t+2}, x)q(x, x_t)}{\int q(x_{t+2}, s)q(s, x_t)\, ds}$$
$$\cdot \left\{ \int g(v_{t+2}; x_{t+2}, v, x)g(v; x, v_t, x_t)\, dv \right\} dx.$$

Now, using

$$q(x', x) = \beta \frac{u'(\xi' - g')}{u'(\xi - g)} f(x', x)$$

above and canceling like terms, we get

(2) $\dfrac{\eta^{(2)}(z_{t+2}, z_t)}{q^{(2)}(x_{t+2}, x_t)}$

$$= \int \frac{f(x_{t+2}, x)f(x, x_t)}{\int f(x_{t+2}, s)f(s, x_t)\, ds}$$
$$\cdot \left\{ \int g(v_{t+2}; x_{t+2}, v, x)g(v; x, v_t, x_t)\, dv \right\} dx.$$

Now we want to claim that the right-hand side of (2) is $g^{(2)}(v_{t+2}; x_{t+2}, v_t, x_t)$.
Recall that

$$h^{(2)}(z_{t+2}, z_t) = \int h(z_{t+2}; z)h(z; z_t)\, dz$$

and $h^{(2)}(z_{t+2}, z_t) = f^{(2)}(x_{t+2}, x_t)g^{(2)}(v_{t+2}; x_{t+2}, v_t, x_t).$

Therefore

$$g^{(2)}(v_{t+2}; x_{t+2}, v_t, x_t)f^{(2)}(x_{t+2}, x_t) = \int h(z_{t+2}; z)h(z; z_t)\, dz,$$

$$g^{(2)}(v_{t+2}; x_{t+2}, v_t, x_t)f^{(2)}(x_{t+2}, x_t)$$
$$= \int f(x_{t+2}, x)f(x, x_t)$$
$$\cdot \left\{ \int g(v_{t+2}; x_{t+2}, v, x)g(v; x, v_t, x_t)\, dv \right\} dx,$$

$$g^{(2)}(v_{t+2}; x_{t+2}, v_t, x_t)$$

$$= \int \frac{f(x_{t+2}, x)f(x, x_t)}{\int f(x_{t+2}, s)f(s, x_t)\, ds}$$

$$\cdot \left\{ \int g(v_{t+2}; x_{t+2}, v, x)g(v; x, v_t, x_t)\, dv \right\} dx.$$

This proves our claim.

Now, supposing that (1) is true for j, we can prove that it is also true for $(j+1)$. The argument is exactly the same as in the case $j = 1$. Use the assumption to get

$$\frac{\eta^{(j+1)}(z_{t+j+1}, z_t)}{q^{(j+1)}(x_{t+j+1}, x_t)}$$

$$= \int \frac{q^{(j)}(x_{t+j+1}, x)q(x, x_t)}{\int q^{(j)}(x_{t+j+1}, s)q(s, x_t)\, ds} \left\{ \int g^{(j)}(v_{t+j}; x_{t+j}, v, x) \right.$$

$$\left. \cdot g(v; x, v_t, x_t)\, dv \right\} dx.$$

Then because

$$q^{(j)}(x_{t+j}, x_t) = \beta^j \frac{u'(\xi_{t+j} - g_{t+j})}{u'(\xi_t - g_t)} f^{(j)}(x_{t+j}, x_t),$$

we get, after canceling like terms,

$$\frac{\eta^{(j+1)}(z_{t+j+1}, z_t)}{q^{(j+1)}(x_{t+j+1}, x_t)}$$

$$= \int \frac{f^{(j)}(x_{t+j+1}, x)f(x, x_t)}{\int f^{(j)}(x_{t+j+1}, s)f(s, x_t)\, ds} \left\{ \int g^{(j)}(v_{t+j}; x_{t+j}, v, x) \right.$$

$$\left. \cdot g(v; x, v_t, x_t)\, dv \right\} dx,$$

where the right-hand side is shown to be $g^{(j+1)}(v_{t+j+1}; x_{t+j+1}, v_t, x_t)$. Now the relevant version of the budget constraint is

(3) $$c_t + \sum_{j=1}^{\infty} \int \eta^{(j)}(z_{t+j}, z_t)c_{t+j}(z_{t+j})\, dz_{t+j}$$

$$\leq (\xi_t - g_t) + \sum_{j=1}^{\infty} \int \eta^{(j)}(z_{t+j}, z_t)[\xi_{t+j} - g_{t+j}]\, dz_{t+j}.$$

Denote $\xi_{t+j} - g_{t+j} = \alpha(x_{t+j})$. Because $\alpha(x_{t+j})$ does not depend on the v component of the state, it follows that

$$\iint \eta^{(j)}(v_{t+j}, x_{t+j}; v_t, x_t)\alpha(x_{t+j}) \, dv_{t+j} \, dx_{t+j}$$
$$= \int q^{(j)}(x_{t+j}, x_t)\alpha(x_{t+j}) \left\{ \int g^{(j)}(v_{t+j}; x_{t+j}, v_t, x_t) \, dv_{t+j} \right\} dx_{t+j}.$$

The integral inside the braces, however, is one. The right-hand side of (3) is just

$$(\xi_t - g_t) + \sum_{j=1}^{\infty} \int q^{(j)}(x_{t+j}, x_t)[\xi_{t+j} - g_{t+j}] \, dx_{t+j}.$$

Therefore the same consumption choices as before are affordable, independent of the government financing decision.

To sum up, this exercise illustrates the general result that increasing the dimensionality of the state vector with objects that are not fundamental does not change the basic results, although it makes the algebra more complicated. It is possible to prove the other propositions of this chapter using the enlarged state vector, provided that the statements about prices are suitably modified.

EXERCISE 5.6   Computing an Equilibrium

Consider a one-nonstorable-good nonstochastic Lucas cash-in-advance economy. A single representative household maximizes $\Sigma_{t=0}^{\infty} \beta^t u(c_t)$, $0 < \beta < 1$, where $u'(c) > 0$, $u''(c) < 0$, $u'(0) = +\infty$. The good is produced by a tree that lasts forever and produces a constant stream of $(\xi > 0)$ units of the consumption good each period. If a household owns s_t shares of the tree, it receives $p_t \xi s_t$ units of currency from the firm during the "shopping stage" of period t. Here p_t is the price level at t. This cash cannot be spent at t but must be carried over into $(t + 1)$. There is a securities trading period at the beginning of t during which taxes are paid and cash and other securities are traded. The household's budget constraints are

$$r_t s_t + \frac{m_t^p}{p_t} + \tau_t + \frac{b_{t+1}^p}{R_t} \leq \theta_t$$

$$\theta_{t+1} = \frac{p_t \xi s_t}{p_{t+1}} + r_{t+1} s_t + b_{t+1}^p + \frac{m_t^p - c_t p_t}{p_{t+1}}$$

$$c_t \leq \frac{m_t^p}{p_t},$$

where c_t is consumption at t, r_t is the price of a claim on the current and all future dollar dividends from a tree (paid during the securities trading period), m_t^p is the household's cash at the close of security trading at t, b_{t+1}^p is the real value at $(t + 1)$ of "tax anticipation" certificates purchased at t, R_t is the rate of return on tax anticipation certificates, τ_t is a lump-sum tax or transfer, and θ_t is real wealth at the beginning of period t.

A government purchases a constant per capita stream of $g_t = g < \xi$ for each $t \geq 0$. These purchases give no utility to private agents. The economy begins with an outstanding stock of unbacked currency of $M_0 = \overline{M}_0$ at the beginning of period zero. The government's budget constraint is

$$g = \tau_t + \frac{b_{t+1}}{R_t} + \frac{M_{t+1} - M_t}{p_t} - b_t, \qquad t \geq 1,$$

and for $t = 0$

$$g = \tau_0 + \frac{b_1}{R_0} + \frac{M_1 - M_0}{p_0}.$$

The government faces the cash-in-advance constraint

$$m_t^g = p_t g_t.$$

The equilibrium condition in the cash market is

$$M_{t+1} = m_t^g + m_t^p.$$

When the economy begins, each household owns one tree and the currency stock M_0. In all questions below assume that

$$M_{t+1} = \mu M_t, \qquad t \geq 1,$$

where $\mu > 1$.

a. Define an equilibrium for this economy.

b. Prove that the following prices are equilibrium ones:

$$r_t = \frac{\beta \xi \mu^{-1}}{1 - \beta}$$

$$R_t = \beta^{-1}$$

$$p_t = \frac{M_1}{\xi} \mu^t.$$

c. Prove the following proposition. Consider an economy with (g, ξ) given and with M_0 given. Let an initial equilibrium be given by $\overline{R}_t, \overline{b}_{t+1}, \overline{M}_{t+1}, \overline{p}_t,$

$\bar{\tau}_t, \bar{c}_t, \bar{r}_t$ for $t \geq 0$. Consider any alternative tax, currency-creation, and borrowing strategies that satisfy

(1) $\qquad \hat{\tau}_0 = \bar{\tau}_0$

(2) $\qquad \dfrac{\hat{b}_1 - \bar{b}_1}{\bar{R}_1} = \dfrac{-(\hat{M}_1 - \bar{M}_0)}{\hat{p}_0} + \dfrac{\bar{M}_1 - \bar{M}_0}{\bar{p}_0}$

(3) $\qquad \dfrac{\hat{b}_{j+1} - \bar{b}_{j+1}}{\bar{R}_1} = \sum_{t=1}^{\infty} \dfrac{(\hat{\tau}_{j+t} - \bar{\tau}_{j+t})}{\bar{R}_1^t}, \qquad$ for all $j \geq 0,$

(4) $\qquad \dfrac{\hat{M}_{t+1}}{\hat{M}_t} = \mu, \qquad t \geq 1.$

Any strategies satisfying (1), (2), and (3) are also equilibria, with

$$\hat{p}_t = \dfrac{\hat{M}_1 \mu^t}{\xi}, \qquad \hat{R}_t = \bar{R}_t = \bar{R}_1 \quad \text{for all } t, \qquad \hat{c}_t = \bar{c}_t, \qquad \hat{r}_t = \bar{r}_t.$$

Interpret this proposition as characterizing the neutrality of open-market operations.

SOLUTION

a. Because the economy is nonstochastic, the natural choice of the space on which an equilibrium is defined corresponds to the space of infinite sequences rather than to the space of stochastic processes. Formally an infinite sequence is a stochastic process of a very special type: each random variable is trivial in the sense that it takes a specific value with probability one.

An equilibrium, then, is a collection of sequences $[\{M_{t+1}\}, \{p_t\}, \{\tau_t\}, \{R_t\}, \{s_t\}, \{r_t\}, \{b_t\}, \{m_t^p\}, \{c_t\}, t \geq 0]$ such that:

i. If private agents are faced with sequences $\{p_t\}$ of prices, $\{r_t\}$ of stock prices, $\{\tau_t\}$ of taxes, and $\{R_t\}$ of rates of return, then the sequences $\{b_t\}$ of "tax anticipation" certificates, $\{m_t^p\}$ of currency, $\{c_t\}$ of consumption, and $\{s_t\}$ of shares solve the following utility maximization problem:

$$\text{maximize } \sum_{t=0}^{\infty} \beta^t u(c_t)$$

$$\text{subject to} \quad r_t s_t + \dfrac{m_t^p}{p_t} + \tau_t + \dfrac{b_{t+1}}{R_t} \leq \theta_t$$

$$\theta_{t+1} = \dfrac{p_t s_t \xi}{p_{t+1}} + r_{t+1} s_t + b_{t+1} + \dfrac{m_t^p - p_t c_t}{p_{t+1}}, \qquad p_t c_t \leq m_t^p, \qquad \theta_0 \text{ given.}$$

ii. The government's choice of $\{M_t\}$, $\{b_t\}$, and $\{\tau_t\}$ satisfies its budget constraint

$$g = \tau_t + \frac{b_{t+1}}{R_t} - b_t + \frac{M_{t+1} - M_t}{p_t}, \qquad t \geq 1$$

$$g = \tau_0 + \frac{b_1}{R_0} + \frac{M_1 - M_0}{p_0}, \quad \text{for } t = 0, \quad \text{where } M_0 = \overline{M}_0 \text{ is given.}$$

The government must also satisfy the cash-in-advance constraint, that is, $p_t g \leq m_t^g$, $t \geq 1$.

iii. Finally we require that all markets clear. This statement is equivalent to

$$M_{t+1} = m_t^g + m_t^p, \qquad c_t + g = \xi, \qquad s_t = 1.$$

b. Using the methods of Chapter 1, *DMT*, we can derive the first-order necessary conditions for a maximum of the individual agent's problem. Then we can use these necessary conditions to find the prices that support the equilibrium allocation, namely $c_t = \xi - g$ for all t. These steps have been already carried out in deriving Equation (5.11), *DMT*. The appropriate nonstochastic version that we use is

$$r_t = \frac{\beta u'(c_{t+1})}{u'(c_t)} \left(r_{t+1} + \xi \frac{M_t}{M_{t+1}} \right).$$

Because $M_{t+1} = \mu M_t$, $c_t = \xi - g$ for all t, we can verify directly that $r_t = \beta \xi / \mu (1 - \beta)$ solves the difference equation[4]

$$r_t = \beta r_{t+1} + \frac{\beta \xi}{\mu}.$$

We use the formula (5.12), *DMT*, to find the price of a risk-free bond. Its nonstochastic version is

$$R_t^{-1} = q = \beta \frac{u'(c_{t+1})}{u'(c_t)} = \beta.$$

Therefore $R_t = \beta^{-1}$.

Finally, because the cash-in-advance constraint is always binding (the

---

4. It is clear that the difference equation has other solutions in which real prices grow exponentially at the rate β^{-1}. It is easy to verify that such a candidate solution cannot be an equilibrium, because the consumer's problem would not be solved by $c_t = \xi - g$, and $s_t = 1$ when faced with such a sequence for r_t. Therefore although it is a well-defined mathematical solution, we discard it on economic grounds.

interest rate R_t is greater than one), we have that

$$p_t \xi = M_{t+1}.$$

Because $M_{t+1} = \mu^t M_1$, we get

$$p_t = \frac{M_1}{\xi} \mu^t.$$

c. The strategy that we follow is typical of the proofs of irrelevance or neutrality propositions. First we show that the conjecture satisfies the government's budget constraint. Then we establish that the private agents' opportunity sets also remain unchanged. Consequently their choices should be the same as before.

From the time zero government's budget constraint we have that

$$0 = (\bar{\tau}_0 - \hat{\tau}_0) + (\bar{b}_1 - \hat{b}_1)\bar{R}_1^{-1} + \frac{\bar{M}_1 - M_0}{\bar{p}_0} - \frac{\hat{M}_1 - M_0}{\hat{p}_0}.$$

The first term on the right-hand side, however, is zero by (1), whereas the last two are equal to zero by the second condition. We now consider the "relevant" (nonstochastic) version of Equation (5.1), *DMT*, which is

$$b_{t+1} R_{t+1}^{-1} = \sum_{j=1}^{\infty} R_1^{-j}[\tau_{t+j} + \xi(1 - \mu^{-1}) - g],$$

where we used the fact that $(M_{t+1} - M_t)/p_t = (1 - \mu^{-1})M_{t+1}/p_t = (1 - \mu^{-1})\xi$ if the cash-in-advance constraint is binding. In this case it is guaranteed to be so, because $\bar{R}_t = \hat{R}_t = \beta^{-1} > 1$ for all t. Finally notice that the flow of seignorage is the same under both policies. This sameness results from the constancy of the rate of growth of currency after period 0 and from the property that in both equilibria the cash-in-advance constraint is binding. The "base" of the inflation tax, M_{t+1}/p_t, is thus guaranteed to equal ξ in both equilibria. By construction the rate $(1 - \mu^{-1})$ is also the same. Consequently revenue or seignorage remains unchanged. The previous condition when evaluated for each policy implies that

$$\hat{b}_{t+1} \bar{R}_{t+1}^{-1} - \bar{b}_{t+1} \bar{R}_{t+1}^{-1} = \sum_{j=1}^{\infty} R_1^{-j}(\hat{\tau}_{t+j} - \bar{\tau}_{t+j}),$$

which is satisfied by assumption. Therefore the new financial strategy is consistent with the government's consumption of g units every period at the original prices.

Next we check that the agent's budget constraints remain unchanged.

Notice that at time zero $\theta_0 \bar{p}_0$ is initial wealth in nominal terms. There is no loss of generality in setting $\theta_0 \bar{p}_0 = M_0$, because we assume that no government bonds are outstanding at that time. Therefore the real value of initial wealth, M_0/p_0, will change with the new policy. We show, however, that this change is exactly offset by the change in the real value of "tax anticipation" certificates issued by the government. First assume that $\bar{r}_t = \hat{r}_t$ for all t. Then we have

$$\bar{r}_0 + \xi - g + \bar{\tau}_0 + \bar{b}_1 \bar{R}_1^{-1} = \frac{M_0}{\bar{p}_0}$$

and $\quad \hat{r}_0 + \xi - g + \hat{\tau}_0 + \hat{b}_1 \bar{R}_1^{-1} = \frac{M_0}{\hat{p}_0},$

where we have used the fact that $m_t^p/p_t = \xi - g$, because the cash-in-advance constraint will be binding.

Subtracting the second from the first, however, we get

$$(\bar{b}_1 - \hat{b}_1)\bar{R}_1^{-1} = \frac{M_0}{\bar{p}_0} - \frac{M_0}{\hat{p}_0}.$$

By the second equation that describes the policy experiment, this formula is satisfied, because $(\hat{M}_1/\hat{p}_0) = (\overline{M}_1/\bar{p}_0) = \xi$. To check the remaining budget constraints we ignore the cash-in-advance constraint (which is satisfied in both equilibria, because $R_t > 1$) and get

$$r_t s_t + \frac{m_t^p}{p_t} + \tau_t + \frac{b_{t+1}}{R_t} \leq \frac{p_{t+1}\xi s_t}{p_t} + r_t s_{t-1} + b_t.$$

In both equilibria, however, we have $m_t^p/p_t = \xi - g$, $s_t = s_{t-1} = 1$, $\bar{r}_t = \hat{r}_t$ (to be verified later), and $p_{t-1}/p_t = \mu^{-1}$. Therefore the budget constraint is

$$(\xi - g) + \tau_t + \frac{b_{t+1}}{R_t} \leq \frac{\xi}{\mu} + b_t.$$

subtracting the caret-bearing budget constraint (at equality) from the macron-bearing budget constraint (also at equality), we have that for both to be satisfied by our conjectured equilibrium quantity it must be that

(1') $\quad (\bar{b}_{t+1} - \hat{b}_{t+1})\bar{R}_1^{-1} + (\bar{\tau}_t - \hat{\tau}_t) = \bar{b}_t - \hat{b}_t.$

We can regard this condition as a difference equation in $x_t = \bar{b}_t - \hat{b}_t$, with a nonhomogeneous part given by $z_t = \bar{\tau}_t - \hat{\tau}_t$. It is straightforward, however, to verify that, by Equation (3) of the description of the policy experiment,

$$x_{t+1}R_1^{-1} = \sum_{j=1}^{\infty} R_1^{-j}z_{t+j}.$$

Then by construction, $\{x_t\}$ satisfies the difference equation (1′). [This statement can be verified by substituting in the "candidate" solution from Equation (3).] The last step is to verify that the prices are as hypothesized. Because the cash-in-advance constraint is binding, we have that

$$\hat{p}_t = \frac{\hat{M}_{t+1}}{\xi}$$

or $\qquad \hat{p}_t = \frac{\hat{M}_1}{\xi}\mu^t.$

Because R_t^{-1} satisfies

$$R_t^{-1} = \frac{\beta u'(c_{t+1})}{u'(c_t)},$$

we have $\bar{R}_t = \hat{R}_t = \beta^{-1}$, because $\hat{c}_t = \bar{c}_t = \xi - g$, all t. Finally $\bar{r}_t$ satisfies

$$\bar{r}_t = \frac{\beta u'(\bar{c}_{t+1})}{u'(\bar{c}_t)}\left(\bar{r}_{t+1} + \frac{\xi \overline{M}_t}{M_{t+1}}\right) = \frac{\beta \bar{r}_{t+1} + \xi}{\mu}.$$

Still, $\overline{M}_t/\overline{M}_{t+1} = \mu^{-1} = \hat{M}_t/\hat{M}_{t+1}$ for $t \geq 0$. Therefore $\hat{r}_t$ satisfies the same equation.

This exercise is a version of Proposition 5.4, *DMT*, where at time zero there is an open-market operation, that is, there is a change in the stock of currency brought about by changing the supply of bonds. At the same time the government changes the future stream of taxes in such a way as to make up for the difference in the real value of the two bond portfolios. This exercise shows that allocations, real stock prices, and inflation remain unchanged, that is, there is a sense in which open-market operations are neutral.

EXERCISE 5.7   Interest on Reserves and Stock Prices

Under the interest-on-reserves scheme described in Proposition 5.6, find a formula for the price $r(x_t)$ of a share in trees at time t.

SOLUTION

The main difference is that, under the scheme on which currency earns interest, the dividends collected at time t, $p_t \xi_t$ earn $R_t p_{t+1}/p_t$ per unit of currency before they can be used for consumption at time $(t + 1)$.

With this change we can follow the same argument used to derive Equation (5.11), *DMT*, to get the following pricing formula:

$$u'(c)r(x) = \int u'(c')[r(x') + R\xi]f(x', x)\, dx',$$

where the left-hand side gives the utility value of giving up $r(x)$ units of consumption. The right-hand side gives the benefits of buying a share. These correspond to the real value of the share at time $(t + 1)$, $r(x_{t+1})$, plus the real value of dividends $p_t \xi_t \alpha_t/p_{t+1}$, where α_t is the interest paid on currency. Because $\alpha_t = R_t p_{t+1}/p_t$, we get that the real value of dividends is $R_t \xi_t$, where $R_t^{-1} = \beta \int [u'(c_{t+1})/u'(c_t)]f(x_{t+1}, x_t)\, dx_{t+1}$. Therefore $r(x_t)$ is such that the benefits from buying a share — measured in utility terms — equal the cost.

EXERCISE 5.8   Incentives for "Private Currencies"

The cash that appears in the model of this chapter is all issued by the government, with the printing of government notes assumed to be costless. Suppose that private agents have access to the same costless technology for printing "notes." Show that, at equilibrium prices for the one-country model of Section 5.1, it is feasible for a safe private bank to issue a private bank note, that is, a piece of paper that can be converted to a specified amount of government currency during any subsequent security trading period. Show that, at the equilibrium prices for the model of Section 5.1, a private bank would have an incentive to issue such notes. Given the full array of markets in state-contingent securities that is assumed to operate in this model, to what forces can we refer in order to interpret the absence of private bank notes in this model?

SOLUTION

We will now show how to set up a private bank that issues notes that can be used to meet the cash-in-advance constraint. For this purpose it suffices to demonstrate that such an activity yields positive profits. Because bank notes can be used to buy goods, their price, say $q(x_t)^{-1}$, must be the same as the price of currency if we are to prevent an obvious arbitrage opportunity. Therefore $q(x_t) = p(x_t)$. Consider the following operation: issue one note at time t. With the proceeds buy a claim to one dollar tomorrow so that the note is fully backed by currency. The cost of buying such insurance is given by a version of Equation (5.12), *DMT*. More precisely, the cost is n_t, where n_t satisfies

$$u'(c_{t+1})n_t = \beta \int u'(c_{t+1}) \frac{p_t}{p_{t+1}} f(x_{t+1}, x_t) \, dx_{t+1}.$$

Then the difference between earnings of issuing a note and the cost of insurance is given by

$$\frac{1}{p_t} - \frac{n_t}{p_t} = \frac{1}{p_t}(1 - n_t).$$

If the risk-free nominal interest rate — in this case it corresponds to $n_t^{-1} - 1$ — is positive, the term $(1 - n_t)$ is also positive. Under these conditions and if there is free entry into the industry of "producing" assets that can be used — as currency is in this model — to buy goods, the prices we used cannot be equilibrium prices. The reason is that the production of bank notes is a constant-returns-to-scale activity that cannot show positive profits in equilibrium.

An equilibrium with valued government currency can be attained if there are legal constraints that prohibit privately issued currencies. These legal restrictions give the government a monopoly over currency issue and protect it from the competitive forces described above.

EXERCISE 5.9   Other Interest-On-Reserve Schemes

Consider three different schemes for paying interest on reserves as in Section 5.5. The first guarantees a real return similar to the return on a risk-free claim to one unit of consumption. This scheme is the one analyzed in Section 5.5 and pays interest on currency at the rate

$$\alpha^1(x_t, x_{t+1}) = R(x_t) \frac{p_{t+1}(x_{t+1})}{p_t(x_t)},$$

where $R(x_t) = [\int q(s, x_t) \, ds]^{-1}$. The second scheme guarantees a real rate of return similar to the rate of growth of the economy. Specifically, $\alpha^2(x_t, x_{t+1})$ is given by

$$\alpha^2(x_t, x_{t+1}) = \frac{\xi_{t+1}}{\xi_t} \frac{p_{t+1}(x_{t+1})}{p_t(x_t)}.$$

Finally, in the third scheme, currency earns a known nominal rate of interest. In particular this nominal rate of interest is set equal to the nominal risk-free rate in an equilibrium where currency does not earn interest. In other words

$$\alpha^3(x_t) = \left[\int g(x_{t+1}, x_t) \frac{p_t(x_t)}{p_{t+1}(x_{t+1})} \, dx_{t+1} \right]^{-1}.$$

Find formulas for the price $r^i(x_t)$ of a share in trees under scheme i. Compare it to the prices under the scheme of Section 5.1 (no interest paid on reserves) and to the price in the economy with no currency of Chapter 3.

SOLUTION

We first derive the price of shares in the economy without currency. As a notational convention we write

$$p_v(x_t) \equiv \sum_{j=0}^{\infty} \int v(x_{t+j}) q^{(j)}(x_{t+j}, x_t) \, dx_{t+j}.$$

Therefore $p_v(x_t)$ is the present value of the stochastic process $\{v(x_t)\}$. From Chapter 5, *DMT*, we have that

$$r(x_t) = \int (r(x_{t+1}) + \xi_{t+1}) q(x_{t+1}, x_t) \, dx_{t+1}$$

$$= \int r(x_{t+1}) q(x_{t+1}, x_t) \, dx_{t+1} + \int \xi_{t+1} q(x_{t+1}, x_t) \, dx_{t+1}.$$

Operating recursively with this formula and using the convention that

$$\int \left[\int r(s) q^{(k)}(s, x) \, ds \right] q^{(n)}(x, z) \, dx = \int r(s) q^{(k+n)}(s, z) \, ds,$$

we have that

$$r(x_t) = \sum_{j=0}^{\infty} \int \xi_{t+j} q^{(j)}(x_{t+j}, x_t) \, dx_{t+j} - \xi_t.$$

Then

$$r(x_t) = p_\xi(x_t) - \xi_t.$$

Next, for the model of Section 5.1, *DMT*, we have derived (see the solution to Exercise 5.1) that

$$r^0(x_t) = p_\xi(x_t) - p_S(x_t) - (\xi_t - S_t),$$

where $S_t = (M_{t+1} - M_t)/p_t$ is seignorage at time t. We now turn to the three interest-on-reserves schemes. The key to pricing assets is to compute exactly the bundle of goods to which a share represents a claim. Recall that under the cash-in-advance constraint the dividends that can actually be used to purchase consumption goods at time $(t + 1)$ are the dividends paid out in currency at time t during the dividend collection session. Because currency earns interest at the rate $\alpha^i(x_t, x_{t+1})$, their nominal value at $(t + 1)$ is $\xi_t p_t \alpha^i(x_t, x_{t+1})$. The real value — in terms of consumption — is $\xi_t p_t \alpha^i(x_t, x_{t+1})/p_{t+1}$. Consequently, $r^i(x_t)$ is the value at time t of the basket of goods to which a share is a claim at time $(t + 1)$, properly priced — or discounted — using the state-contingent prices. Then

$$r^i(x_t) = \int \left[r^i(x_{t+1}) + \frac{\xi_t p_t}{p_{t+1}} \alpha^i(x_t, x_{t+1}) \right] q(x_{t+1}, x_t) \, dx_{t+1}$$

$$= \int r^i(x_{t+1}) q(x_{t+1}, x_t) \, dx_{t+1}$$

$$+ \int \frac{\xi_t p_t}{p_{t+1}} \alpha^i(x_t, x_{t+1}) q(x_{t+1}, x_t) \, dx_{t+1}, \qquad i = 1, 2, 3.$$

Thus we see that, for $i = 1$, $(\xi_t p_t/p_{t+1})\alpha^1(x_t, x_{t+1}) = \xi_t R(x_t)$. Thus

$$r^1(x_t) = \int r^1(x_{t+1}) q(x_{t+1}, x_t) \, dx_{t+1} + \xi_t R(x_t) \int q(x_{t+1}, x_t) \, dx_{t+1}$$

$$= \int r^1(x_{t+1}) q(x_{t+1}, x_t) \, dx_{t+1} + \xi_t.$$

By repeatedly iterating on this equation we get

$$r^1(x_t) = p_\xi(x_t).$$

Next, for $i = 2$, we have that $(\xi_t p_t/p_{t+1})\alpha^2(x_t, x_{t+1}) = \xi_{t+1}$. Therefore

$$r^2(x_t) = \int [r^2(x_{t+1}) + \xi_{t+1}] q(x_{t+1}, x_t) \, dx_{t+1}.$$

This pricing formula coincides with the one derived for the economy without currency. Then we know that

$$r^2(x_t) = p_\xi(x_t) - \xi_t.$$

Finally

$$\frac{\xi_t p_t}{p_{t+1}} \alpha^3(x_t) = \frac{\xi_t}{p_{t+1}} \left(\frac{1}{\int [q(s, x_t)/p_{t+1}] \, ds} \right)$$

Therefore

$$r^3(x_t) = \int r^3(x_{t+1})q(x_{t+1}, x_t)\, dx_{t+1}$$

$$+ \left(\frac{\xi_t}{\int [q(s, x_t)/p_{t+1}]\, ds} \right) \int \frac{1}{p_{t+1}} q(x_{t+1}, x_t)\, dx_{t+1}$$

or $r^3(x_t) = \int r^3(x_{t+1})q(x_{t+1}, x_t)\, dx_{t+1} + \xi_t.$

As a result

$$r^3(x_t) = p_\xi(x_t).$$

Notice that

$$r^0(x_t) = r(x_t) - [p_S(x_t) - S_t].$$

Then if $p_S(x_t) - S_t > 0$, the price of a share in "trees" under the cash-in-advance scheme with no interest being paid on reserves is lower than the price of the same capital asset in a no-currency economy. On the other hand, no matter whether the government guarantees a real or a nominal return, the price of trees with this interest-on-reserves scheme is higher than in the economy without currency [$p_\xi(x_t) > p_\xi(x_t) - \xi_t$]. If the government were to pay interest at the "rate of growth," the price of the capital asset would be the same as in the economy without currency.

To sum up, we have shown that, in general, when interest is paid on currency holdings, the value of trees goes up. The intuitive reasoning is that in this cash-in-advance economy ownership of a tree is equivalent to a claim to currency (and not to goods). When no interest is paid, however, currency is taxed through the "inflation tax." The payment of interest on cash holdings is one way of reducing the inflation tax, and consequently under such a scheme the present value of any nominal claim (in this case a tree) goes up.

EXERCISE 5.10   Stock Prices and Inflation

Consider a one-country version of Lucas's cash-in-advance model. The household's preferences are

(1) $E \sum_{t=0}^{\infty} \beta^t \ln c_t, \qquad 0 < \beta < 1.$

Government purchases $g_t = 0$ for all t. The endowment of the one good ξ_t is Markov.

The stock of currency evolves according to the Markov law

$$(2) \qquad \frac{M_{t+1}}{M_{t+2}} = \rho \frac{M_t}{M_{t+1}} + \epsilon_{t+1}, \qquad 0 < \rho < 1,$$

where ϵ_{t+1} is a serially independent random process distributed independently of M_t/M_{t+1} and ϵ_{t+1} has bounded support on the interval $[\epsilon, \bar{\epsilon}]$. The currency changes through lump-sum transfers and taxes. Define

$$\bar{x} = \frac{\bar{\epsilon}}{1-\rho} \quad \text{and} \quad x = \frac{\epsilon}{1-\rho}.$$

Notice that, if M_t/M_{t+1} is in $[x, \bar{x}]$, then M_{t+j}/M_{t+j+1} are in $[x, \bar{x}]$ for all j.

The timing of transactions remains exactly as in Lucas's model. In particular, a share in a tree purchased during the securities trading session at t represents a claim to the dividends payable in currency from t on.

a. Assume that M_0/M_1 belongs to $[x, \bar{x}]$ and that $\bar{x} < 1/\beta\rho$. Show that the strong form of the quantity theory holds, that is,

$$p_t = \frac{M_{t+1}}{\xi_t}.$$

b. Let r_t be the price of trees at time t, denominated in units of the consumption good at t. Assume that M_0/M_1 belongs to $[x, \bar{x}]$ and that $\bar{x} < 1/\beta\rho$. Show that

$$r_t = \xi_t \cdot \frac{\beta\rho}{1-\rho\beta} \cdot \frac{M_t}{M_{t+1}}.$$

c. Describe a sense in which an increase in the rate of growth of currency increases the rate of inflation and decreases the price of trees.

d. Interpret the dependence of trees (stock prices) on the rate of currency creation. How does an increase in the rate of growth of currency, and the attendant effects on the price of trees and the rate of inflation, affect the welfare of the representative consumer?

SOLUTION

a. To show that the cash-in-advance constraint is always binding we will show that an asset that has the same risk characteristics as currency—one-period risk-free nominal bonds—has a higher return. If this is the case no agent will choose to hold more currency than is needed for current purchases. Consequently the strong form of the quantity theory will hold.

To price a risk-free bond that pays R_t units of currency tomorrow for each bond of one dollar of nominal value today we use a version of the asset-pricing Equation (5.5), *DMT*. The real price today of such an asset is $1/p_t$. The resale value tomorrow is zero (it is a one-period bond), whereas dividends are—in time $(t+1)$ consumption goods—R_t/p_{t+1}. Therefore in equilibrium we must have

$$u'(c_t)\frac{1}{p_t} = \beta E_t\left\{u'(c_{t+1})\frac{R_t}{p_{t+1}}\right\}.$$

We guess that the strong form of the quantity theory holds, $p_t = M_{t+1}/\xi_t$; then we verify that under the guess $R_t > 1$. This procedure is sufficient to verify our conjecture, because bonds are a safe asset with a higher nominal return than currency. Using the fact that $u'(c) = 1/c$ and our conjecture, we get

$$1 = \beta R_t E_t\left\{\frac{M_{t+1}}{M_{t+2}}\right\} = \beta R_t \rho \frac{M_t}{M_{t+1}}.$$

Therefore

$$R_t = \frac{M_{t+1}}{M_t}\frac{1}{\beta\rho}.$$

Still, $R_t > 1$ requires that

$$\frac{1}{\beta\rho} > \frac{M_t}{M_{t+1}}.$$

This condition is guaranteed, however, by our assumptions on the process generating M_t/M_{t+1}.

   b. The Euler equation associated with the purchase of trees is

$$r_t u'(c_t) = \beta E_t\{u'(c_{t+1})r_{t+1}\}$$
$$+ \beta E_t\left\{u'(c_{t+1})\xi_t\frac{p_t}{p_{t+1}}\right\}.$$

Substitute into the Euler equation the equilibrium consumption $c_t = \xi_t$, the formula $u'(c_t) = c_t^{-1}$, and the equilibrium condition that $p_t = M_{t+1}/\xi_t$ to obtain

$$\frac{r_t}{\xi_t} = \beta E_t\left\{\frac{r_{t+1}}{\xi_{t+1}}\right\} + \beta E_t\frac{M_{t+1}}{M_{t+2}}.$$

By repeated iteration it can be verified that the stationary solution of this difference equation is

$$\frac{r_t}{\xi_t} = \sum_{j=1}^{\infty} \beta^j E_t \frac{M_{t+j}}{M_{t+j+1}}.$$

Given the Markov law for M_t/M_{t+1}, we obtain

$$\frac{r_t}{\xi_t} = \frac{\beta\rho}{1-\beta\rho} \frac{M_t}{M_{t+1}}.$$

c. The inverse of the equilibrium gross inflation rate is

$$\frac{p_{t-1}}{p_t} = \frac{M_t}{M_{t+1}} \frac{\xi_t}{\xi_{t-1}}.$$

Evidently, given ρ, an increase in M_t/M_{t+1} (a decrease in the rate of currency creation) raises both p_{t-1}/p_t and r_t. Note that

$$\frac{d}{d\rho}\left(\frac{\beta\rho}{1-\beta\rho}\right) > 0,$$

so that an increase in ρ increases r_t, given ξ_t and M_t/M_{t+1}. An increase in ρ is associated with *lower* future rates of currency growth, given M_t/M_{t+1}. Higher future rates of currency growth thus drive current tree prices downward.

   d. Tree prices depend on the current and future rates of currency creation because dividends are payable in currency. The value of this dividend stream in terms of current consumption goods depends on current and future price levels, which in turn depend on the process generating currency.

   Welfare of the representative agent, as measured by (5.7), *DMT,* is unaffected by alterations in the process generating M_t/M_{t+1} and the resulting changes in the p_t process. The equilibrium consumption allocation remains $c_t = \xi_t$. The price of trees r_t is affected by changes in the M_t/M_{t+1} process, as is the rate of return on trees. The representative household is compensated for these changes, however, by alterations in the stream of lump-sum taxes (or subsidies) used to generate currency changes.

References and Suggested Readings

Clower, Robert W. 1967. A reconsideration of the microfoundations of monetary theory. *Western Economic Journal* 6:1–9.

Friedman, Milton. 1960. *A Program for Monetary Stability.* Bronx: Fordham University Press.

Hall, Robert E. 1983. Optimal fiduciary monetary systems. *Journal of Monetary Economics* 12(1):33–50.

Kareken, John H., and Neil Wallace. 1981. On the indeterminancy of equilibrium exchange rates. *Quarterly Journal of Economics* 96(2):207–222.

Liviatan, Nissan. 1984. Tight money and inflation. *Journal of Monetary Economics* 13(1):5–15.

Lucas, Robert E., Jr. 1978. Asset prices in an exchange economy. *Econometrica* 42(2):1429–45.

——— 1980. Equilibrium in a pure currency economy. *Economic Inquiry* 18(2):203–220. (Reprinted in *Models of Monetary Economies,* ed. J. H. Kareken and N. Wallace, pp. 131–146. Minneapolis: Federal Reserve Bank of Minneapolis, 1980.)

——— 1982. Interest rates and currency prices in a two-country world. *Journal of Monetary Economics* 10(3):335–359.

Lucas, Robert E., Jr., and Nancy L. Stokey. 1983. Optimal fiscal and monetary policy in an economy without capital. *Journal of Monetary Economics* 12(1):55–93.

——— 1985. Money and interest in a cash-in-advance economy. Working Paper 1618. National Bureau of Economic Research, Chicago.

McCallum, Bennett T. 1984. Are bond-financed deficits inflationary? A Ricardian analysis. *Journal of Political Economy* 92(1):123–135.

Peled, Dan. 1985. Stochastic inflation and government provision of indexed bonds. *Journal of Monetary Economics* 15(3):291–308.

Sargent, Thomas J., and Neil Wallace. 1981. Some unpleasant monetarist arithmetic. Federal Reserve Bank of Minneapolis *Quarterly Review* 5(3):1–17.

——— 1984. Interest on reserves. *Journal of Monetary Economics* 15(3):279–290.

Yun, Y. Eugene. 1985. Business cycles in a cash-in-advance model. University of Minnesota, Minneapolis.

6 | Credit and Currency with Long-Lived Agents

EXERCISE 6.1   Value of Unbacked Currency

Prove that, in the $T = +\infty$ version of the model of Section 6.3 in which private loan markets are permitted to operate and $N^A = N^B$, there exists no equilibrium in which unbacked currency is valued.

SOLUTION

To prove that equilibrium with valued fiat currency does not exist, we show that "real" currency holdings grow too fast. The intuition underlying this result is that the competitive equilibrium without unbacked currency is Pareto optimal for the environment that we analyze. When one more asset is added to the menu of securities that can be traded, we do not expect the new allocation to differ from the Pareto-optimal allocation achieved in the previous equilibrium, because all possible gains from trade had been exhausted. By an argument similar to that used in Section 6.6, *DMT,* we shall show that, if fiat currency were to be valued, then the sequence $\{p_t\}$ would be decreasing at a geometric rate. Because the supply of currency is constant, real money balances would be growing without bound. Therefore we would have a situation in which financial wealth was growing fast while consumption remained bounded. Because this cannot be optimal for the agents, we cannot have an equilibrium with valued fiat currency. To state this argument formally, consider the maximization problem faced by individual h:

$$\max \sum_{t=0}^{\infty} \beta^t u(c_t^h)$$

by the choice of sequences $\{c_t^h\}$, $\{l_t^h\}$, $\{m_t^h\}$ that satisfy

$$c_t^h + l_t^h + \frac{m_t^h}{p_t} \leq y_t^h + [1 + r(t-1)]l_{t-1}^h + \frac{m_{t-1}^h}{p_t},$$

$$m_t^h \geq 0, \qquad \text{all } t, \qquad m_{-1}^h, \, l_{-1}^h \text{ given.}$$

The maximization is performed taking the sequences $\{1 + r(t)\}$ and $\{p_t\}$ as given. Notice that for any known sequence $\{p_t\}$ we can say that the agent chooses a sequence $\{q_t^h\}$ instead of $\{m_t^h\}$, where $q_t^h \equiv m_t^h/p_t$.

To solve the maximization problem, we form the Lagrangian

$$J = \sum_{t=0}^{\infty} \beta^t \{ u(c_t^h) + \lambda_t^h [y_t^h + [1 + r(t-1)]l_{t-1}^h$$

$$+ q_{t-1}^h \frac{p_{t-1}}{p_t} - c_t^h - l_t^h - q_t^h] \},$$

where $\{\lambda_t^h\}$ is a sequence of nonnegative Lagrange multipliers. The first-order conditions are

$$\beta^t \{ u'(c_t^h) - \lambda_t^h \} \leq 0, \qquad = \quad \text{if } c_t^h > 0, \qquad t = 0, 1, \ldots$$
$$-\beta^t \lambda_t^h + \beta^{t+1} [1 + r(t)]\lambda_{t+1}^h = 0, \qquad t = 0, 1, \ldots$$

$$-\beta^t \lambda_t^h + \beta^{t+1} \frac{p_t}{p_{t+1}} \lambda_{t+1}^h \leq 0, \qquad = \quad \text{if } q_t^h > 0, \qquad t = 0, 1, \ldots$$

$$c_t^h + l_t^h + q_t^h \leq y_t^h + [1 + r(t-1)]\, l_{t-1}^h + q_{t-1}^h \frac{p_{t-1}}{p_t},$$

$$t = 0, 1, \ldots$$

and the "transversality conditions"

$$\lim_{T \to \infty} \beta^T \lambda_T^h l_T^h = 0, \qquad \lim_{T \to \infty} \beta^T \lambda_T^h q_T^h = 0.$$

Our strategy is to assume that an equilibrium with valued fiat currency exists, that is, $q_t = q_t^A + q_t^B > 0$ and to derive a contradiction from this assumption. In particular we will show that the last transversality condition is violated for either A or B. Because this condition is necessary for a maximum of the individual's problem, this is a violation of the assumption that an equilibrium exists.

Assume that the utility function has enough curvature near zero that $c_t^h > 0$, $\forall (h, t)$. Then $u'(c_t^h) = \lambda_t^h$. The implication is that

$$\frac{u'(c_{t+1}^A)}{u'(c_t^A)} = \frac{\lambda_{t+1}^A}{\lambda_t^A} = \frac{1}{\beta[1 + r(t)]} = \frac{\lambda_{t+1}^B}{\lambda_t^B} = \frac{u'(c_{t+1}^B)}{u'(c_t^B)}.$$

Using this equality and the assumption of market equilibrium, $c_t^A + c_t^B = 1$,

$\forall\ t \geq 0$, we have

$$\frac{u'(c_{t+1}^A)}{u'(c_t^A)} = \frac{u'(1 - c_{t+1}^A)}{u'(1 - c_t^A)}.$$

Letting $h(x) \equiv u'(x)/u'(1-x)$, we can rewrite the equality as

$$h(c_{t+1}^A) = h(c_t^A).$$

Notice, under the assumption of strict concavity of $u(\,\cdot\,)$, that $h(\,\cdot\,)$ has an inverse. Therefore

$$h(c_{t+1}^A) = h(c_t^A), \quad \text{iff } c_{t+1}^A = c_t^A.$$

This provision establishes that, if a competitive equilibrium exists, agents completely smooth out their consumption streams. This result is not surprising, as it was established in Section 6.2, *DMT*, that optimal allocations are constant and that with a loan market the competitive equilibrium is optimal. Notice that this statement implies $\lambda_t^h = \lambda^h, \forall\ t$. If currency is held by agent h at t, we have that

$$\lambda_{t+1}^h \beta \frac{p_t}{p_{t+1}} = \lambda_t^h \quad \text{or} \quad p_{t+1} = \beta p_t.$$

Because in any monetary equilibrium either $m_t^A > 0$ or $m_t^B > 0$ for all t, we have established that prices decline at a geometric rate β. It follows that

$$q_t \equiv \frac{p_{t-1}}{p_t} q_{t-1},$$

which implies that

$$q_t = \beta^{-1} q_{t-1}, \quad \text{or} \quad q_t = \beta^{-t} q_0 \quad \text{and} \quad q_0 > 0.$$

In particular, notice that for any constant k

$$\lim_{T \to \infty} \beta^T k q_T = k q_0.$$

Now suppose that the transversality condition for agent A is satisfied, that is,

(1) $$\lim_{T \to \infty} \beta^T \lambda^A q_T^A = 0.$$

We want to argue that the implication is that the corresponding condition for B cannot be satisfied. We note that assumption (1) implies

$$\lim_{T \to \infty} \beta^T \lambda^B q_T^B = \lim_{T \to \infty} \beta^T \lambda^B [q_T - q_T^A] = \lim_{T \to \infty} \lambda^B \beta^T q_T - \lim_{T \to \infty} \lambda^B \beta^T q_T^A$$

$$= \lim_{T \to \infty} \lambda^B \beta^T q_T = \lambda^B q_0 > 0.$$

This statement violates part of the definition of equilibrium, namely utility maximization. Consequently we have derived a contradiction by assuming that there exists an equilibrium with valued fiat currency.

EXERCISE 6.2   Computing Equilibrium Interest Rates

Suppose that there are N^A agents with endowment stream $\{y_t^A\}$, $t = 0, \ldots,$ T, and N^B agents with endowment stream $\{y_t^B\}$, $t = 0, \ldots, T$. We require that $y_t^h \geq 0$ but otherwise leave the streams of endowments unrestricted. Assume that the preferences of all agents are described by $\Sigma_{t=0}^T \beta^t u(c_t^h)$, where

$$u(c_t) = u_0 + u_1 c_t - (u_2/2)c_t^2, \qquad u_1, u_2 > 0.$$

Compute the sequence of equilibrium one-period interest rates for the consumption loans model of Section 6.2, and show that it is given by

$$1 + r(t-1) = \frac{(N^A + N^B)u_1 - u_2(N^A y_{t-1}^A + N^B y_{t-1}^B)}{\beta[(N^A + N^B)u_1 - u_2(N^A y_t^A + N^B y_t^B)]}$$

for $t = 1, 2, \ldots, T$.

Hints.

a. Formulate each agent's problem as a discrete-time calculus-of-variations problem using the methods of Sargent (1979, chap. 9) and using l_t^h as agent h's state variable, or as a dynamic programming problem. Obtain the Euler equations. (See Section 1.4 on the way to derive the Euler equations in a dynamic programming setup.)

b. Multiply agent A's Euler equation for l_t^A by N^A and add it to N^B times agent B's Euler equation for l_t^B.

c. Impose the equilibrium condition that $N^A l_t^A + N^B l_t^B = 0$ for $t = 0, \ldots, T$, and solve for $1 + r(t-1)$.

SOLUTION

We let the reader follow the hints. Here an alternative—but totally equivalent—approach is adopted. This line uses the Lagrange multiplier approach described in Section 1.6, *DMT*. The individual maximization problem is

$$\max \sum_{t=0}^T \beta^t \left[u_0 + u_1 c_t^h - \frac{u_2}{2} (c_t^h)^2 \right],$$

subject to $c_t^h \geq 0$, $t = 0, 1, \ldots, T$, and

$$c_t^h + l_t^h \leq y_t^h + [1 + r(t-1)]l_{t-1}^h, \qquad l_T^h \geq 0.$$

The last condition simply reflects the fact that, if borrowing and lending were not constrained in the last period, agents would demand loans in every period in order always to consume at their bliss point $\hat{c}_t^h = u_1/u_2$. To rule this out as a feasible allocation, making the competitive problem interesting, we assume $(N^A + N^B)u_1/u_2 > N^A y_t^A + N^B y_t^B$, $\forall\ t$.

We form the Lagrangian

$$J = \sum_{t=0}^{T} \beta^t \left\{ u_0 + u_1 c_t^h - \frac{u_2}{2} (c_t^h)^2 + \lambda_t^h \right. \\ \left. \cdot [y_t^h + [1 + r(t-1)]l_{t-1}^h - c_t^h - l_t^h] \right\}.$$

The first-order necessary conditions (and the sufficient conditions in this case) are

$$\beta^t \{u_1 - u_2 c_t^h - \lambda_t^h\} \leq 0, \qquad = \text{ if } c_t^h > 0, \qquad t = 0, \ldots, T$$
$$-\beta^t \lambda_t^h + [1 + r(t)]\beta^{t+1}\lambda_{t+1}^h = 0, \qquad t = 0, \ldots, T-1.$$

Assume that the solution is interior. Then multiplying the first equation by N^h and summing over h, we get

$$(N^A + N^B)u_1 - u_2(N^A c_t^A + N^B c_T^B) = N^A \lambda_t^A + N^B \lambda_t^B.$$

Proceeding in the same manner with the second equation, we obtain

(1) $$N^A \lambda_t^A + N^B \lambda_t^B = [1 + r(t)]\beta(N^A \lambda_{t+1}^A + N^B \lambda_{t+1}^B).$$

Notice that we are implicitly assuming that all agents of type h end up with the same consumption bundle. This need not be the case when otherwise similar agents have different "endowments" of initial loans l_{-1}^h. It is clear that we could still add up the marginal conditions; instead of getting terms of the form $N^A c_t^A + N^B c_t^B$, we would get a term like $\Sigma_{h\in H} c_t^h$, where H is the set of "names" in the economy. For the purpose of this exercise, our symmetry assumption is harmless, as we care about aggregates no matter how they are obtained. Notice also that, in equilibrium, total consumption, $N^A c_t^A + N^B c_t^B$, must equal total income, $N^A y_t^A + N^B y_t^B$. When we make this substitution, it turns out that

$$N^A \lambda_t^A + N^B \lambda_t^B = (N^A + N^B)u_1 - u_2(N^A y_t^A + N^B y_t^B).$$

Using this result in Equation (1), it follows that

$$(N^A + N^B)u_1 - u_2(N^A y_t^A + N^B y_t^B)$$
$$= [1 + r(t)]\beta\{(N^A + N^B)u_1 - u_2(N^A y_{t+1}^A + N^B y_{t+1}^B)\}.$$

This is the desired result.

Finally it is important to observe that the method that allowed us to price an asset (risk-free loans) in an economy with heterogeneous consumers without taking into account the distribution of income does not generalize. In our procedure it was crucial that all agents have the same preferences and that the marginal utility be linear in consumption. This scenario allowed us to aggregate over individuals. It is a good exercise to consider a nonquadratic function and to verify that, in general, the distribution of income does influence the rate of interest.

EXERCISE 6.3   "Self-Insurance" and the Permanent Income Theory

Consider the following modification of the model of Section 6.3. Assume that $N^A = N^B$, that $T = +\infty$, and that y_t^A for $t = 0, 1, \ldots$ is now a sequence of independently and identically distributed random variables, each of which is distributed uniformly on the interval $[0, 1]$. Assume that $y_t^B = 1 - y_t^A$, so that y_t^B is also uniformly distributed on $[0, 1]$. Notice that there is no aggregate risk, although there is risk for each individual. An agent of type h seeks to maximize

$$E_0 \sum_{t=0}^{\infty} \beta^t u(c_t^h),$$

where E_t is the mathematical expectation operator conditional on $(y_t^h,$ $y_{t-1}^h, \ldots, y_0^h)$, $u(c_t) = u_0 + u_1 c_t - \dfrac{u_2}{2} c_t^2$, and $0 < \beta < 1$. Let there be a market in perfectly safe one-period consumption loans, with a one-period gross interest rate of $[1 + r(t)]$ between periods t and $(t + 1)$. The agent's budget constraint in period t is $c_t^h + l_t^h \le y_t^h + [1 + r(t - 1)]l_{t-1}^h$, with boundary conditions

$$\lim_{T \to \infty} E_t \phi(T, t) l_t^h = 0, \qquad l_{-1}^h = 0, \quad \text{where}$$

$$\phi(T, t) = \left(\prod_{s=1}^{T} [1 + r(t + s - 1)] \right)^{-1}.$$

The flow budget constraint with these terminal conditions can be solved to give

(a)
$$c_z^h + E_z \sum_{t=1}^{\infty} c_{t+z}^h \left(\prod_{s=1}^{t} [1 + r(z + s - 1)] \right)^{-1}$$

$$= y_z^h + E_z \sum_{t=1}^{\infty} y_{t+z}^h \left(\prod_{s=1}^{t} [1 + r(z + s - 1)] \right)^{-1}$$

$$+ l_{z-1}^h [1 + r(z - 1)],$$

$$z = 0, 1, 2, \ldots$$

The equilibrium condition for the model can be expressed as either

$$N^A l_t^A + N^A l_t^B = 0$$

or $c_t^A + c_t^B = 1$ for $t = 0, 1, \ldots$

Prove that an equilibrium is given by

(b)
$$\frac{1}{1 + r(t)} = \beta, \qquad t = 0, 1, \ldots$$

(c)
$$c_t^h = \frac{1}{2} + \frac{1 - \beta}{\beta} l_{t-1}^h + (1 - \beta)\left(y_t^h - \frac{1}{2} \right), \qquad t = 0, 1, \ldots,$$

$$h = A, B.$$

Hint. Obtain the stochastic Euler equations, using the methods of Section 1.3 or Sargent (1979, chap. 14). Notice that given (b), (c) satisfies (a) and the stochastic Euler equations and also implies market clearing.

Notice that the interest rate is certain, despite the appearance of randomness in the model. Notice also that (c) is a version of the "permanent income" theory. The agent's permanent income is

$$\frac{1}{2} + \frac{1 - \beta}{\beta} l_{t-1}^h = \frac{1}{2} + r(t - 1)l_{t-1}^h,$$

which equals the sum of Ey_t^h for all t plus the expected interested income from his initial assets of l_{t-1}^h. The agent's transitory income in period t is $(y_t^h - 1/2)$. The marginal propensity to consume out of permanent income is unity, whereas the marginal propensity to consume out of transitory income is $(1 - \beta)$.

SOLUTION

We follow the hint and consider the agent's problem, namely,

$$\max E_0 \sum_{t=0}^{\infty} \beta^t u(c_t^h)$$

subject to $c_t^h + l_t^h \leq y_t^h + [1 + r(t-1)]l_{t-1}^h$

and $\lim_{T \to \infty} E_t \phi(T, t)l_T^h = 0, \; l_{-1}^h = 0.$

We assume that u_1 is large enough to have $u_1 - u_2 > 0$. This provision guarantees a positive marginal utility and allows us to substitute the flow budget constraint into the utility function to get

$$\max E_0 \sum_{t=0}^{\infty} \beta^t \left\{ u_0 + u_1[y_t^h + [1 + r(t-1)]l_{t-1}^h - l_t^h] \right.$$
$$\left. - \frac{u_2}{2} [y_t^h + [1 + r(t-1)]l_{t-1}^h - l_t^h]^2 \right\}.$$

Recall that, at time t, l_t^h is to be chosen and that the information set includes $r(t)$. This situation amounts to an assumption about the markets that are open at each date. Let $Ey_t^h = \bar{y}$. Notice that the assumptions that $y_t^B = 1 - y_t^A$ and y_t^A is distributed uniformly on $[0, 1]$ imply that $Ey_t^A = Ey_t^B = 1/2$. The Euler equation for our optimization problem is

$$-u_1 + u_2[y_t^h + [1 + r(t-1)]l_{t-1}^h - l_t^h] + \beta u_1[1 + r(t)]$$
$$+ \{-\beta u_2 \bar{y} - \beta u_2[1 + r(t)]l_t^h + \beta u_2 E_t l_{t+1}^h\}[1 + r(t)] = 0.$$

We want to impose market clearing. In this setup with $N^B = N^A$ and all agents of a given type being alike, we solve for a symmetric equilibrium, that is, for one in which all individuals of a given type receive the same allocation. This symmetric equilibrium is characterized by $l_t^A + l_t^B = 0$. In particular, the implication is $E_t l_{t+1}^A + E_t l_{t+1}^B = 0$. Adding the previous Euler equation over $h = A, B$, we get

$$-2u_1 + u_2(y_t^A + y_t^B) + 2\beta u_1[1 + r(t)]$$
$$- \beta u_2[1 + r(t)](E_t y_{t+1}^A + E_t y_{t+1}^B) = 0$$

or $-2u_1 + u_2 - [1 + r(t)]\beta(-2u_1 + u_2) = 0,$

which implies that

$$1 + r(t) = \beta^{-1} \; \forall \, t,$$

because $u_2 - 2u_1 \neq 0$. The strategy now is, given the market-determined rate of interest, to solve for the agent's optimal decision rules. For this purpose we use the nonstochastic version of the Euler equation to get

$$l^h_{t+1} - (1 + \beta^{-1})l^h_t + \beta^{-1}l^h_{t-1} = y^h_{t+1} - y^h_t, \qquad t \geq 0.$$

This is a second-order difference equation in l^h_t with a "driving process" given by $(y^h_{t+1} - y^h_t)$. To find a solution to such an equation, we ordinarily use two initial conditions. In this case we have only one initial condition, which is of the form $l^h_{-1} = 0$. The transversality condition $\lim_{T \to \infty} E_t \phi(T, t)l^h_T = \lim_{T \to \infty} E_t \beta^{T-t} l^h_T = 0$, however, requires that the expected rate of growth of l^h_t be bounded strictly below β^{-1}, as otherwise we would not get convergence of the sequence $E_t \beta^{T-t} l^h_T$ as needed.

Using lag operator notation we can write the previous difference equation as

$$[1 - (1 + \beta^{-1})L + \beta^{-1}L^2]l^h_{t+1} = y^h_{t+1} - y^h_t,$$

where we define $LX_t \equiv X_{t-1}$. The polynomial in the lag operator can be factored as

$$(1 - \lambda_1 L)(1 - \lambda_2 L)l^h_{t+1} = y^h_{t+1} - y^h_t,$$

where $\lambda_1 = 1$ and $\lambda_2 = \beta^{-1}$.

Notice that $(1 - \lambda_i L)X_t = X_t - \lambda_i LX_t = X_t - \lambda_i X_{t-1}$. A solution to the above second-order difference equation is a function mapping the integers and the driving process into values of l^h_t. We will show that there are many such functions but that only one satisfies $l^h_{-1} = 0$ and the restrictions that the budget constraint imposes on the rate of growth of one-period loans.

We first transform the second-order difference equation into a first-order difference equation, as these can easily be solved by simply iterating. (The reader familiar with difference equations and how to impose a transversality condition on the solution path may ignore the following paragraphs and simply check the solution. An analysis of difference equations using lag operators that deals with these questions can be found in Sargent (1979), especially chapters 9 and 11.) Denote by $z^i_{t+1} = (1 - \lambda_i L)l^h_{t+1}$. With this notation the difference equation can be written as

$$(1 - \lambda_2 L)z^1_{t+1} = y^h_{t+1} - y^h_t \quad \text{or} \quad (1 - \lambda_1 L)z^2_{t+1} = y^h_{t+1} - y^h_t.$$

We will analyze the possible solutions to each of these "versions" of the difference equation. Although there are many solutions of this Euler equation, only one satisfies the initial condition and the terminal condition, as we shall show by studying all of the possible solutions. We can iterate either forward or backward on $(1 - \lambda_j L)z_{t+1}^i = y_{t+1}^h - y_t^h$. If we go backward we get

$$z_{t+1}^i = \lambda_j z_t^i + y_{t+1}^h - y_t^h \quad \text{or} \quad z_1^i = \lambda_j z_0^i + y_1^h - y_0^h.$$

In the case $\lambda_j = \beta^{-1}$ and $z_t^i = l_t^h - l_{t-1}^h$, just pick the first t such that $l_t^h \neq l_{t-1}^h$. Notice that, unless $y_t^h = y_{t-1}^h$, such t exists. Denote it by τ. Then for $T > \tau$ we have

$$z_T = \left(\frac{1}{\beta}\right)^{T-\tau} z_\tau^i + \sum_{s=0}^{T} \left(\frac{1}{\beta}\right)^{T-s} (y_{\tau+s}^h - y_{\tau-1+s}^h).$$

For any $\tau \leq t \leq T$, it is true that

$$\beta^T z_T = \beta^\tau z_\tau^i + \sum_{s=0}^{T} \left(\frac{1}{\beta}\right)^{-s} (y_{\tau+s}^h - y_{\tau-1+s}^h) \quad \text{and}$$

$$E_t \beta^T z_T = \beta^\tau z_\tau^i + \sum_{s=0}^{t-\tau} \left(\frac{1}{\beta}\right)^{-s} (y_{\tau+s}^h - y_{\tau-1+s}^h).$$

The right-hand side does not depend on T. Therefore the limit as $T \to \infty$ is not zero if z_τ^i is not zero, which contradicts $\lim_{T\to\infty} E_t \beta^T l_t^h = 0$.

Take the case $\lambda_j = 1$ and $z_t^i = l_t^h - \beta^{-1} l_{t-1}^h$. Denote $\hat{l}_t^h \equiv \beta^t l_t^h$. Then the transversality condition requires that $\lim_{T\to\infty} E_t \hat{l}_T^h = 0$. The difference equation is now

$$l_t^h - \beta^{-1} l_{t-1}^h = l_{t-1}^h - \beta^{-1} l_{t-2}^h + y_t^h - y_{t-1}^h$$

or $\quad \hat{l}_t^h - \hat{l}_{t-1}^h = \beta(\hat{l}_{t-1}^h - \hat{l}_{t-2}^h) + \beta^t (y_t^h - y_{t-1}^h).$

This equation holds for $t \geq 1$, with $\hat{l}_{-1}^h = 0$. Let τ be the first t such that $\hat{l}_t^h \neq 0$. Denote $\beta^t (y_t^h - y_{t-1}^h) \equiv n_t^h$. Then $\hat{l}_{\tau+1}^h = (1 + \beta)\hat{l}_\tau^h + n_{\tau+1}^h$. We iterate to get

$$\hat{l}_{\tau+k}^h = \left(\sum_{j=0}^{k} \beta^j\right) \hat{l}_\tau^h + \left(\sum_{j=0}^{k-1} \beta^j\right) n_{\tau+1}^h + \cdots$$

$$+ \left(\sum_{j=0}^{k-s} \beta^j\right) n_{\tau+s}^h + \cdots + n_{\tau+k}^h.$$

Let $T = \tau + k$, and $t = \tau + s$, $s < k$. Notice that $E_t n_v^h = 0$, $\forall\, v > t + 1$. Also denote $d_N \equiv \sum_{j=0}^{N} \beta^j$. Then

$$E_t \hat{l}_T^h = d_{T-\tau} \hat{l}_\tau^h + d_{T-\tau-1} n_{\tau+1}^h + \cdots$$

$$+ d_{T-\tau-s} n_{\tau+s}^h - d_{T-\tau-s-1} y_{\tau+s}^h.$$

Notice that, for every j, $\lim_{T\to\infty} d_{T-j} = 1/(1 - \beta)$. Taking limits on both sides, we obtain

$$\lim_{T \to \infty} E_t \beta^T l_T^h = \frac{1}{1-\beta} \{\beta^\tau l_\tau^h + n_{\tau+1}^h + \cdots + n_{\tau+s}^h - y_{\tau+s}^h\}.$$

This is in general nonzero for some t. Consequently both backward solutions violate the transversality condition in the end.

We look now at the forward solution, which is

$$z_t^i = \lambda_j^{-1}(z_{t+1}^i + y_t^h - y_{t+1}^h) \quad \text{or}$$
$$z_t^i = \lambda_j^{-1}[\lambda_j^{-1}(z_{t+2}^i + y_{t+1}^h - y_{t+2}^h) + y_t^h - y_{t+1}^h].$$

After iterating k times, we obtain

$$z_t^i = \lambda_j^{-k} z_{t+k}^i + \sum_{s=0}^{k-1} \lambda_j^{s+1}(y_{t+s}^h - y_{t+1+s}^h).$$

Take first the case $\lambda_j = \lambda_1 = 1$. Taking the expectation conditional on information available at t on both sides, we get

$$E_t z_t^i = z_t^i = E_t z_{t+k}^i + \left(y_t - \frac{1}{2}\right), \forall \, k.$$

Denote $E_t z_{t+k}^i = \bar{z}_t^i, \, k = 1, 2, \ldots$. Let τ be a t such that $l_\tau^i \neq 0$. Then

$$l_{\tau+1}^h = \frac{1}{\beta} l_\tau + \bar{z}_{\tau+1}^i + y_{\tau+1} - \frac{1}{2}.$$

Iterating on this equation

$$l_{\tau+k}^h = \left(\frac{1}{\beta}\right)^k l_\tau^h + \sum_{s=1}^{k} \left(\frac{1}{\beta}\right)^{k-s} \bar{z}_{\tau+s}^i$$
$$+ \sum_{s=1}^{k} \left(\frac{1}{\beta}\right)^{k-s} (y_{\tau+s}^h - y_{\tau+s+1}^h).$$

Let $\tau + k = T$ and $\tau \le t < T$. Then as $E_t \bar{z}_s^i = \bar{z}_t^i, \forall \, s \ge t$,

$$E_t \beta^T l_T^h = \beta^\tau l_\tau^h + \beta^T \sum_{s=1}^{t-\tau} \left(\frac{1}{\beta}\right)^{T-\tau-s} \bar{z}_{\tau+s}^i$$
$$+ \beta^T \bar{z}_t^i \sum_{s=t-\tau+1}^{T-\tau} \left(\frac{1}{\beta}\right)^{T-\tau-s} + \beta^T \sum_{s=1}^{t-\tau-1} \left(\frac{1}{\beta}\right)^{T-\tau-s}$$
$$\cdot (y_{\tau+s}^h - y_{\tau+s+1}^h) + \beta^T \left(\frac{1}{\beta}\right)^{T-t} \left(y_t^h - \frac{1}{2}\right).$$

Taking limits as $T \to \infty$ on both sides, it follows that

$$\lim_{T \to \infty} E_t \beta^T l_T^h = \beta^\tau l_\tau^h + \sum_{s=1}^{t-\tau} \beta^{\tau+s} \bar{z}_{\tau+s}^i$$

$$+ \sum_{s=1}^{t-\tau-1} \beta^{\tau+s}(y_{\tau+s}^h - y_{\tau+1+s}^h) + \bar{z}_t^i \frac{\beta^{t+1}}{1 - \beta}$$

$$+ \beta^t \left(y_t^h - \frac{1}{2} \right).$$

It is clear that there is no reason why this solution should guarantee that the transversality condition is satisfied. Then we are left with only one possibility, namely $\lambda_j = \beta^{-1}$. In this case

$$z_t^1 = \beta^k z_{t+k}^1 + \sum_{s=0}^{k-1} \beta^{s+1}(y_{t+s}^h - y_{t+1+s}^h).$$

First taking expectations conditional on information available at t on both sides and then taking limits as k goes to infinity, we get

$$z_t^1 = \lim_{k \to \infty} E_t \beta^k z_{t+k}^1 + \beta \left(y_t^h - \frac{1}{2} \right).$$

We impose the transversality condition to get

$$z_t^1 = l_t^h - l_{t-1}^h + \beta \left(y_t^h - \frac{1}{2} \right) \quad \text{or} \quad l_t^h = l_{t-1}^h + \beta \left(y_t^h - \frac{1}{2} \right).$$

This function, after we have imposed $l_{-1}^h = 0$, satisfies the Euler equation and the transversality condition by construction and hence is a solution. As we have already shown that every other candidate that satisfies the Euler equation violates either the initial condition or the condition on the growth rate of l_t^h, it follows that this is the unique solution to our problem.

Using the solution on the "flow" budget constraint we get

$$c_t^h = \frac{1}{2} + \frac{1 - \beta}{\beta} l_{t-1}^h + (1 - \beta) \left(y_t^h - \frac{1}{2} \right),$$

$$t = 0, 1, \dots, \quad h = A, B,$$

which is the desired result.

EXERCISE 6.4   The Distribution of Currency

Consider the model of Section 6.6 with $T = +\infty$ and with $N^A = N^B$. Keep all aspects of the model as in Section 6.6 except for the initial stocks of currency.

Let each type A agent begin with $m_{-1}^A = m/2$ units of currency and each type B agent begin with $m_{-1}^B = m/2$ units of currency.

a. Find equilibrium consumption allocations and a price path in which currency is valued. How is currency redistributed over time in this equilibrium?

b. How do this equilibrium consumption allocation and price path compare with those computed in Section 6.6?

SOLUTION

a. Because the environment is very similar to that of Section 6.7, *DMT*, we closely follow the argument presented in the text. We either assume the "turnpike" interpretation of Section 6.8, *DMT*, or directly rule out the existence of a loan market. The problem faced by individual h is

$$\max \sum_{t=0}^{\infty} \beta^t u(c_t^h)$$

by choice of sequences $\{c_t^h\}, \{m_t^h\}$ that satisfy

$$c_t^h + \frac{m_t^h}{p_t} \le y_t^h - z_t^h + \frac{m_{t-1}^h}{p_t}, \qquad m_t^h \ge 0,$$

where y_t^h is the endowment sequence. For $h = A$, this sequence is $\{1 + m/(2p_0), 0, 1, 0, 1, \ldots \}$, whereas for $h = B$ the sequence is $\{m/(2p_0), 1, 0, 1, 0, \ldots \}$. In period zero each agent has a claim to half of the existing money supply. As in Section 6.7, *DMT*, z_t^h is the amount of taxes paid by agent h at time t. The following pattern of taxes is used

$$z_t^A = \begin{cases} 1 - \lambda, & t \text{ even} \\ 0, & t \text{ odd.} \end{cases}$$

$$z_t^B = \begin{cases} 0, & t \text{ even} \\ 1 - \mu, & t \text{ odd,} \end{cases}$$

where λ and μ are chosen to satisfy $0 < \lambda, \mu < 1$, and also

$$\frac{\lambda}{1 + \beta} + \frac{\mu}{1 + \beta} = 1$$

To solve the maximization problem, we form the Lagrangian

$$J = \sum_{t=0}^{\infty} \beta^t \left\{ u(c_t^h) + \lambda_t^h \left[y_t^h - z_t^h + \frac{m_{t-1}^h}{p_t} - \frac{m_t^h}{p_t} - c_t^h \right] \right\},$$

where λ_t^h is a sequence of nonnegative Lagrange multipliers. The first-order conditions are

$$\beta^t\{u'(c_t^h) - \lambda_t^h\} \le 0, \qquad = 0 \quad \text{if } c_t^h > 0, \qquad t = 0, 1, \ldots$$

$$\frac{-\beta^t\lambda_t^h}{p_t} + \frac{\beta^{t+1}\lambda_{t+1}^h}{p_{t+1}} \le 0, \qquad = 0 \quad \text{if } m_t^h > 0, \qquad t = 0, 1, \ldots$$

$$c_t^h + \frac{m_t^h}{p_t} \le y_t^h - z_t^h + \frac{m_{t-1}^h}{p_t}, \qquad t = 0, 1, \ldots$$

$m_{-1}^h = 0$, $h = A, B$, and the transversality condition

$$\lim_{T\to\infty} \beta^T\lambda_T^h \frac{m_T^h}{p_T} = 0.$$

As in Section 6.7, *DMT*, we make the following conjectures. An agent of type h will have a positive demand for currency only during the periods in which she has positive endowment. In other words $m_t^A = m_t^s$ for t even, and $m_t^B = m_t^s$ for t odd, where m_t^s is money supply at time t. We also conjecture that $c_t^h = c^h$ for all t, that is, consumption is constant over time. We proceed with the conjecture, and at the end we verify that it holds. If $c_t^h = c^h > 0$, then $\lambda_t^h = \lambda^h > 0$. Therefore, because $m_t^h > 0$ for all t and some h, the second condition is satisfied at equality for either $h = A$ or $h = B$. Consequently the implication is that

$$\beta^t\lambda^h\left(\frac{-1}{p_t} + \frac{\beta}{p_{t+1}}\right) = 0, \quad \text{or} \quad p_{t+1} = \beta p_t, \qquad t = 0, 1, \ldots$$

Then under the conjectured equilibrium there is "deflation" at the rate β. From the budget constraint we get

$$m_t^h = \begin{cases} p_t(y_t^h - z_t^h - c_t^h) & \text{if } y_t^h > 0 \\ 0 & \text{otherwise} \end{cases}$$

More precisely

$$m_t^A = \begin{cases} p_0[\lambda + m/2p_0 - c^A] & \text{at } t = 0 \\ p_t[\lambda - c^A] & t \text{ even}, \qquad t \ne 0 \\ 0 & t \text{ odd} \end{cases}$$

$$m_t^B = \begin{cases} p_t(\mu - c^B) & t \text{ odd} \\ 0 & t \text{ even} \end{cases}$$

Finally, because the government uses tax proceeds to retire currency from circulation, the process followed by the currency supply is

$$m_t^s = m_{t-1}^s - p_t(z_t^A + z_t^B), \qquad t = 0, 1, \ldots,$$

with $m_{-1}^s = m$ given.

To characterize the equilibrium fully we need to compute c^A, c^B, and p_0. Once we have p_0 we obtain p_t from $p_t = \beta^t p_0$. To find the endogenous variables we use three equilibrium conditions:

(1) $\qquad m_0^s = m - p_0(1 - \lambda) = p_0(\lambda - c^A) + \dfrac{m}{2} = m_0^A$

(2) $\qquad m_1^s = m_0^s - p_1(1 - \mu) = p_1(\mu - c^B) = m_1^B$

(3) $\qquad c^A + c^B = 1.$

If we use $p_1 = \beta p_0$ the system (1)–(3) contains three equations and three unknowns. Its solution is given by

$$c^A = \frac{1 + \lambda}{2 + \beta}, \qquad c^B = \frac{\mu}{2 + \beta}, \qquad p_0 = \frac{(2 + \beta)m}{2\mu}.$$

We now verify that this candidate is indeed a solution. Because by construction the first three of the necessary conditions for a maximum are satisfied, we only have to check that the transversality condition is not violated. For $t \geq 1$, we have that m_t^h / p_t is a sequence of constants and zeros. Because $\lambda_t^h = \lambda^h$, the transversality condition is satisfied.

b. Notice that in the equilibrium of Section 6.7, *DMT*, we had $c^A = \lambda/(1 + \beta)$ and $c^B = \mu/(1 + \beta)$. Therefore in the equilibrium of this model, consumption of a type A agent is higher, whereas consumption of the type B agent is lower. The reason is the differences in income distribution. In this model a type A agent is endowed at time zero with half of the money supply. This wealth effect increases her permanent consumption. On the other hand, both economies share the same rate of deflation: prices decrease at the rate β. The initial price level p_0 is different. It turns out that in this economy the price level is lower than in the economy of Section 6.7, *DMT*.

EXERCISE 6.5   Rate-of-Return Dominance

Consider a version of the turnpike model of Section 6.8 modified as follows: two agents travel in the same direction and can therefore engage in intertemporal trades. These agents share the same preferences but have different endowments. East-heading agents: agents 1 and 2 have endowment streams given by

$$y_t^1 = 1, \qquad t = 0, 1, \ldots$$

$$y_t^2 = \begin{cases} 0, & t \text{ even} \\ w, & t \text{ odd}. \end{cases}$$

West-heading agents: agents 3 and 4 have endowments given by

$$y_t^3 = 1, \qquad t = 0, 1, \ldots$$

$$y_t^4 = \begin{cases} w, & t \text{ even} \\ 0, & t \text{ odd.} \end{cases}$$

Preferences are given by $\Sigma \beta^t u(c_t^h)$, where $u(c) = (c^{1-\rho} - 1)/(1 - \rho)$.

a. Assume that there is no outside debt. Compute the competitive equilibrium of this model

b. Now endow agent 2 with m units of currency. Specify under what conditions there exists an equilibrium in which currency is valued and the price level is constant.

c. Compare the rates of return on different assets—currency and loans—faced by east- and west-heading agents. What accounts for the difference?

d. Argue that neither the part (a) equilibrium nor the part (b) equilibrium is optimal when we restrict ourselves to allocations that treat all agents of a given type identically.

SOLUTION

a. The following solution is based on an exercise prepared by Shinichi Watanabe (personal communication). The problem faced by agent h is

$$\max \sum_{t=0}^{\infty} \beta^t u(c_t^h)$$

subject to $c_t^h + l_t^h \leq y_t^h + [1 + r(t-1)]l_{t-1}^h, \; l_{-1}^h = 0.$

Because l_t^h is unrestricted we can write a single budget constraint that leaves the agent with the same opportunity set. We can therefore regard agent h as solving the following problem:

$$\max \sum_{t=0}^{\infty} \beta^t u(c_t^h)$$

subject to $\sum_{t=0}^{\infty} p_t c_t^h \leq W^h,$

where W^h is wealth and is given by $W^h = \sum_{t=0}^{\infty} p_t y_t^h$. In this formulation p_t is the price of consumption at time t (in the location where this agent is going to be) in terms of some numeraire. We can choose consumption at time zero as numeraire and then set $p_0 = 1$. Notice that with this normalization $p_t = \prod_{j=0}^{t-1}[1 + r(j)]^{-1}$. The first-order necessary conditions for the maximization problem are

$$\beta^t u'(c_t^h) \le \lambda^h p_t, \; = 0 \quad \text{if } c_t^h > 0, \qquad t = 0, 1, \ldots$$

and $\quad \displaystyle\sum_{t=0}^{\infty} p_t c_t^h = W^h.$

Because each pair of agents faces the same environment every two periods, we hypothesize that the solution is periodic. In particular, we look for a solution of the following type

$$c_t^h = \begin{cases} c_0^h, & t \text{ even} \\ c_1^h, & t \text{ odd}. \end{cases}$$

Under this guess it follows that

$$p_{2n} = \beta^{2n} p_0 = \beta^{2n} \qquad p_{2n+1} = \beta^{2n} p_1.$$

In other words, the two-period discount factor is β^2. Also from the first-order conditions we get

$$\frac{u'(c_0^h)}{\beta u'(c_1^h)} = \frac{1}{p_1}$$

or $\qquad c_1^h = c_0^h \left(\dfrac{\beta}{p_1} \right)^{1/\rho},$

and $\qquad c_0^h (1 + \beta^2 + \beta^4 + \cdots)$
$$+ \, c_1^h (p_1 + \beta^2 p_1 + \beta^4 p_1 + \cdots) = W^h.$$

With these conditions we can derive explicit solutions for the demand functions c_t^h. These are

$$c_0^h = \frac{(1 - \beta^2) W^h}{1 + \beta^{1/\rho} p_1^{1-1/\rho}}$$

$$c_1^h = \frac{(\beta/p_1)^{1/\rho}(1 - \beta^2) W^h}{1 + \beta^{1/\rho} p_1^{1-1/\rho}}.$$

We first analyze the equilibrium of the east-heading agents. For $h = 1$ we get that $W^h = (1 + p_1)/(1 - \beta^2)$, whereas for $h = 2$, $W^h = w p_1/(1 - \beta^2)$. By Walras's law we need to impose only one equilibrium condition. We choose to solve for $c_0^1 + c_0^2 = 1$. Then this condition is equivalent to

$$\frac{1 + p_1}{1 + \beta^{1/\rho} p_1^{1-1/\rho}} + \frac{w_1 p_1}{1 + \beta^{1/\rho} p_1^{1-1/\rho}} = 1.$$

The solution is

$$p_1 = \beta(1 + w)^{-\rho}.$$

Therefore the sequence of prices faced by these agents is

$$\{1, \beta(1 + w)^{-\rho}, \beta^2, \beta^3(1 + w)^{-\rho}, \beta^4, \ldots \}.$$

Alternatively, the sequence of one-period interest rates is

$$\{[1 + r^e(t)]\} = \left\{ \frac{(1 + w)^\rho}{\beta}, \frac{1}{\beta(1 + w)^\rho}, \frac{(1 + w)^\rho}{\beta}, \frac{1}{\beta(1 + w)^\rho}, \cdots \right\}$$

The competitive allocation is

$$c_t^1 = \begin{cases} \dfrac{1 + \beta(1 + w)^{-\rho}}{1 + (1 + w)\beta(1 + w)^{-\rho}}, & t \text{ even} \\[3mm] \dfrac{(1 + w)[1 + \beta(1 + w)^{-\rho}]}{1 + (1 + w)\beta(1 + w)^{-\rho}}, & t \text{ odd} \end{cases}$$

$$c_t^2 = \begin{cases} \dfrac{w\beta(1 + w)^{-\rho}}{1 + (1 + w)\beta(1 + w)^{-\rho}}, & t \text{ even} \\[3mm] \dfrac{(1 + w)w\beta(1 + w)^{-\rho}}{1 + (1 + w)\beta(1 + w)^{-\rho}}, & t \text{ odd.} \end{cases}$$

If we perform the same calculations for west-heading agents, we see that the sequence of one-period interest rates is given by

$$\{[1 + r^0(t)]\} = \left\{ \frac{1}{\beta(1 + w)^\rho}, \frac{(1 + w)^\rho}{\beta}, \frac{1}{\beta(1 + w)^\rho}, \cdots \right\}.$$

The competitive allocation is

$$c_t^3 = \begin{cases} \dfrac{1 + \beta(1 + w)^\rho}{1 + (1 + w)^{-1}\beta(1 + w)^\rho}, & t \text{ even} \\[3mm] \dfrac{(1 + w)^{-1}[1 + \beta(1 + w)^\rho]}{1 + (1 + w)^{-1}\beta(1 + w)^\rho}, & t \text{ odd} \end{cases}$$

$$c_t^4 = \begin{cases} \dfrac{w}{1 + (1 + w)^{-1}\beta(1 + w)^\rho}, & t \text{ even} \\[3mm] \dfrac{(1 + w)^{-1}w}{1 + (1 + w)^{-1}\beta(1 + w)^\rho}, & t \text{ odd.} \end{cases}$$

Notice that, at any given date t, four agents (one of each type) meet at a given trading post. If we did not distinguish between private debt issued by east- or west-heading agents, we would find that in this economy similar assets sell for different prices. In other words, the rates of interest at which these agents make intertemporal trades are different. The key to understanding this paradox is to realize that private debt issued by, say, east-heading agents is very different from private debt issued by west-heading agents, because if an east-heading agent were to buy an IOU issued by a west-heading individual, he would never be able to redeem it: the pattern of meetings is such that neither he nor anybody else he will meet in the future will be able to meet the issuer. The spatial separation (a very specific pattern of meetings) is therefore the force that explains the differences in rates of return faced by east- and west-heading agents.

b. We now endow agent 2 — the agent who has zero endowment at time zero — with m units of currency. Notice that, because loans between agents who move in the same direction remain unrestricted, currency cannot dominate private debt in rate of return if both currency and loans are being held. It is possible, however, for the rate of return facing, say, east-heading agents at a given time to exceed one (the rate of return of currency under a constant-price-level equilibrium) if neither agent is holding currency, that is, if both agents are at a corner solution. This is the type of situation for which we will look. The problem faced by private agents in a competitive equilibrium is exactly the same as in part (a). The only difference is that the level of agent 2's wealth must be increased by m/p: the value of real currency holdings that play the role of a time zero endowment.

Notice that at $t = 0$ east-heading agents faced a rate of return greater than one $[1 + r^e(0) = (1 + w)^\rho/\beta > 1]$. Because currency will have a rate of return of one, we hypothesize that neither agent 1 nor agent 2 will hold currency from period 1 to period 2. It must therefore be the case that agent 2 sells his currency holdings to either agent 3 or agent 4. Inasmuch as agents heading in the same direction face the same rate of return — and if both assets (currency and private loans) are held, they must bear the same rate of return — it follows that the composition of individual portfolios is indeterminate. It may be helpful, however, to imagine that agent 4 — who has an endowment of w — buys the currency and takes it to the next trading post. At time $t = 1$, agent 4 will "look like" agent 2 at $t = 0$. He will have an endowment of m units of currency and zero of the good. On the other hand, he will meet a type 2 agent who, at $t = 1$, resembles a type 4 agent at $t = 0$: he has no currency (he sold it during the previous period) and has an endowment of w units of the consumption good.

We hypothesize that in even periods type 4 agents hold currency that they sell the following period to type 2 agents. These in turn sell it back to the next type 4 agent that they meet. With this pattern in mind, it follows that $(p_1^0)^{-1}$, the rate of return faced by west-heading agents at time zero, must equal the rate of return on currency, which is one, whereas $(p_1^e)^{-1}$, the rate faced by east-heading agents at time zero, must be at least one.

Let s_t^h be savings of agent h at time t. Then $s_t^h = y_t^h - c_t^h$. Under our conjecture we have

$$s_0^1 + s_0^2 = 0$$
$$s_0^3 + s_0^4 = q,$$

where $q = m/p > 0$.

Notice that s_0^2 is given by

$$s_0^2 = q - \frac{(1 - \beta^2)q + p_1^e w}{1 + \beta^{1/\rho}p_1^{e(1-1/\rho)}},$$

because agent 2 is endowed with currency. Then to compute an equilibrium, we impose $p_1^0 = 1$, and we need to find $q > 0$ and $p_1^e \le 1$ that solve

$$s_0^1 + s_0^2 = \frac{\beta^{1/\rho}p_1^{e(1-1/\rho)} - p_1^e + q\beta^2 + q\beta^{1/\rho}p_1^{e(1-1/\rho)} - p_1^e w}{1 + \beta^{1/\rho}p_1^{e(1-1/\rho)}} = 0$$

$$s_0^3 + s_0^4 = \frac{(1 + w)\beta^{1/\rho}p_1^{0(1-1/\rho)} - p_1^0}{1 + \beta^{1/\rho}p_1^{0(1-1/\rho)}} = q > 0.$$

Because $p_1^0 = 1$, it follows that $q > 0$ if and only if $(1 + w)\beta^{1/\rho} - 1 > 0$. This condition, however, is equivalent to $1 + r^0(0) = 1/\beta(1 + w)^\rho < 1$, the interest rate faced by the west-heading agents in the nonmonetary equilibrium must be less than one. To complete the proof that our candidate is indeed an equilibrium, we must show that there is a $p_1^e \le 1$ that solves the first equilibrium condition. It is straightforward to verify that $p_1^e = \beta^2$ is a solution. We generated that guess in the following way: because $c_0^h = c_2^h = \cdots = c_{2n}^h$, $n = 0, 1, \ldots$, we know that the two-period rate of return is β^{-2}. Because between periods 1 and 2 the east-heading agents will hold the currency, it follows that $1 + r^e(1) = 1$. On the other hand, however, a simple arbitrage argument shows that the two-period rate of return equals the product of the corresponding one-period rates, that is,

$$[1 + r^e(0)][1 + r^e(1)] = \beta^{-2}.$$

Therefore $p_1^e = [1 + r^e(0)^{-1}] = \beta^2$. We can then display the sequence of rates of return faced by east- and west-heading agents in this equilibrium

$$\{1 + r^e(t)\} = \{\beta^{-2}, 1, \beta^{-2}, 1, \beta^{-2}, \ldots\}$$
$$\{1 + r^0(t)\} = \{1, \beta^{-2}, 1, \beta^{-2}, \ldots\}.$$

The equilibrium allocation is

$$
c_t^1 = \begin{cases} \dfrac{1 + \beta^2}{1 + \beta^{(2-1/\rho)}}, & t \text{ even} \\[3mm] \dfrac{\beta^{-1/\rho}(1 + \beta^2)}{1 + \beta^{(2-1/\rho)}}, & t \text{ odd.} \end{cases}
$$

$$
c_t^2 = \begin{cases} \dfrac{(1 - \beta^2)[(1 + w)\beta^{1/\rho} - 1] + \beta^2 w(1 + \beta^{1/\rho})}{(1 + \beta^{1/\rho})(1 + \beta^{(2-1/\rho)})}, & t \text{ even} \\[3mm] \dfrac{\beta^{-1/\rho}(1 - \beta^2)[(1 + w)\beta^{1/\rho} - 1] + \beta^{(2-1/\rho)}w(1 + \beta^{1/\rho})}{(1 + \beta^{1/\rho})(1 + \beta^{(2-1/\rho)})}, & t \text{ odd} \end{cases}
$$

$$
c_t^3 = \begin{cases} \dfrac{2}{1 + \beta^{1/\rho}}, & t \text{ even} \\[3mm] \dfrac{2\beta^{1/\rho}}{1 + \beta^{1/\rho}}, & t \text{ odd} \end{cases}
$$

$$
c_t^4 = \begin{cases} \dfrac{w}{1 + \beta^{1/\rho}}, & t \text{ even} \\[3mm] \dfrac{\beta^{1/\rho}w}{1 + \beta^{1/\rho}}, & t \text{ odd} \end{cases}
$$

Finally, notice that the value of p—the price level—can be computed from

$$
\frac{m}{p} = \frac{(1 + w)\beta^{1/\rho} - 1}{1 + \beta^{1/\rho}}.
$$

In this equilibrium the price level is proportional to the amount of currency.

c. At $t = 0$, assets held by west-heading agents—currency and loans—bear a unit rate of return. On the other hand, east-heading agents do not hold currency, because this is dominated in rate of return by private debt, which has a rate of return equal to β^{-2}. At $t = 1$, of course, the roles of east- and west-heading agents are reversed, with east-heading agents facing a rate of return of one and west-heading individuals facing a rate of return of β^{-2}. The basic reason for the differences in rates of return is that, at time zero, say, the endowment pattern of east-heading agents is such that the aggregate demand for savings is relatively low. On the other hand, west-heading agents are relatively well endowed at time zero and are willing to buy the currency held by east-heading agents. Therefore, because these two groups of agents will never meet again, all they can trade is the currency. One group turns out to end up in a corner solution, and it is therefore possible to observe the rate-of-return dominance.

Notice that the rate of return on private loans issued by east-heading agents at time zero is lower in the equilibrium with valued currency, because $\beta^{-2} < (1 + w)^\rho \beta^{-1}$. The basic reason is that in the equilibrium with valued currency the borrower, agent 2, has a higher endowment of time zero good. This characteristic reduces the demand for loans and consequently decreases the rate of interest.

d. If we follow the same arguments given in Section 6.2, *DMT,* it is easy to establish that optimal allocations that treat all agents of a given type identically must be constant sequences. The underlying intuition is fairly straightforward. In each period each agent is going to be at a point where the aggregate endowment is constant and equal to $(2 + w)$. Therefore—under the symmetry assumption—it is possible to offer each agent a constant stream of consumption. Because the utility function is strictly concave, a constant sequence is preferred to any varying sequence of the same present value. It is therefore possible to have constant sequences "dominate" time-varying sequences (in our case periodic sequences). In both equilibria the allocations are time varying and hence not optimal. Moreover it is not hard to check that the equilibrium with valued currency does not Pareto dominate the autarkic equilibrium. To verify that it does not, compute the utility of each agent under the competitive allocation. Denote this value by u^h, $h = 1, \ldots , 4$. Then after some algebraic manipulation it can be shown that $du^1/dp_1 < 0$ whenever $p_1 < \beta$, and $du^4/dp_1 < 0$. Because for agent 1 p increases [from $\beta/(1 + w)^\rho$ to β^2] and for agent 4 decreases [from $\beta(1 + w)^\rho$ to one], their utilities move in different directions. Finally notice that as β approaches one the allocations converge to a constant sequence. The reason is that when β goes to one there is no rate-of-return dominance, and therefore all agents face the same rate of return every period.

References and Suggested Readings

Bewley, Truman. 1980. The optimum quantity of money. In *Models of Monetary Economies,* ed. J. H. Kareken and N. Wallace, pp. 169–210. Minneapolis: Federal Reserve Bank of Minneapolis.

Friedman, Milton. 1969. The optimum quantity of money. In *The Optimum Quantity of Money and Other Essays,* pp. 1–50. Chicago: Aldine.

Lucas, Robert E., Jr. 1980. Equilibrium in a pure currency economy. In *Models of Monetary Economies,* ed. J. H. Kareken and N. Wallace, pp. 131–146. Minneapolis: Federal Reserve Bank of Minneapolis.

Sargent, Thomas J. 1979. *Macroeconomic Theory.* New York: Academic Press.

Townsend, Robert. 1980. Models of money with spatially separated agents. In *Models of Monetary Economies,* ed. J. H. Kareken and N. Wallace, pp. 265–304. Minneapolis: Federal Reserve Bank of Minneapolis.

7 | Credit and Currency with Overlapping Generations

EXERCISE 7.1   Credit Controls

Consider the following overlapping-generations model. At each date $t \geq 1$ there appear N two-period-lived young people, said to be of generation t, who live and consume during periods t and $(t + 1)$. At time $t = 1$ there exist N old people who are endowed with $H(0)$ units of paper "dollars," which they offer to supply inelastically to the young of generation 1 in exchange for goods. Let $p(t)$ be the price of the one good in the model, measured in dollars per time t good. For each $t \geq 1$, $N/2$ members of generation t are endowed with $y > 0$ units of the good at t and 0 units at $(t + 1)$, whereas the remaining $N/2$ members of generation t are endowed with 0 units of the good at t and $y > 0$ units when they are old. All members of all generations have the same utility function:

$$u[c_t^h(t), c_t^h(t + 1)] = \ln c_t^h(t) + \ln c_t^h(t + 1),$$

where $c_t^h(s)$ is the consumption of agent h of generation t in period s. The old at $t = 1$ simply maximize $c_0^h(1)$. The consumption good is nonstorable. The currency supply is constant through time, so $H(t) = H(0)$, $t \geq 1$.

a. Define a competitive equilibrium without valued currency for this model. Who trades what with whom?

b. Compute the nonvalued-currency competitive equilibrium values of the gross return on consumption loans, the consumption allocation of the old at $t = 1$, and that of the "borrowers" and "lenders" for $t \geq 1$.

c. Define a competitive equilibrium with valued currency. Who trades what with whom?

d. Prove that for this economy there does not exist a competitive equilibrium with valued currency.

e. Now suppose that the government imposes the restriction that $l_t^h(t)[1 + r(t)] \geq -y/4$, where $l_t^h(t)[1 + r(t)]$ represents claims on $(t + 1)$-period consumption purchased (if positive) or sold (if negative) by household h of generation t. This is a restriction on the amount of borrowing. For an equilibrium without valued currency, compute the consumption allocation and the gross rate of return on consumption loans.

f. In the setup of (e), show that there exists an equilibrium with valued currency in which the price level obeys the quantity theory equation $p(t) = qH(0)/N$. Find a formula for the undetermined coefficient q. Compute the consumption allocation and the equilibrium rate of return on consumption loans.

g. Are lenders better off in economy (b) or economy (f)? What about borrowers? What about the old of period 1 (generation 0)?

SOLUTION

a. We first describe the problem faced by the young of generation t. This problem is

$$\max_{c_t^h(t),\, c_t^h(t+1),\, l_t^h(t),\, m_t^h(t)} u^h(c_t^h(t),\, c_t^h(t+1))$$

subject to $c_t^h(t) + l_t^h(t) + \dfrac{m_t^h(t)}{p(t)} \leq w_t^h(t)$

$$c_t^h(t+1) \leq w_t^h(t+1) + [1 + r(t)]l_t^h(t) + \dfrac{m_t^h(t)}{p(t+1)},$$

$$[c_t^h(t),\, c_t^h(t+1),\, m_t^h(t)] \geq 0.$$

Let $c_t^h = [c_t^h(t), c_t^h(t+1)]$ and denote by $c_t = (c_t^1, \ldots, c_t^N)$ the consumption vector of generation t. We use c_0 to denote second-period consumption of the generation that is old at $t = 1$. A sequence $c = \{c_t\}_{t=0}^{\infty}$ is called an allocation. We are now ready to define an equilibrium. A competitive equilibrium without valued fiat money is a sequence $\{1/p(t)\}_{t=1}^{\infty}$ identically equal to zero, a sequence $\{r(t)\}_{t=1}^{\infty}$, and an allocation c that satisfies two conditions.

(i) Given $r(t)$, c_t^h solves the agents' maximization problem for every h and $t \geq 1$.

(ii) Given c_t^h, we know that $l_t^h(t) = w_t^h(t) - c_t^h(t)$. Market clearing requires

that

$$\sum_{h=1}^{N} l_t^h(t) = 0, \qquad t = 1, 2, \ldots$$

In this economy with only one good at each date, the only possible trades are intertemporal ones, that is, exchanges of consumption in one period for consumption in some other period. No intergenerational trades are possible. At any time t, an "old" agent cares only about consumption. This agent would be willing to buy the good but has nothing to offer to a young agent in exchange. Therefore no exchanges can be made. Intragenerational trades will occur in equilibrium. The utility function is such that agents want consumption over time to be smooth. Endowments vary across time, however, and are asymmetric across agents, making room for exchange of loans. Agents who are well endowed during their first period of life will be willing to give up some consumption when they are young in exchange for goods in their second period of life. Agents who are well endowed when they are old will be willing to accept those trades.

b. Solving the competitive problem for the Cobb-Douglas utility function we find that

$$s_t^h(t) \equiv w_t^h(t) - c_t^h(t) = \frac{1}{2}\left[w_t^h(t) - \frac{w_t^h(t+1)}{1+r(t)}\right].$$

In the nonvalued-currency equilibrium, $s_t^h(t) = l_t^h(t)$. To compute the rate of interest that clears the market for consumption loans, we need to determine the aggregate savings function. For an agent endowed $(y, 0)$, savings are $y/2$. As there are $N/2$ agents of this type, their aggregate demand is given by $Ny/4$. For an agent endowed $(0, y)$, the savings are $-y/(2[1 + r(t)])$. Total savings for this group are $-(Ny/4)[1 + r(t)]^{-1}$. The aggregate per capita savings function of the economy is

$$f[1 + r(t)] \equiv \frac{1}{4}\left[y - \frac{y}{1+r(t)}\right].$$

We defined an equilibrium as a sequence $\{r(t)\}$ and c, satisfying utility maximization and market clearing. Then the first part—utility maximization—is embedded already in $f(\cdot)$, whereas market clearing requires that

$$\frac{1}{N}\sum_{h=1}^{N} l_t^h(t) = f[1 + r(t)] = 0.$$

The unique solution to this condition is $r(t) = 0$, for all t, corresponding to a gross rate of return of one. To compute the equilibrium allocation, recall that it can be obtained from

$$c_t^h(t) = w_t^h(t) - l_t^h(t), \qquad c_t^h(t+1) = w_t^h(t+1) + [1 + r(t)]l_t^h(t).$$

For a lender—an agent endowed $(y, 0)$—we obtain $l_t^h(t) = y/2$. Consequently, $c_t^h(t) = y/2$, $c_t^h(t+1) = y/2$, $h = 1, \ldots, N/2$, and $t \geq 1$. In the case of a borrower—an individual endowed $(0, y)$—we obtain $l_t^h(t) = -y/2$. Therefore $c_t^h(t) = y/2$, $c_t^h(t+1) = y/2$, $h = N/2 + 1, \ldots, N$, and $t \geq 1$. The old at $t = 1$, that is, the members of generation zero, consume their endowments of the one good.

c. Notice that our definition of the competitive problem faced by the young is general enough to incorporate the maximization exercise that is solved in an equilibrium with valued currency. As in (a), define $m_t = [m_t^1(t), \ldots, m_t^N(t)]$, $m = \{m_t\}_{t=1}^{\infty}$. Then a competitive equilibrium with valued fiat currency is a pair of sequences $\{r(t)\}_{t=1}^{\infty}$ and $\{p(t)\}_{t=1}^{\infty}$ with $p(t)$ finite and greater than zero $\forall t$, an allocation c, and a sequence m such that

(i) Given $r(t)$ and $p(t)$, c_t^h and $m_t^h(t)$ solve the maximization problem defined in (a), for $h = 1, \ldots, N, t \geq 1$.
(ii) Given the choices of individual agents, markets clear, that is,

$$\sum_{h=1}^{N} l_t^h(t) + \sum_{h=1}^{N} \frac{m_t^h(t)}{p(t)} = \frac{H(t)}{p(t)}, \qquad t \geq 1.$$

This last condition is equivalent to the condition that the market for the consumption good clears.

In this equilibrium, there occur the same kinds of trades as in the equilibrium without valued fiat currency, because no markets have been shut. The fact that there is a "new" market, however—the market for currency—permits additional exchanges to be made. In this equilibrium, the "old" at each t have something that is valuable to the young—currency. The "young" are willing to give up some of the good at t in exchange for currency, because they know that next period—when they are the "old"—they will be able to exchange currency for goods. It is still true that agents engage in trade for the sole purpose of making the time pattern of consumption different (in general, also smoother) than the time pattern of endowments.

d. To prove the nonexistence results, we proceed by contradiction. From the first-order condition of the utility maximization problem we obtain

$$c_t^h(t): \quad u_1^h[c_t^h(t), c_t^h(t+1)] - \lambda_{1t}^h \leq 0, \qquad = 0 \quad \text{if } c_t^h(t) > 0$$
$$c_t^h(t+1): \quad u_2^h[c_t^h(t), c_t^h(t+1)] - \lambda_{2t}^h \leq 0, \qquad = 0 \quad \text{if } c_t^h(t+1) > 0$$
$$l_t^h(t): \quad -\lambda_{1t}^h + [1 + r(t)]\lambda_{2t}^h = 0$$

$$m_t^h(t). \quad -\frac{1}{p(t)}\lambda_{1t}^h + \lambda_{2t}^h\frac{1}{p(t+1)} \leq 0, \qquad = 0 \quad \text{if } m_t^h(t) > 0,$$

where λ_{1t}^h and λ_{2t}^h are nonnegative Lagrange multipliers.

Because the definition of an equilibrium with valued currency requires that $m_t^h(t) > 0$ for some h and for every t, we have that, for that h [assuming that $c_t^h(t)$ and $c_t^h(t+1)$ are strictly positive, which is true in any equilibrium],

$$1 + r(t) = \frac{p(t)}{p(t+1)}.$$

This arbitrage condition must hold in equilibrium.

Notice that as both assets—loans and currency—have the same rate of return and are equally safe, individuals are indifferent about the composition of their portfolios, because assets are held to profit only from the intertemporal shifts of consumption that they allow, and because, if a valued currency equilibrium exists, both assets must offer exactly the same intertemporal terms of trade. Consequently, agents should not care which asset they hold. We can therefore view each agent as choosing "savings": $s_t^h(t) = l_t^h(t) + m_t^h(t)/p(t)$. The equilibrium aggregate composition of "savings" is determined not from the asset demand side but from the restriction that markets clear. Formally the choice of $s_t^h(t)$ is no different from the choice of $l_t^h(t)$ that we analyzed in (b).

We first derive a contradiction from the assumption that an equilibrium exists in a somewhat more general setup. Subsequently we analyze the particular case that constitutes the present exercise.

Given $1 + r(t) = p(t)/p(t+1)$, it is clear that $s_t^h(t)$ depends on $1 + r(t)$ [or $p(t)/p(t+1)$]. If we denote this function as $s_t^h(t) = f^h[1 + r(t)]$, and

$$\frac{1}{N}\sum_{h=1}^{N} s_t^h(t) = \frac{1}{N}\sum_{h=1}^{N} f^h[1 + r(t)] = f[1 + r(t)],$$

then the equilibrium condition (ii) instructs us to set $r(t)$ such that

$$f[1 + r(t)] = \frac{H(t)}{p(t)N}$$

or $f[1 + r(t)]p(t) = \dfrac{H(t)}{N} = \dfrac{H(t+1)}{N}$

$$= p(t+1)f[1 + r(t+1)].$$

Hence

$$f[1 + r(t+1)] = [1 + r(t)]f[1 + r(t)].$$

We have shown that, in an equilibrium where currency is not valued, $r(t) = 0$, that is, $f(1) = 0$. Moreover, if $f(\cdot)$ is increasing in $r(t)$ (an assumption satisfied in this exercise), we have that $H(t)/p(t)N > 0$ implies $r(t) > 0$. If we set $r(t) > 0$, then $[1 + r(t)]f[1 + r(t)] > f[1 + r(t)] > 0$. Hence $r(t+1) > r(t)$ because $f[1 + r(t+1)] = [1 + r(t)]f[1 + r(t)]$. Thus we see that, if we start with any $r(1) > 0$, the sequence $\{r(t)\}$ generated under the assumption that an equilibrium with valued fiat currency exists is increasing. Now at every t, $f[1 + r(t)] = H(t)/p(t)N$ has a natural interpretation as the amount of time t good that the "old" at t consume in excess of their endowment. In this economy total resources are finite (actually they are constant), so $f[1 + r(t)]$ must be bounded, that is,

$$f[1 + r(t)] \le B, \quad \text{some } B > 0.$$

Because $f(\cdot)$ is an increasing function of $r(t)$, however, we have that $[1 + r(t)]f[1 + r(t)]$ grows without bound. Inasmuch as $f[1 + r(t+1)] = [1 + r(t)]f[1 + r(t)]$, this is a contradiction.

Notice that the "key" element in the argument is that $r(1) > 0$. Without this inequality we would not have been able to show that $\{r(t)\}$ is increasing. Yet $r(1) > 0$ is an implication of $p(1) > 0$ and the requirement that the per capita excess saving function be equal to $H(1)/p(1)N$.

In our case, we have

$$f[1 + r(t)] = \frac{1}{4}\left[y - \frac{y}{1 + r(t)}\right].$$

Using $1 + r(t) = p(t)/p(t+1)$ and $f[1 + r(t)] = H(0)/p(t)N$, we have

$$\frac{y}{4}[p(t) - p(t+1)] = H(0)N \quad \text{or} \quad p(t+1) = p(t) - \frac{4H(0)}{Ny}.$$

Hence for any finite $p(1) > 0$, the sequence $p(t)$ is decreasing with constant decrements of size $4H(0)/Ny$. Consequently, no matter how high $p(1)$ is, there exists a finite T such that $p(t) < 0$, $\forall\, t \ge T$. This series of statements contradicts our definition of equilibrium.

e. To analyze this form of credit limit, we solve the same problem as in (a) supplemented by the constraint $l_t^h(t)[1 + r(t)] \geq -y/4$. Clearly for the first group—the natural lenders—the new constraint is not going to be binding, and $f^h[1 + r(t)] = y/2, h = 1, \ldots, N/2$. For the borrowers, the constraint is binding. Recall that the "unconstrained" problem for this group gives $m_t^h(t) = 0$ and $l_t^h(t) = -y/(2[1 + r(t)])$. Then no matter what $r(t)$ is, we have $[1 + r(t)]l_t^h(t) = -y/2 < -y/4$. Hence borrowers will be effectively constrained, and $[1 + r(t)]l_t^h(t) = -y/4$. This equation gives a new savings schedule equal to

$$f^h[1 + r(t)] = \frac{-y}{4[1 + r(t)]}, \qquad h = \frac{N}{2} + 1, \ldots, N.$$

In an equilibrium where currency is not valued, $1/p(t) = 0 \; \forall \; t$, and the relevant market-clearing condition is (ii) in (a),

$$\frac{1}{N} \sum_{h=1}^{N} f^h[1 + r(t)] \equiv f[1 + r(t)] = 0.$$

Substituting the "new" functions $f^h(\cdot)$, we have

$$f[1 + r(t)] = \frac{y}{4} \left\{ 1 - \frac{1}{2[1 + r(t)]} \right\}.$$

Then the equilibrium rate is $r(t) = -1/2$. As in (b), we can compute c_t^h, given $s_t^h(t)$ and the endowment to get

$$c_t^h = \left(\frac{y}{2}, \frac{y}{4} \right), \qquad h = 1, \ldots, \frac{N}{2},$$

$$c_t^h = \left(\frac{y}{2}, \frac{3y}{4} \right), \qquad h = \frac{N}{2} + 1, \ldots, N.$$

It is clear that as expected, because the interest rate decreased, borrowers are better off and lenders worse off. The welfare of the old at $t = 1$ remains unchanged, as they do not trade with any generation born at $t = 1$ or later.

f. The savings function that we derived in (e) remains unchanged. The relevant equilibrium conditions are

$$f[1 + r(t)] = H(t)/[p(t)N], \qquad t = 1, 2, \ldots,$$
$$1 + r(t) = p(t)/p(t + 1), \qquad t = 1, 2, \ldots$$

Given $H(t) = H(0)$ and the particular form of $f(\cdot)$, the equilibrium price sequence must satisfy the difference equation

$$p(t + 1) = 2p(t) - \frac{8H(0)}{Ny}.$$

One possible solution to this difference equation (for which we do not have "initial conditions") is a constant $p(t)$. Then $p(t) = p* = 8H(0)/Ny$ is a solution. If we write the quantity equation as

$$p(t) = qH/N,$$

it follows that $q = 8/y$.

It is not hard to see that, if $p(1) < p*$, the corresponding $\{p(t)\}$ sequence cannot be an equilibrium, because there is a finite T_1 such that $\forall t \geq T_1$, $p(t) < 0$. On the other hand, if $p(1) > p*$, we can establish—given the linearity of the difference equation—that $p(t) > p(t-1)$ $\forall t \geq 2$ and that $p(t) \to \infty$. This is still an equilibrium with valued fiat currency, but as $H(t)/p(t)N \to 0$ in equilibrium, we must have that $f[1 + r(t)] \to 0$ and consequently that the equilibrium allocation converges to the allocation of the equilibrium in which currency is not valued. For the "stationary" equilibrium $p(t) = p*$, we compute c_t^h as in (b) to get

$$c_t^h = \left(\frac{y}{2}, \frac{y}{2}\right), \qquad h = 1, \ldots, \frac{N}{2},$$

$$c_t^h = \left(\frac{y}{4}, \frac{3y}{4}\right), \qquad h = \frac{N}{2} + 1, \ldots, N.$$

Because $1 + r(t) = p(t)/p(t+1) = p*/p* = 1$, we get $r(t) = 0$.

g. Lenders face the same constraints in economies (b) and (f), because the rate of return is in both cases zero, and the constraint on borrowing is not effective for them. Consequently, their welfare level must be the same.

The initial old are better off in economy (f), because their endowment is more highly valued. In economy (b) the value of their endowment of $H(0)$ is zero, whereas in economy (f) this value is $H(0)/p* > 0$. Their consumption can therefore be higher. Because for the old the ranking according to consumption and welfare is the same, we conclude that the old at $t = 1$ are better off in (f). Finally borrowers are worse off in economy (f). They cannot be better off, because in both cases the rate of return is the same, but they face an additional constraint in economy (f), which can only shrink their choice set. [This argument depends heavily on the fact that the rate of return is the same. If that were not the case, the conclusion would not follow. For a counterexample, consider economy (e). In its environment borrowers are more constrained than in (b), but the rate of interest is sufficiently low to allow them to achieve a higher level of welfare.] To establish that borrowers in economy (f) are actually worse off, we use strict convexity and symmetry of preferences. By strict convexity we mean that if $u(x_1) = u(x_2)$, $x_1 \neq x_2$, then

$$u(x^\lambda) > u(x_1) = u(x_2),$$

where $x^\lambda = \lambda x_1 + (1 - \lambda)x_2$, $\qquad 0 < \lambda < 1$.

By "symmetry" we mean

$$u(c_1, c_2) = u(c_2, c_1), \qquad \forall \, (c_1, c_2) > 0.$$

In economy (b) borrowers completely smooth out consumption over their life span. The consumption bundle is $c_t^h = (\hat{c}, \hat{c})$, where $\hat{c} = y/2$. In economy (f) they consume $c_t^h = (c_1, c_2)$, where $c_1 = y/4$ and $c_2 = 3y/4$. Then we have $u(c_1, c_2) = u(c_2, c_1)$. Define

$$\tilde{c}_1 = \lambda c_1 + (1 - \lambda)c_2, \qquad \tilde{c}_2 = \lambda c_2 + (1 - \lambda)c_1.$$

By strictly convexity of preferences

$$u(\tilde{c}_1, \tilde{c}_2) > u(c_1, c_2) = u(c_2, c_1)$$

for any $0 < \lambda < 1$. Choose $\lambda = 1/2$ to get $\tilde{c}_1 = \hat{c}$ and $\tilde{c}_2 = \hat{c}$. This statement completes the proof.

EXERCISE 7.2   Inside Money and Real Bills

Consider the following overlapping-generations model of two-period-lived people. At each date $t \geq 1$ there are born N_1 individuals of type 1 who are endowed with $y > 0$ units of the consumption good when they are young and zero units when they are old; there are also born N_2 individuals of type 2 who are endowed with zero units of the consumption good when they are young and $Y > 0$ units when they are old. The consumption good is nonstorable. At time $t = 1$, there are N old people, all of the same type, each endowed with zero units of the consumption good and H_0/N units of unbacked paper called "fiat currency." The populations of type 1 and 2 individuals, N_1 and N_2, remain constant for all $t \geq 1$. The young of each generation are identical in preferences and maximize the utility function $\ln c_t^h(t) + \ln c_t^h(t + 1)$ where $c_t^h(s)$ is consumption in the sth period of a member h of generation t.

a. Consider the equilibrium without valued currency (that is, the equilibrium in which there is no trade between generations). Let $[1 + r(t)]$ be the gross rate of return on consumption loans. Find a formula for $[1 + r(t)]$ as a function of N_1, N_2, y, and Y.

b. Suppose that N_1, N_2, y, and Y are such that $[1 + r(t)] > 1$ in the equilibrium without valued currency. Then prove that there can exist no quantity-theory-style equilibrium where fiat currency is valued and where the price level $p(t)$ obeys the quantity theory equation $p(t) = q \cdot H_0$, where q is a positive constant and $p(t)$ is measured in units of currency per unit good.

c. Suppose that N_1, N_2, y, and Y are such that in the nonvalued-currency equilibrium, $1 + r(t) < 1$. Prove that there exists an equilibrium in which fiat currency is valued and that there obtains the quantity theory equation $p(t) = q \cdot H_0$, where q is a constant. Construct an argument to show that the equilibrium with valued currency is not Pareto superior to the nonvalued-currency equilibrium.

d. Suppose that N_1, N_2, y, and Y are such that, in the above nonvalued-currency economy, $[1 + r(t)] < 1$, so that there exists an equilibrium in which fiat currency is valued. Let $\bar{p}$ be the stationary equilibrium price level in that economy. Now consider an alternative economy, identical with the preceding one in all respects except for the following feature: a government each period purchases a constant amount L_g of consumption loans and pays for them by issuing debt on itself, called "inside money" M_I, in the amount $M_I(t) = L_g \cdot p(t)$. The government never retires the inside money, using the proceeds of the loans to finance new purchases of consumption loans in subsequent periods. The quantity of outside money, or currency, remains H_0, whereas the "total high-power money" is now $H_0 + M_I(t)$.

(i) Show that in this economy there exists a valued-currency equilibrium in which the price level is constant over time at $p(t) = \bar{p}$, or equivalently, as in the economy in (c), $p(t) = qH_0$.
(ii) Explain why government purchases of private debt are not inflationary in this economy.
(iii) In standard macroeconomic models, once-and-for-all government open-market operations in private debt normally affect real variables and/or the price level. What accounts for the difference between those models and the one in this problem?

SOLUTION

a. The problem solved by the young of generation $t \geq 1$ is

$$\max_{c_t^h(t), c_t^h(t+1), s_t^h(t)} u^h[c_t^h(t), c_t^h(t+1)]$$

subject to $c_t^h(t) + s_t^h(t) \leq w_t^h(t)$,
$$c_t^h(t+1) \leq w_t^h(t+1) + [1 + r(t)]s_t^h(t),$$

where $s_t^h(t)$ is interpreted as savings, measured in time t consumption good, and $[1 + r(t)]$ is the rate of return on savings. Given any desired amount of savings, an agent has to choose the composition of his portfolio. If two assets are available—loans and currency—we have that $s_t^h(t) = l_t^h(t) + m_t^h(t)/p(t)$. Let the rate of return on consumption loans be $[1 + r(t)]$. Next period the value of the portfolio $l_t^h(t) + m_t^h(t)/p(t)$ will be $[1 + r(t)]l_t^h(t) + m_t^h(t)p(t)/[p(t+1)p(t)]$. In an equilibrium with valued currency $1/p(t) > 0$ and $m_t^h(t) > 0$ for some h; consequently, currency cannot be dominated by loans—otherwise no agent would hold currency—and both assets have the same rate of return $p(t)/p(t+1) = 1 + r(t)$. Therefore, the value of the portfolio in terms of $(t + 1)$ good can be written as $[1 + r(t)][l_t^h(t) + m_t^h(t)/p(t)] = [1 + r(t)]s_t^h(t)$. Clearly, in an equilibrium where currency is not valued, $1/p(t) = 0$, and the same formulation in terms of $s_t^h(t)$ is applicable.

For the logarithmic utility function, the first-order conditions yield

$$s_t^h(t) = f^h[1 + r(t)] = \frac{1}{2}\left[w_t^h(t) - \frac{w_t^h(t+1)}{1 + r(t)}\right].$$

Let

$$f[1 + r(t)] \equiv \frac{1}{N_1 + N_2}\sum_{h=1}^{N_1+N_2} f^h[1 + r(t)]$$

$$= \frac{1}{2}\left[(1 - \alpha)y - \frac{\alpha Y}{1 + r(t)}\right],$$

where $\quad 1 - \alpha = \dfrac{N_1}{N_1 + N_2}\quad$ and $\quad \alpha = \dfrac{N_2}{N_1 + N_2}$.

In an equilibrium in which currency is not valued, the relevant equilibrium condition is that the market for (intragenerational) loans clears, that is,

$$f[1 + r(t)] = 0.$$

Using the particular form of $f[1 + r(t)]$, we get that the unique rate of return that clears the market is given by

$$1 + r(t) = \frac{N_2 Y}{N_1 y}.$$

b. We give a proof of a more general result, namely, that no equilibrium with valued currency can exist—either quantity-theory style or not—for an even larger class of economies. To do so we assume that $f[1 + r(t)]$ is monotone increasing and continuous, an assumption that is clearly satisfied by the $f(\cdot)$ function we derived.

If the rate of return that clears the market in the nonmonetary equilibrium, say r_1, is greater than zero, we have

$$f(1 + r_1) = 0.$$

In an equilibrium such that currency is valued, we have

$$f[1 + r(t)] = \frac{H_0}{\overline{N}p(t)} > 0, \quad \text{all } t, \quad \text{where } \overline{N} = N_1 + N_2.$$

Given

$$1 + r(t) = \frac{p(t)}{p(t + 1)},$$

the implication is that

$$f[1 + r(t + 1)] = [1 + r(t)]f[1 + r(t)], \qquad r(t) > r_1 > 0.$$

Then notice that $r(1) > r_1$ implies $f[1 + r(2)] > f[1 + r(1)]$, which in turn implies $r(2) > r(1)$. Proceeding in this manner, we establish that the sequence of rates of return that can potentially be equilibrium rates of return is monotone increasing. Then it either converges to some $\bar{r}$ or diverges. We now prove that it cannot converge. By continuity of $f(\cdot)$, we have that if $r(t) \to \bar{r}$ then $f[1 + r(t)] \to f(1 + \bar{r})$. Then as t goes to infinity, we have

$$f(1 + \bar{r}) = (1 + \bar{r})f(1 + \bar{r}).$$

Yet $\bar{r} \geq r(t) > r_1 > 0$, which yields a contradiction. Therefore the sequence $\{r(t)\}$ goes to infinity. But this contradicts the assumption that an equilibrium exists, because $f[1 + r(t)]$ is bounded by, say, total endowments, whereas $[1 + r(t)]f[1 + r(t)]$ is going to infinity as $t \to \infty$. Consequently, we cannot have equality for all t.

For the example at hand, we can show this result by simply establishing that no matter how large $p(1)$ is, the sequence $\{p(t)\}$ generated by the equilibrium condition contains negative terms for all $t \geq T$, T finite.

The condition $f[1 + r(t)] = H_0/\overline{N}p(t)$ corresponds to $(1/2)\{(1 - \alpha)y - \alpha Y/[1 + r(t)]\} = H_0/\overline{N}p(t)$, whereas $1 + r(t) > 1$ in a nonvalued-currency equilibrium is simply $N_2 Y/N_1 y > 1$. Using $1 + r(t) = p(t)/p(t + 1)$, we get

$$(1 - \alpha)yp(t) - \alpha Yp(t + 1) = \frac{2H_0}{\overline{N}}$$

or

$$p(t + 1) = \frac{N_1 y}{N_2 Y} p(t) - \frac{2H_0}{N_2 Y}$$

Let

$$\frac{N_1 y}{N_2 Y} = \phi.$$

Then

$$p(t+1) = \phi^t p(1) - \frac{2H_0}{N_2 Y} \sum_{j=0}^{t-1} \phi^j.$$

Because $0 < \phi < 1$, however, for t large the first term becomes negligible, whereas the second term converges to $-2H_0/[N_2 Y(1 - \phi)]$, a negative number. Therefore, for large t, $p(t)$ must be negative.

c. As in (b), we can first show that this result obtains in greater generality. Assume, as before, that $f(\cdot)$ is increasing and continuous. We are given that

$$f(1 + r_1) = 0 \quad \text{and} \quad r_1 < 0.$$

By continuity and monotonicity, we have that $f(1) > 0$. Then let $p(t) = \bar{p} = H_0/f(1)\bar{N}$. It is easy to verify that the conditions for existence of an equilibrium with valued currency are satisfied by construction. For the example, we want a constant solution to

$$p(t+1) = \frac{N_1 y}{N_2 Y} p(t) - \frac{2H_0}{N_2 Y}$$

where $\quad \dfrac{N_1 y}{N_2 Y} > 1.$

Such a solution is

$$p(t) = p = \frac{2H_0}{N_1 y - N_2 Y} > 0, \quad \text{and} \quad 1 + r(t) = 1.$$

To argue that the equilibrium with valued currency does not Pareto dominate the equilibrium where currency is valueless, it suffices to show that at least one agent is worse off. We do so for the type 2 agents, that is, for borrowers. The basic idea is that when the rate of interest increases — and the rate of return in the equilibrium with valued currency is higher than the rate of return in the equilibrium without valued currency — borrowers are worse off.

Given a rate of interest r, we say that an agent is a borrower if argmax $u[w_1 - s, w_2 + (1 + r)s] < 0$. Let s_i be the solution to the maximization problem when the rate of interest is r_i. Assume that $r_1 > r_2$ and that s_1 and s_2

are negative (the agent is a borrower). Then

$$u[w_1 - s_1, w_2 + (1 + r_2)s_1] \leq u[w_1 - s_2, w_2 + (1 + r_2)s_2],$$

given that the optimal choice is s_2 when $r = r_2$. Still, $u(w_1 - s_1, w_2 + [1 + r_1]s_1) < u[w_1 - s_1, w_2 + (1 + r_2)s_1]$, given $s_1 < 0$, $r_1 > r_2$, and monotonicity of $u(\cdot)$. This statement proves the proposition. In terms of the example, pick an agent of type 2 endowed $(0, Y)$. This agent will always borrow, and the logarithmic utility function is monotone increasing. Consequently the previous result applies.

d. i. The basic argument that explains this sort of irrelevance result is that the gross composition of individual portfolios is not determinate. Consider, for example, an individual who, at the going rate of return, wants to "save" ten dollars. This agent should be indifferent among portfolios that consist of $(10 + l)$ assets or loans acquired and l debts or loans granted, for any l. This result implies that, if the government wants to increase its demand for "loans," private agents will be willing to supply those "loans" and simultaneously to "borrow" in another market—the market for currency, for example—so that their net asset position remains unchanged.

Given the government policy, the "new" per capita aggregate demand is $L_g/N + f[1 + r(t)]$. Equilibrium requires that excess demand for loans, that is, excess savings, be equal to net supply of assets, which is $M_I(t)/p(t) + H/p(t)$. Let $\bar{p}$ be the price we found in (c), that is,

$$f(1) = \frac{H}{N\bar{p}}.$$

If $p(t) = \bar{p}$ is an equilibrium, we must have $M_I(t) = M_I = Lg\bar{p}$, and

$$\frac{L_g}{N} + f(1) = \frac{H}{N\bar{p}} + \frac{M_I}{N\bar{p}}.$$

This is the case if and only if $L_g = M_I/\bar{p}$—exactly the condition we are given. Hence the conjecture is verified.

ii. Notice that in this setup it is a little bit arbitrary to call M_I money. We can think of M_I as liabilities of a financial intermediary that are fully backed by real loans. In this sense there is no creation of new currency, because the "new" asset inherits all the characteristics of the real loans by which it is backed. Therefore such a trivial operation—an exchange of names—cannot have any effects.

iii. In standard macro models we usually assume that money and bonds are "different" assets, different enough for us to start out with well-defined demands for each. In the model we are analyzing, we have a well-defined demand for savings but *not* for each asset that can potentially be part of those savings. Actually, in our model, in an equilibrium with valued currency, agents are completely indifferent between portfolios that contain only bonds and portfolios that contain only currency, because the rate of return is the same.

We could alter our model in at least two ways to obtain well-defined demands for each asset. First, we could suppose that, even though bonds have a higher return, currency is held because of some legal restrictions. Second, in the absence of legal restrictions there are perhaps sources of demand other than the stream of goods that assets can buy. Currency-in-the-utility-function and cash-in-advance models are examples of such approaches.

It seems possible to imagine a transactions technology that makes money and bonds "different." This technology must be rich enough to rule out private intermediation that produces "moneylike" assets backed by bonds. In some sense, these situations can be interpreted either as some form of legal restriction or as arising from the assumption that the government and the private sector have different technologies for producing "currencylike" assets. In either case, we would also have obtained nonneutrality of an open-market operation.

EXERCISE 7.3   Social Security and the Price Level

Consider an economy ("economy I") that consists of overlapping generations of two-period-lived people. At each date $t \geq 1$ there are born a constant number N of young people, who desire to consume both when they are young, at t, and when they are old, at $(t + 1)$. Each young person has the utility function $\ln c_t(t) + \ln c_t(t + 1)$, where $c_s(t)$ is time t consumption of an agent born at s. For all dates $t \geq 1$, young people are endowed with $y > 0$ units of a single nonstorable consumption good when they are young and zero units when they are old. In addition, at time $t = 1$ there are N old people endowed in the aggregate with H units of unbacked fiat currency. Let $p(t)$ be the nominal price level at t, denominated in dollars per time t good.

a. Define and compute an equilibrium with valued fiat currency for this economy. Argue that it exists and is unique. Now consider a second economy ("economy II") that is identical to the above economy except that economy II possesses a social security system. In particular, at each date $t \geq 1$, the government taxes $\tau > 0$ units of the time t consumption good away from each young person and at the same time gives τ units of the time t consumption good to each old person then alive.

b. Does economy II possess an equilibrium with valued fiat currency? Describe the restrictions on the parameter τ, if any, that are needed to ensure the existence of such an equilibrium.

c. If an equilibrium with valued fiat currency exists, is it unique?

d. Consider the *stationary* equilibrium with valued fiat currency. Is it unique? Describe how the value of currency or price level would vary across economies with differences in the size of the social security system, as measured by τ.

SOLUTION

a. We first define an equilibrium with valued currency as a pair of sequences $\{p(t)\}_{t=1}^{\infty}$ and $\{r(t)\}_{t=1}^{\infty}$, with $p(t) > 0$ and finite, all t; and an allocation $c = \{c_t^h\}_{t=1}^{\infty}$ such that

(i) $1 + r(t) = p(t)/p(t + 1)$.

(ii) Given $\{p(t)\}$ and $\{r(t)\}$, each agent h of generation t chooses savings, $s_t^h(t)$, and lifetime consumption $c_t^h = [c_t^h(t), c_t^h(t + 1)]$ to solve

$$\max_{c_t^h(t), c_t^h(t+1), s_t^h(t)} u^h[c_t^h(t), c_t^h(t + 1)]$$

$$\text{subject to} \quad c_t^h(t) + s_t^h(t) \leq w_t^h(t),$$
$$c_t^h(t + 1) \leq w_t^h(t + 1) + [1 + r(t)]s_t^h(t).$$

Denote

$$f^h[1 + r(t)] \equiv w_t^h(t) - c_t^h(t).$$

(iii) Market clearing requires that

$$\frac{1}{N} \sum_{h=1}^{N} f^h[1 + r(t)] \equiv f[1 + r(t)] = \frac{H(t)}{p(t)N}, \qquad t = 1, 2, \ldots$$

Notice that condition (i) requires that neither currency nor private loans dominate the other in rate of return. This is a consequence of utility maximization. If an agent holds both loans and currency, then the two must have equal rates of return. If not, the budget set can clearly be enlarged by holding only one asset, namely the one with the higher rate of return.

It is easy to derive $f^h(\cdot)$ for the Cobb-Douglas utility function. It turns out to be

$$f^h[1 + r(t)] = \frac{1}{2}\left[w_t^h(t) - \frac{w_t^h(t + 1)}{1 + r(t)}\right].$$

For economy I, we have $w_t^h(t) = y$ and $w_t^h(t + 1) = 0$. Then

$$f[1 + r(t)] = \frac{y}{2}.$$

Still, (iii) requires $f[1 + r(t)] = H/p(t)N$. Hence the unique solution is $p(t) = 2H/Ny$, and $r(t) = 0$,

This condition establishes existence—because $p(t) > 0$—and uniqueness.

b. To compute an equilibrium for economy II, we note that this second economy shares the characteristics of economy I except for one, namely the endowment pattern. In this economy, part of the first-period endowment is taxed away by the government. The effective or disposable first-period endowment is then $w_t^h(t) = y - \tau$. On the other hand, agents receive a transfer in their second period of life that can formally be considered an endowment. Consequently we set $w_t^h(t + 1) = \tau$.

The definition of equilibrium remains unchanged. For this "new" economy, we can compute that $f[1 + r(t)] = (1/2)(y - \tau - \tau/[1 + r(t)])$.

We know that a valued-currency equilibrium with a gross rate of interest strictly greater than one cannot exist. To see this point, suppose that $1 + r(t) = 1 + r_1 > 1$. We have $p(t)/p(t + 1) = 1 + r(t)$, however, or $p(t + 1) = (1 + r_1)^{-1}p(t)$. Hence prices decrease in this economy. On the other hand, aggregate real currency balances $H/p(t)$, are growing without bound. [It is easy to see that they grow exponentially at the rate $(1 + r_1)$.] This statement violates condition (iii) in the definition of equilibrium, because the left-hand side—savings—is bounded by the level of first-period endowments. Then it is clear that, if moving τ affects the "admissible" values $r(t)$, we will probably have to rule out some τ to guarantee the existence of an equilibrium.

In any equilibrium with valued currency, $f[1 + r(t)] > 0$. For this economy that condition is

$$\frac{1}{2}\left[(y - \tau) - \frac{\tau}{1 + r(t)}\right] > 0,$$

or equivalently

$$1 + r(t) > \frac{\tau}{y - \tau}.$$

We have argued, however, that in an equilibrium with valued currency the rate of return cannot be bounded below by a number strictly greater than one. Therefore, we cannot have $\tau/(y - \tau) > 1$. This situation requires that $\tau \le y/2$. The case $\tau = y/2$ can be handled similarly, as we now see. Notice that, if $1 + r(t) = 1$, then $f^h[1 + r(t)] = 0$. Hence we need $1 + r(t) > 1$. We also have to rule out the possibility of a sequence of terms $r(t)$ that has strictly positive components but that converges to zero. To do so, we show that if $r(1) > 0$—a necessary condition for $H/p(1) > 0$—the sequence $r(t)$ goes to infinity. We have that

$$\frac{y}{2}\left[1 - \frac{1}{1 + r(t)}\right] = \frac{H}{p(t)N} = \frac{H}{p(t + 1)N}[1 + r(t)]$$

$$= \frac{y}{2[1 + r(t)]}\left[1 - \frac{1}{1 + r(t + 1)}\right].$$

Rearranging terms we get

$$r(t + 1) = \frac{r(t)}{1 - r(t)}.$$

It is easy to see that, if $r(1) > 0$, then $r(2) > r(1)$. The sequence $\{r(t)\}$ is increasing (actually it diverges, but we do not need such a strong result) and hence $\{1 + r(t)\}$ cannot converge to one.

To recapitulate, we learned that if $\tau \ge y/2$ there cannot be an equilibrium with valued fiat currency. Now it is simple to establish that for any $\tau < y/2$ there exists at least one such equilibrium. We prove this claim by simply constructing one. Notice that if $\tau < y/2$, then $f(1) > 0$. Pick $p(t) = \bar{p} = f(1)^{-1}H/N$, and this is an equilibrium.

The restrictions on the parameters of the economy—basically the relative size of first- and second-period endowments—that are needed for an equilibrium with valued fiat currency to exist have a natural economic interpretation. Recall that condition (iii) of the definition of equilibrium requires that the economy save a positive amount. Moreover we know that aggregate average savings must occur at rates of return that are less than or equal to one. Young individuals—the only potential savers—will save positive amounts only to increase their consumption in the second period of their life. If their lifetime endowments are tilted toward their second period (in other words, if τ is large), then at "low" interest rates there will be no positive excess savings and hence no valued fiat currency.

This interpretation readily suggests that a model to generate nonexistence of an equilibrium with valued fiat money can be devised by increasing the number of borrowers to the point where the "average" agent does not want to have positive savings at rates of return smaller than or equal to one.

c. In this section, we argue that there are many equilibria with valued currency. The conditions for existence are

$$\frac{1}{2}\left(w_1 - \frac{w_2}{1+r(t)}\right) = \frac{H}{p(t)N},$$

$$1 + r(t) = \frac{p(t)}{p(t+1)}, \qquad p(t) > 0, \quad \text{all } t,$$

where $w_1 = y - \tau$, $w_2 = \tau$, and $w_1 > w_2$, because $\tau < y/2$. Making the appropriate substitutions, we can reduce the condition for existence to finding a solution to the following difference equation

$$p(t)w_1 - w_2 p(t+1) = \frac{2H}{N} \quad \text{or} \quad p(t+1) = \frac{w_1}{w_2} p(t) - \frac{2H}{Nw_2}.$$

Notice that we are not given an initial condition. Therefore many different functions mapping the positive integers into real numbers can be solutions of that difference equation. One of them is precisely that found in (b), that is, a constant price.

$$p(t) = \bar{p} = \frac{2H}{N(w_1 - w_2)}.$$

We can now parameterize the set of solutions by the initial value $p(1)$. Basically, we care about two sets: (1) the set of paths $\{p(t)\}$ such that $p(1) < \bar{p}$ and (2) the set of paths $\{p(t)\}$ such that $p(1) > \bar{p}$. We want to argue that no element of the first set can be an equilibrium and that any element of the second is, that is, that there is a continuum of equilibria.

First, given the definition of $\bar{p}$, we can rearrange the difference equation to read

$$p(t+1) - \bar{p} = \frac{w_1}{w_2} [p(t) - \bar{p}].$$

This is a first-order homogeneous difference equation in the variable $Z_t \equiv p(t) - \bar{p}$. For any initial condition Z_1, the solution is

$$Z_{t+1} = \left(\frac{w_1}{w_2}\right)^t Z_1, \qquad \frac{w_1}{w_2} > 1.$$

Then if $Z_1 < 0$—that is, $p(1) < \bar{p}$—Z_t decreases without bound, and for some finite T, $Z_t < -\bar{p}$ for all $t \geq T$. The implication is that $p(t) < 0$, which contradicts the definition of equilibrium.

If we pick $p(1)$ in the second set, $Z_1 = p(1) - \bar{p} > 0$. Then as t grows, Z_t

also grows, that is, $p(t)$ diverges. Yet this *is* an equilibrium. Nothing prevents prices from going to infinity in our definition of equilibrium with valued currency. Clearly, "real" currency balances, $H/p(t)$, are converging to zero. The rate of return is also converging to the rate of return of the nonvalued-currency equilibrium, and the consumption allocation converges to the equilibrium allocation of the economy without currency. The equilibrium is not "stationary," in the sense that the allocations depend on time even in a purely stationary physical endowment.

d. We have already argued that there is only one equilibrium with constant rate of return, namely the one that obtains when $p(t) = \bar{p}$, all t.

Now if we analyze different economies indexed by τ, it is clear from our findings in (b) that, if $\tau_1 > \tau_2$, which corresponds to $w_1^1 < w_1^2$ and $w_2^1 > w_2^2$, we have

$$\bar{p}_1 = \frac{2H}{N(w_1^1 - w_2^1)} > \bar{p}_2 = \frac{2H}{N(w_1^2 - w_2^2)}.$$

One interpretation of this result is that, the more "important" the social security system ($\tau_1 > \tau_2$), the less important are private savings as a way of providing consumption in the second period of life. Consequently the value of those savings must be smaller ($H/\bar{p}_1 < H/\bar{p}_2$).

For these economies a social security system is a perfect substitute for private savings in the sense that per capita second-period consumption is $y/2$ regardless of τ.

EXERCISE 7.4   Seignorage

Consider an economy consisting of overlapping generations of two-period-lived agents. At each date $t \geq 1$, there are born N_1 "lenders" who are endowed with $\alpha > 0$ units of the single consumption good when they are young and zero units when they are old. At each date $t \geq 1$, there are also born N_2 "borrowers" who are endowed with zero units of the consumption good when they are young and $\beta > 0$ units when they are old. The good is non-storable, and N_1 and N_2 are constant through time. The economy starts at time 1, at which time there are N old people who are in the aggregate endowed with $H(0)$ units of unbacked, intrinsically worthless pieces of paper called dollars. Assume that α, β, N_1, and N_2 are such that

$$\frac{N_2\beta}{N_1\alpha} < 1.$$

Assume that everyone has preferences

$$u[c_t^h(t), c_t^h(t+1)] = \ln c_t^h(t) + \ln c_t^h(t+1),$$

where $c_t^h(s)$ is consumption of time s good of agent h born at time t.

a. Compute the equilibrium interest rate on consumption loans in the equilibrium without valued currency.

b. Construct a *brief* argument to establish whether or not the equilibrium without valued currency is Pareto optimal.

The economy also contains a government that purchases and destroys G_t units of the good in period t, $t \geq 1$. The government finances its purchases entirely by currency creation. That is, at time t,

$$G_t = \frac{H(t) - H(t-1)}{p(t)},$$

where $[H(t) - H(t-1)]$ is the additional dollars printed by the government at t and $p(t)$ is the price level at t. The government is assumed to increase $H(t)$ according to

$$H(t) = zH(t-1), \qquad z \geq 1,$$

where z is a constant for all time $t \geq 1$.

At time t, old people who carried over $H(t-1)$ dollars between $(t-1)$ and t offer these $H(t-1)$ dollars in exchange for time t goods. Also at t the government offers $H(t) - H(t-1)$ dollars for goods, so that $H(t)$ is the total supply of dollars at time t, to be carried over by the young into time $(t+1)$.

c. Assume that $1/z > N_2\beta/N_1\alpha$. Show that under this assumption there exists a continuum of equilibria with valued currency.

d. Display the unique stationary equilibrium with valued currency in the form of a "quantity theory" equation. Compute the equilibrium rate of return on currency and consumption loans.

e. Argue that if $1/z < N_2\beta/N_1\alpha$, then there exists no valued-currency equilibrium. Interpret this result. (Hint: Look at the rate of return on consumption loans in the equilibrium without valued currency.)

f. Find the value of z that *maximizes* the government's G_t in a stationary equilibrium. Compare this with the largest value of z that is compatible with the existence of a valued-currency equilibrium.

SOLUTION

a. Given the logarithmic structure of preferences, it is easy to show that the solution to the problem

$$\max_{c_t^h(t), c_t^h(t+1), s_t^h(t)} u^h[c_t^h(t), c_t^h(t+1)]$$

subject to $\quad c_t^h(t) + s_t^h(t) \le w_t^h(t),$
$$c_t^h(t+1) \le w_t^h(t+1) + [1 + r(t)]s_t^h(t)$$

is a savings function of the form

$$s_t^h(t) \equiv f^h[1 + r(t)] = \frac{1}{2}\left[w_t^h(t) - \frac{w_t^h(t+1)}{1 + r(t)}\right]$$

where, as usual, savings is to be understood as the sum of loans $l_t^h(t)$ and "real" currency holdings $m_t^h(t)/p(t)$. It has also been proved in the text that, if $m_t^h(t) > 0$, then $p(t)/p(t+1) = 1 + r(t)$, and hence there is no loss of generality in assuming a single rate of return on savings.

In an equilibrium without valued currency, $1/p(t) = 0$, all t. Then an equilibrium is a sequence $\{r(t)\}, t = 1, 2, \ldots$, and an allocation $[\{c_{t-1}^h(t)\}, h = 1, \ldots, N, t = 1, 2, \ldots]$ such that

$$f[1 + r(t)] = \frac{1}{N_1 + N_2}\sum_{h=1}^{N_1+N_2} f^h[1 + r(t)] = 0.$$

In this environment there are N_1 agents with savings function $\alpha/2$, and N_2 agents with savings function $-\beta/2[1 + r(t)]$. Denoting $k = N_1/(N_1 + N_2)$, average aggregate savings are

$$f[1 + r(t)] = \frac{1}{2}\left[k\alpha - \frac{(1 - k)\beta}{1 + r(t)}\right], \quad \text{and} \quad f[1 + r(t)] = 0$$

implies $\quad 1 + r(t) = \dfrac{(1 - k)\beta}{k\alpha} = \dfrac{N_2\beta}{N_1\alpha} < 1.$

b. We want to argue that, because the rate of return is lower than the rate of growth, the equilibrium allocation is not Pareto optimal. To prove this point it suffices to display another allocation that is Pareto superior, that is, that is feasible and increases the utility level of at least one agent in the economy without decreasing the utility of others.

A typical "lender" consumes $c^L = (\alpha/2, N_2\beta\alpha/N_1\alpha 2)$, whereas a "borrower" consumes $c^B = (\beta N_1\alpha/2N_2\beta, \beta/2)$. The new allocation that we are going to construct gives borrowers exactly the same lifetime consumption as the competitive equilibrium. In the competitive allocation, lenders' total consumption is

$$N_1\frac{\alpha}{2} + N_1\left(\frac{N_2\beta}{N_1\alpha}\frac{\alpha}{2}\right) = \frac{1}{2}(N_1\alpha + N_2\beta).$$

An allocation that is stationary (all generations indexed $t \geq 1$ get the same lifetime consumption) and treats all lenders symmetrically must satisfy

$$N_1 \hat{c}_1 + N_1 \hat{c}_2 \leq \frac{1}{2}(N_1 \alpha + N_2 \beta).$$

In particular, we can write $\hat{c}_1 = c_1^L - \delta$ and $\hat{c}_2 = c_2^L + \delta$. This guarantees that feasibility is satisfied. The utility derived from the competitive bundle is $u(c_1^L, c_2^L)$. The maximal utility that is consistent with feasibility and keeping the consumption of the initial old at least at the original level can be obtained by setting δ so that

$$\delta = \operatorname*{argmax}_{\delta \geq 0} u(c_1^L - \delta, c_2^L + \delta).$$

If the solution is $\delta > 0$, strict quasi-concavity of $u(\,\cdot\,)$ implies that $u(\hat{c}_1, \hat{c}_2) > u(c_1^L, c_2^L)$. That the solution is indeed positive can be established from the first-order condition of the maximization problem that requires

$$\frac{u_2(c_1^L - \delta, c_2^L + \delta)}{u_1(c_1^L - \delta, c_2^L + \delta)} = 1.$$

In a competitive equilibrium

$$\frac{u_2(c_1^L, c_2^L)}{u_1(c_1^L, c_2^L)} = \frac{1}{1 + r(t)} = \frac{N_1 \alpha}{N_2 \beta} > 1.$$

Still,

$$\frac{u_2(c_1^L - \delta, c_2^L + \delta)}{u_1(c_1^L - \delta, c_2^L + \delta)} \to 0 \quad \text{as} \quad \delta \to c_1^L$$

and goes to infinity as $\delta \to -c_2^L$. Moreover, u_2/u_1 is monotone decreasing. Then if

$$\frac{u_2(c_1^L - \delta, c_2^L + \delta)}{u_1(c_1^L - \delta, c_2^L + \delta)} = 1,$$

it must be that $\delta > 0$. This conclusion shows that the "new" allocation makes all lenders better off, increases the consumption of the old at $t = 1$, and gives the borrowers the same consumption that they get in the competitive equilibrium. Consequently we have found an allocation that is Pareto superior (although *not* Pareto optimal) to the competitive allocation. Therefore the latter cannot be Pareto optimal.

c. An equilibrium with valued fiat currency is a pair of sequences $\{r(t)\}$ and $\{p(t)\}$, $p(t) > 0$, all t; and an allocation $[\{c_{t-1}^h(t)\}, h = 1, \ldots, N_1 + N_2,$

$t = 1, 2, \ldots]$ such that

(1) $\qquad f[1 + r(t)] = \dfrac{H(t)}{p(t)(N_1 + N_2)}, \qquad t = 1, 2, \ldots$

(2) $\qquad 1 + r(t) = \dfrac{p(t)}{p(t + 1)}.$

We can reduce the two equations to

$$\frac{1}{2}\left[k\alpha - (1 - k)\beta \frac{p(t + 1)}{p(t)} \right] = \frac{H(t)}{p(t)(N_1 + N_2)}$$

or $\qquad p(t + 1) = \dfrac{k\alpha}{(1 - k)\beta} p(t) - \dfrac{2H(0)}{(1 - k)\beta} \dfrac{z^t}{(N_1 + N_2)}.$

Define

$$\hat{p}(t) = \frac{p(t)}{z^t}.$$

Then

(3) $\qquad \hat{p}(t + 1) = \dfrac{N_1\alpha}{N_2\beta} \hat{p}(t) - \dfrac{2H(0)}{(1 - k)\beta z(N_1 + N_2)}.$

Notice that there is a one-to-one correspondence between solutions $\{\hat{p}(t)\}$ and $\{p(t)\}$. In particular, if for some parameter values $\hat{p}(t) < 0$ for some t, for those values $p(t) < 0$ in the same set of values t.

Assume that $1/z > N_2\beta/N_1\alpha$. Then define

$$\bar{p} = \frac{2H(0)}{N_1\alpha - N_2\beta z}.$$

Clearly, $\hat{p}(t) = \bar{p}$ is a solution to (3), which means that $p(t) = z^t\bar{p}$ is an equilibrium price sequence. By simple iteration it follows that, if $\hat{p}(1) > \bar{p}$, then the sequence $\{\hat{p}(t)\}$ is positive and diverges. Correspondingly, the sequence $\{p(t)\}$, with initial condition $p(1) = \hat{p}(1)z$ and given by $p(t) = z^t\hat{p}(t)$, also diverges, but this in no way contradicts our definition of equilibrium. In this equilibrium, "real" currency balances $H(t)/p(t)$ are converging to zero. The rate of return on loans and the consumption allocation converge to the values we computed in (a).

d. We have already done much of the work. Notice that an equilibrium is stationary if the consumption allocation does not depend on time. For the environment of this exercise, such an equilibrium requires that the interest rate be constant. In such an equilibrium

$$f[1 + r(t)] = f(1 + r) = \frac{H(t)}{p(t)}, \quad \text{all } t.$$

Then

$$\frac{H(t)}{p(t)} = \frac{H(t + 1)}{p(t + 1)} = \frac{zH(t)}{p(t + 1)}.$$

This equality requires $p(t + 1) = zp(t)$ and $1 + r = p(t)/p(t + 1) = 1/z$. Recall, however, that we have already found an equilibrium where prices grow at the rate z. This is given by $p(t) = z^t \bar{p}$. This is the unique path $\{p(t)\}$ that satisfies the difference equation and gives $1 + r(t) = 1/z$, all t.

e. If $1/z < N_2\beta/N_1\alpha$, we can write (3) as

$$\hat{p}(t + 1) = \phi\hat{p}(t) - \frac{2H(0)}{N_2\beta z}, \quad \phi = N_1\alpha/N_2\beta z < 1.$$

Iterating on this equation, we get

$$\hat{p}(t) = \phi^{t-1}\hat{p}(1) - \frac{2H(0)}{N_2\beta z} \frac{1 - \phi^{t-1}}{1 - \phi}.$$

Then, because $0 < \phi < 1$, it is clear that, no matter how high $\hat{p}(1)$ is, there exists a finite T such that for every $t \geq T$, $\hat{p}(t) < 0$. This statement in turn implies that $p(t) < 0$, which contradicts the definition of equilibrium. This nonexistence result clearly puts a bound to z, that is, currency supply cannot grow too fast. It shows that, for an equilibrium with valued fiat currency to exist, it is necessary that the "stationary rate of return" $1/z$ be greater than the rate of return that obtains when currency is not valued, $N_2\beta/N_1\alpha$. The result illustrated here holds for this class of models, namely that, if an equilibrium with valued currency exists, then the rate of return is greater than the rate that clears the market for loans when currency has no value.

f. In this section, we compare different stationary equilibria. In any of these equilibria, average real currency balances are constant, and we can write

$$\frac{G(z)}{N} = \frac{H(t + 1) - H(t)}{Np(t + 1)}$$

$$= \frac{H(t + 1)}{Np(t + 1)} - \frac{p(t)}{p(t + 1)} \frac{H(t)}{Np(t)} = f\left(\frac{1}{z}\right)\left(1 - \frac{1}{z}\right).$$

For the economy of this exercise, we have

$$\frac{G(z)}{N} = \frac{1}{2} [k\alpha - (1-k)\beta z] \left(1 - \frac{1}{z}\right).$$

It is clear that, if $G(z) > 0$, we need $z > 1$. On the other hand, to guarantee existence of an equilibrium, $z < N_1\alpha/N_2\beta$. The value of z that maximizes G solves

$$\max_{1 < z < N_1\alpha/N_2\beta} \frac{1}{2} [k\alpha - (1-k)\beta z] \left(1 - \frac{1}{z}\right).$$

This is a concave program. The solution is given by any z within the feasible set that satisfies the first-order condition. Such a z is $(N_1\alpha/N_2\beta)^{1/2}$. Notice that the value of z, or steady-state inflation, that maximizes government revenue from inflation is not the largest z for which an equilibrium with valued currency exists. The underlying intuition is simple: this largest feasible z maximizes the rate at which real currency balances are taxed. A higher z, however, reduces real money balances or the "base" of the inflation tax. The optimal choice balances the effects of the higher tax rate against the lower base on which the inflation tax is levied.

EXERCISE 7.5   Oscillating Physical Returns

Consider an overlapping-generations model with $N(t) = N(0) > 0$ for $t \geq 1$. Let the net rate of return on storage $\rho(t)$ be given by the periodic sequence

$$\rho(t) = \begin{cases} \rho(1) > 0, & \text{for } t \text{ odd} \\ \rho(2) < 0, & \text{for } t \text{ even}, \end{cases}$$

with $[1 + \rho(1)] \cdot [1 + \rho(2)] < 1$. Let the per capita saving function be $f[1 + r(t)]$ for $r(t) > \rho(t)$. Let the saving function satisfy $f'[1 + r(t)] > 0$ for $r(t) > \rho(t)$ and

$$\lim_{\substack{r(t) \to \rho(2) \\ r(t) > \rho(2)}} f[1 + r(t)] > 0.$$

Let there be a fixed stock of government-supplied unbacked currency in the amount H that is initially in the hands of the old people at $t = 1$. Assume that $G(t) = 0$ for all $t \geq 1$ and $H(t) = H$ for all $t \geq 1$.

a. Describe the equilibrium in which currency is valueless. Compute the equilibrium rate of return on loans and the equilibrium amounts of storage.

b. Let $p(t)$ be the price level and $K(t)$ the storage amount at t. Prove that there exists a stationary or periodic equilibrium of the form

$$p(t) = \begin{cases} p(1), & t \text{ odd} \\ p(2), & t \text{ even,} \end{cases}$$

with $0 < p(2) < p(1) < \infty$, and with $K(t) = K(1) > 0$ for t odd and $K(t) = 0$ for t even,

c. Assume that all agents are identical, so that $f[1 + r(t)]$ is the saving function of the representative agent. Prove that the equilibrium in (b) Pareto dominates the equilibrium in (a).

d. (Optional.) Indicate in what sense the assumption that

$$\lim_{\substack{r(t) \to p(2) \\ r(t) > p(2)}} f[1 + r(t)] > 0$$

is necessary for the existence proof to go through. Notice that this statement is *not* equivalent to saying that without that assumption an equilibrium does not exist. It just says that without the assumption we cannot establish existence.

e. (Optional.) Prove that no equilibrium exists with valued currency and with zero storage at every t, that is, $K(t) = 0$ for all t.

f. (Optional.) Prove that there exists a continuum of equilibria with valued currency and such that $K(t) > 0$ for all t. These equilibria are such that they all "converge" to the equilibrium computed in part (a). This argument establishes nonuniqueness of the result in (b).

g. (Optional.) Prove that there exist no equilibria such that $K(t) = 0$ and $r(t - 1) = p(2)$ if t odd.

SOLUTION

a. We define an equilibrium in which currency is valueless as a pair of sequences $\{r(t)\}$, $\{K(t) \geq 0\}$ and the associated consumption allocation such that

(i) $f[1 + r(t)] = \dfrac{K(t)}{N(t)} \geq 0$

(ii) $K(t)[r(t) - p(t)] = 0$.

The first condition simply states that excess saving in this economy takes the form of capital or storage. The second guarantees that, when $K(t)$ is positive, the rates of return on consumption loans and storage are equal.

We now characterize the equilibrium. Denote by

(1) $\qquad f[1 + p(2)] = \max_{\substack{r(t) \to p(2) \\ r(t) > p(2)}} f[1 + r(t)].$

Then we conjecture that the equilibrium takes the form

$$r(t) = \begin{cases} p(1) & \text{if } t \text{ is odd} \\ p(2) & \text{if } t \text{ is even} \end{cases}$$

$$K(t) = \begin{cases} K_1 & \text{if } t \text{ is odd} \\ K_2 & \text{if } t \text{ is even,} \end{cases}$$

where K_1 and K_2 are given by

$$K_i = Nf[1 + p(i)], \qquad i = 1, 2.$$

Notice that $p(1) > p(2)$ and the assumption of an increasing and continuous $f(\cdot)$ for values of $r(t)$ greater than $p(2)$ guarantees that $f[1 + p(1)]$ is well defined and greater than zero. In this equilibrium $\{K(t)\}$ is a periodic sequence and is positive for all t.

b. We define a competitive equilibrium with valued fiat currency as sequences $\{p(t)\}$, $\{r(t)\}$, $\{K(t) \geq 0\}$ and an associated consumption allocation that satisfy

(i) $0 < p(t) < \infty$,   all t

(ii) $\dfrac{p(t)}{p(t+1)} = 1 + r(t)$

and $r(t) \geq p(1)$ if t is odd, $r(t) \geq p(2)$ if t is even

(iii) $Nf[1 + r(t)] = K(t) + \dfrac{H}{p(t)}$, $K(t) \geq 0$, $K(t)[r(t) - p(t)] = 0$.

We now establish existence of an equilibrium with the desired features. Let t be odd, and choose $1 + r(t) = 1 + p(1) = p_1/p_2$. Then

$$1 + r(t+1) = \frac{p_2}{p_1} = [1 + p(1)]^{-1} > 1 + p(2),$$

because $[1 + p(1)][1 + p(2)] < 1$.

Therefore, under this assumption, for t even, $1 + r(t) > 1 + p(2)$ and $K(t) = 0$.

We have then

$$Nf(1 + p(1)) = K_1 + \frac{H}{p_1}, \qquad t \text{ odd}$$

$$Nf\left(\frac{p_2}{p_1}\right) = \frac{H}{p_2}, \qquad t \text{ even}$$

and $\quad p_2 = [1 + \rho(1)]^{-1} p_1$.

Because $f[1 + \rho(2)] > 0$, $p_2/p_1 = [1 + \rho(1)]^{-1} > [1 + \rho(2)]$, and $f(\,\cdot\,)$ is monotone increasing, we have that

$$f([1 + \rho(1)]^{-1}) > 0.$$

Define

$$p_2 = \frac{H}{Nf([1 + \rho(1)]^{-1})}$$

Then

$$p_1 = [1 + \rho(1)]p_2 = \frac{[1 + \rho(1)]H}{Nf([1 + \rho(1)]^{-1})}$$

Consequently

$$\frac{H}{p_1} = \frac{Nf([1 + \rho(1)]^{-1})}{1 + \rho(1)}.$$

It remains to be proved that, given our choices of p_1, p_2, and the rates of return, we can find a nonnegative K_1 such that

$$K_1 = Nf[1 + \rho(1)] - \frac{H}{p_1} = N\left\{f[1 + \rho(1)] - \frac{f([1 + \rho(1)]^{-1})}{1 + \rho(1)}\right\}.$$

Monotonicity of $f(\,\cdot\,)$ and $1 + \rho(1) > [1 + \rho(1)]^{-1}$, however, guarantee that $K_1 > 0$. By construction our candidate equilibrium satisfies (i)–(iii). This statement completes the proof.

c. If all agents are alike and savings are positive in equilibrium, then every individual is a lender. Consequently, it suffices to show that lenders are better off when the rate of return increases, because when t is odd the rate of return coincides with that of the equilibrium where currency is valueless, whereas at even dates, $p_2/p_1 > 1 + \rho(2)$, that is, the rate of return is higher. An individual is a lender if

$$\operatorname*{argmax}_s u[w_1 - s, w_2 + (1 + r)s] > 0.$$

We claim that, if utility is increasing in each good, s_1 and s_2 are optimal choices when the interest rates are r_1 and r_2, respectively; and s_1, s_2 positive, then $r_1 > r_2$ implies

$$u[w_1 - s_1, w_2 + (1 + r_1)s_1] > u[w_1 - s_2, w_2 + (1 + r_2)s_2].$$

The proof is a simple revealed-preference argument. By the assumption of utility maximization,

$$u[w_1 - s_1, w_2 + (1 + r_1)s_1] \geq u[w_1 - s_2, w_2 + (1 + r_1)s_2].$$

Because s_2 is positive, $r_1 > r_2$, and utility is strictly increasing,

$$u[w_1 - s_2, w_2 + (1 + r_1)s_2] > u[w_1 - s_2, w_2 + (1 + r_2)s_2].$$

d. In part (b), the condition (1) was used to establish that $f(p_2/p_1) > 0$, that is, that currency is valued when t is even. The logic of the argument was the following. Because $f(\cdot)$ is increasing and $p_2/p_1 > 1 + \rho(2)$, it follows that $f(p_2/p_1) > f[1 + \rho(2)]$.

It is clear that without this condition we could not have established that $f(p_2/p_1) > 0$. That condition, however, is not necessary for existence of an equilibrium (although it is used in the preceding proof of existence) in the sense that it is possible that $f(p_2/p_1) > 0$ even if $f[1 + \rho(2)] < 0$. This is hardly surprising, because it is usually very hard to find conditions that are necessary for the existence of an equilibrium apart from some arbitrage relations.

e. We prove this result by contradiction. Assume that an equilibrium with $K(t) = 0$, all t, exists. Then for all t, $Nf[1 + r(t)] = H/p(t)$. Then using that equilibrium condition at t, $(t + 1)$, and $(t + 2)$, we get

$$f[1 + r(t)][1 + r(t)] = f[1 + r(t + 1)],$$
$$f[1 + r(t + 1)][1 + r(t + 1)] = f[1 + r(t + 2)].$$

Combining these two conditions, we get

$$f[1 + r(t)][1 + r(t)][1 + r(t + 1)] = f[1 + r(t + 2)].$$

Let $g(\cdot)$ be the inverse function of $f(\cdot)$. This function exists for all $r(t) > \rho(2)$. Moreover, as $f(\cdot)$ is monotone increasing, so is $g(\cdot)$. Then we have that $1 + r(t + 1) = g([1 + r(t)]f[1 + r(t)])$. Consequently

$$f[1 + r(t + 2)] = g([1 + r(t)]f[1 + r(t)])[1 + r(t)]f[1 + r(t)].$$

Let t be odd. Then we know $r(t) \geq \rho(1) > 0$.

We now establish that the sequence $\{r(t), r(t + 2), r(t + 4), \ldots\}$ is increasing and unbounded above. Because

$$r(t) > 0, \qquad g([1 + r(t)]f[1 + r(t)]) > g(f[1 + r(t)]).$$

Still,

$$g(f[1 + r(t)]) \equiv 1 + r(t)$$

by definition of $g(\cdot)$. Then $f[1 + r(t + 2)] > [1 + r(t)]^2 f[1 + r(t)]$, which implies $1 + r(t + 2) > 1 + r(t)$, because $f(\cdot)$ is monotone increasing. The sequence $\{r(t), t \text{ odd}\}$ is thus monotone increasing; therefore it either converges to some $\bar{r}$ or diverges.

Suppose it converges to $\bar{r}$. Then it must be true—by continuity of $f(\cdot)$ and $g(\cdot)$—that

$$f(1 + \bar{r}) = g[(1 + \bar{r})f(1 + \bar{r})](1 + \bar{r})f(1 + \bar{r})$$

or, because $\bar{r} > 0$,

$$f(1 + \bar{r}) > (1 + \bar{r})^2 f(1 + \bar{r}) > f(1 + \bar{r}),$$

which is a contradiction; then the sequence goes to infinity. Now consider the sequence $\{r(t + 1), r(t + 3), r(t + 5), \ldots\}$, where t is odd.

$$1 + r(t + 1) = \frac{f[1 + r(t + 2)]}{[1 + r(t)]f[1 + r(t)]}.$$

Now $r(t + 2j) \to \infty$ as $j \to \infty$ implies that the denominator goes to infinity. Average aggregate savings, however, are bounded—say by total first-period endowments—and the implication is that the numerator is bounded. The immediate consequence is that $1 + r(t + 2j + 1)$ goes to zero as j goes to infinity, but this statement contradicts the assumption that an equilibrium exists, because a necessary condition for existence is $r(t + 2j + 1) \geq \rho(2) > 0$, all t even, and $j \geq 0$.

f. We want to show that there exists a continuum of equilibria with valued currency. By doing so we will establish that the one described in (b) is not unique. We conjecture that there exist equilibria in which $K(t) > 0$, all t. Under this conjecture we must have $r(t) = \rho(1)$ at t odd and $r(t) = \rho(2)$ at t even. If t is odd,

$$Nf[1 + \rho(1)] = K(t) + \frac{H}{\rho(t)}, \qquad \rho(t + 1) = [1 + \rho(1)]^{-1}\rho(t).$$

If $(t + 1)$ is even,

$$Nf[1 + \rho(2)] = K(t + 1) + \frac{H}{\rho(t + 1)}.$$

Then

$$Nf[1 + \rho(2)] = K(t + 1) + [1 + \rho(1)]\{Nf[1 + \rho(1)] - K(t)\}$$

or $\quad Nf[1 + \rho(2)] - [1 + \rho(1)]Nf[1 + \rho(1)]$
$\qquad = K(t + 1) - [1 + \rho(1)]K(t).$

This equilibrium condition implies that $\{K(t)\}$ obeys the following difference equation, when t is odd:

$$K(t + 1) = [1 + p(1)]K(t) + Nf[1 + p(2)]$$
$$- [1 + p(1)]Nf[1 + p(1)].$$

Now

$$K(t + 2) = Nf[1 + p(1)] - \frac{H}{p(t + 2)}.$$

If t is odd, we know that $p(t + 2) = [1 + p(1)]^{-1}[1 + p(2)]^{-1}p(t)$. Consequently

$$K(t + 2) = Nf[1 + p(1)]$$
$$- [1 + p(1)][1 + p(2)]\{Nf[1 + p(1)] - K(t)\}$$

or $$K(t + 2) = [1 + p(1)][1 + p(2)]K(t)$$
$$+ Nf[1 + p(1)]\{1 - [1 + p(1)][1 + p(2)]\}.$$

Recall that, by assumption, $[1 + p(1)][1 + p(2)] < 1$. Therefore it follows that $K(t) = K_1 = Nf[1 + p(1)]$ is a stationary point of the above difference equation.

We can similarly find the difference equation that governs the sequence $\{K(t + 1), K(t + 3), \ldots\}$, for t odd. This is given by

$$K(t + 3) = [1 + p(1)][1 + p(2)]K(t + 1)$$
$$+ \{1 - [1 + p(1)][1 + p(2)]\}Nf[1 + p(2)].$$

A stationary point of this difference equation is $K(t) = K_2 = Nf[1 + p(2)]$.

The question of existence reduces to the question of whether it is possible to find a nonnegative sequence $\{K(t)\}$ such that $K(t) \leq Nf[1 + p(t)]$ and such that the even and the odd terms satisfy the two difference equations. The answer is affirmative. We ask the reader to check that each of the two difference equations is stable in the sense that, for any initial condition, $K(t) < Nf[1 + p(t)]$. The sequence $K(t)$ converges to $Nf[1 + p(t)]$ from below; that is, convergence is monotone.

We now show how to generate those equilibria. First, pick any $K(1)$ in the interval

$$Nf[1 + p(1)] - \frac{Nf[1 + p(2)]}{1 + p(1)} < K(1) < Nf[1 + p(1)].$$

Given H, this $K(1)$ determines $p(1)$. Now $K(2)$ is given by $K(2) = Nf[1 + p(2)] - H[1 + p(1)]/p(1)$. The reader can verify that, given our initial choice of $K(1)$, it turns out that $0 < K(2) < Nf[1 + p(2)]$. With these two initial values, we can use the first difference equation to get $\{K(3), K(5), \ldots\}$ from $K(1)$, whereas the second difference equation gives $\{K(4), K(6), \ldots\}$. Then, given $[1 + p(1)][1 + p(2)] < 1$, we have that $\{K(t), t \text{ odd}\}$ converges to K_1, and $\{K(t), t \text{ even}\}$ converges to K_2. Also $p(t+2) = [1 + p(1)]^{-1}[1 + p(2)]^{-1}p(t)$, t even; therefore, $H/p(t)$ converges to zero [this is another way of seeing that $K(t) \to K_i$, $i = 1, 2$, depending on whether t is odd or even, because this is the equilibrium when $H/p(t) = 0$]. Because we can construct an equilibrium from any value of $K(1)$ in the specified interval, we established that a continuum of equilibria exists.

g. To prove this result, assume that $K(t) = 0$ for some t odd, $t > 1$. Suppose that $r(t - 1) = p(2)$. Then at $(t - 1)$ we have

$$Nf[1 + p(2)] = K(t - 1) + \frac{H}{p(t-1)}, \qquad K(t-1) \geq 0.$$

Then, at t,

$$Nf[1 + r(t)] = \frac{H}{p(t)} = \frac{[1 + p(2)]H}{p(t-1)}$$
$$Nf[1 + r(t)] = [1 + p(2)]\{Nf[1 + p(2)] - K(t-1)\}.$$

The equation $K(t) = 0$, however, implies that $r(t) \geq p(1) > p(2)$. Hence $f[1 + r(t)] > f[1 + p(2)]$. Because $p(2) < 0$, the two conditions are contradictory.

EXERCISE 7.6 Indeterminacy of Exchange Rates

Consider a two-country, one-nonstorable-good, overlapping-generations model of two-period-lived agents. In country i there is a constant number N_i of young people born at each $t \geq 1$. Agents in both countries have the common preferences $u[c_t^h(t), c_t^h(t + 1)] = \ln c_t^h(t) + \ln c_t^h(t + 1)$. The per capita endowments in country i are time invariant and are given by $[\Sigma w_t^h(t)/N_1, \Sigma w_t^h(t + 1)/N_1] = (\alpha_1, \alpha_2)$ for country 1, and by $[\Sigma w_t^h(t)/N_2, \Sigma w_t^h(t + 1)/N_2] = (\beta_1, \beta_2)$ for country 2. At time 0, the old of country i are endowed with $H_i(0)$ units of inconvertible currency. The currency of country 1 is called "pounds," whereas the currency of country 2 is called "dollars." The government of country i makes the currency supply grow according to $H_i(t) = z_i H_i(t - 1)$ for $t \geq 1$, where $z_i \geq 1$. The currency is used to finance government purchases of the good. No explicit taxes are imposed, and the government budget constraints are $G_i(t) = [H_i(t) - H_i(t - 1)]/$

$p_i(t)$, where $p_i(t)$ is the price level in country i's currency. Define the exchange rate as $e(t) = p_1(t)/p_2(t)$.

Consider a free-trade, flexible-exchange-rate regime in which agents in the two countries are permitted freely to borrow and to lend to each other and to hold each other's currency.

a. Write down the condition for equilibrium in the world currency-consumption loans market.

b. Prove that $[(\beta_2 N_2 + \alpha_2 N_1)/(\beta_1 N_2 + \alpha_1 N_1)] < 1$ is a necessary condition for the existence of an equilibrium with valued currency if $z_1 \geq 1$ and $z_2 \geq 1$.

c. Find conditions on $(z_1, z_2, \alpha_1, \alpha_2, N_1, N_2, \beta_1, \beta_2)$ such that there exists an equilibrium in which

(i) both countries' currencies are valued
(ii) country 1's currency is valued but there exists no equilibrium in which country 2's currency is valued.

d. Under conditions in which an equilibrium exists, with both currencies being valued, prove that any constant exchange rate $e(t) = e$, $t \geq 1$ in the interval $(0, \infty)$ is an equilibrium exchange rate.

e. Give a formula for:

(i) the balance of trade
(ii) the balance of payments.

SOLUTION

a. We first introduce some notation and derive some preliminary results. Let $M(t)$ be the world money supply measured in pounds, or $M(t) = H_1(t) + e(t)H_2(t)$. Notice that $M(t)/p_1(t) = H_1(t)/p_1(t) + H_2(t)/p_2(t)$, given $e(t) = p_1(t)/p_2(t)$. If $e(t) = e$, all t, then

$$M(t + 1) = z_1 H_1(t) + e z_2 H_2(t).$$

Define

$$\sigma(t) \equiv \frac{M(t + 1)}{M(t)}$$

and

$$\lambda(t) \equiv \frac{H_1(t)}{H_1(t) + e H_2(t)}.$$

Then it follows that

$$\sigma(t) = z_1 \lambda(t) + [1 - \lambda(t)]z_2.$$

This expression says that the rate of growth of the world money supply is a weighted average of the rate of growth of the individual countries' currency supplies. Notice that the weights depend on the particular value of e that obtains. Given the money supply rule, we can write $\lambda(t)$ as itself a function of the initial currency supplies, the exchange rate, and z_1 and z_2:

$$\lambda(t) = \frac{(z_1/z_2)^t \Pi_1(0)}{H_1(0)(z_1/z_2)^t + eH_2(0)}.$$

For any $0 < e < \infty$, as t goes to infinity, $\lambda(t)$ behaves according to

$$\lim_{t \to \infty} \lambda(t) = \begin{cases} 1 & \text{if } \frac{z_1}{z_2} > 1 \\ H_1(0)/[H_1(0) + eH_2(0)] & \text{if } z_1 = z_2 \\ 0 & \text{if } \frac{z_1}{z_2} < 1. \end{cases}$$

Notice that, if $z_1 = z_2$, then $\sigma(t) = z_1 = z_2$, all t. It is clear that $\min(z_1, z_2) \leq \sigma(t) \leq \max(z_1, z_2)$ all t; and that $\lim_{t \to \infty} \sigma(t) = \max(z_1, z_2)$.

Consider the problem faced by an individual agent of country k ($k = 1, 2$). As usual, if more than one asset is held, there must be no rate-of-return dominance among the assets that appear in the savings portfolios. This requirement translates into the condition that

$$1 + r(t) = \frac{p_1(t)}{p_1(t+1)} = \frac{p_2(t)}{p_2(t+1)}.$$

This condition can be rearranged to read

$$e(t) \equiv \frac{p_1(t)}{p_2(t)} = \frac{p_1(t+1)}{p_2(t+1)} \equiv e(t+1).$$

Therefore, if both currencies are held, the exchange rate is constant. For the logarithmic utility function, it is straightforward to derive that the solution to the optimization problem faced by an individual, that is,

$$\max_{c_t^h(t), c_t^h(t+1), s_t^h(t)} u^h[c_t^h(t), c_t^h(t+1)]$$

subject to $$c_t^h(t) + s_t^h(t) \leq w_t^h(t),$$
$$c_t^h(t) \leq w_t^h(t+1) + [1 + r(t)]s_t^h(t)$$

yields a saving function of the form

$$f^h[1 + r(t)] = \frac{1}{2}\left[w_t^h(t) - \frac{w_t^h(t+1)}{1 + r(t)} \right].$$

Aggregating over the young of each country, we get that the per capita saving functions in each country are given by

$$f^1[1 + r(t)] = \frac{1}{2}\left[\alpha_1 - \frac{\alpha_2}{1 + r(t)}\right] \quad \text{for country 1}$$

and $$f^2[1 + r(t)] = \frac{1}{2}\left[\beta_1 - \frac{\beta_2}{1 + r(t)}\right] \quad \text{for country 2.}$$

The world per capita savings function is then

$$f[1 + r(t)] \equiv \frac{N_1}{N_1 + N_2} f^1[1 + r(t)] + \frac{N_2}{N_1 + N_2} f^2[1 + r(t)].$$

We define an equilibrium as a set of sequences $\{p_1(t)\}$, $\{p_2(t)\}$, $\{r(t)\}$, and $\{e(t)\}$ and the allocation associated with the individual savings functions such that

(i) $0 < p_i(t) < \infty$ if country i currency is valued, otherwise $1/p_i(t) = 0$, $i = 1, 2$.

(ii) $e(t) = p_1(t)/p_2(t)$ if both currencies are valued. If country 2 currency is not valued, then $e(t) = 0$; if country 1 currency is not valued, set $1/e(t) = 0$.

(iii) $f[1 + r(t)] = M(t)/p_1(t)$ if country 1 currency is valued. If not, simply express world money supply in dollars instead of pounds and use $p_2(t)$ as the relevant price level.

For the present example, condition (iii) is

$$\frac{1}{2}\left[(N_1\alpha_1 + N_2\beta_1) - \frac{(N_1\alpha_2 + N_2\beta_2)}{1 + r(t)}\right] = \frac{M(t)}{p_1(t)}.$$

Using $1 + r(t) = p_1(t)/p_1(t + 1)$, we can rewrite the above equation to get

$$p_1(t + 1) = \frac{N_1\alpha_1 + N_2\beta_1}{N_1\alpha_2 + N_2\beta_2} p_1(t) - \frac{2M(t)}{N_1\alpha_2 + N_2\beta_2}.$$

b. We want to use the difference equation that determines equilibrium prices to prove this result. For any $p_1(1)$, we have that

$$p_1(t) = \phi^{t-1} p_1(1) - \frac{2M(1)}{N_1\alpha_2 + N_2\beta_2} \sum_{j=1}^{t-1} \phi^{t-j-1} \prod_{k=1}^{j} \sigma(k)$$

where $$\phi = \frac{N_1\alpha_1 + N_2\beta_1}{N_1\alpha_2 + N_2\beta_2}.$$

Then it is clear that a necessary condition for existence is $\phi > 1$. For if $\phi \le 1$, the first term does not increase, whereas $\sigma(k) \ge 1$, all k; consequently, the second term — which grows at least linearly in t — eventually dominates, implying $p_1(t) < 0$, all $t \ge T$, for some T finite.

c. i. The difference equation that governs prices can be rewritten as

$$p_1(t) = \phi^{t-1} \left\{ p_1(1) - \frac{2M(1)}{N_1 \alpha_2 + N_2 \beta_2} \sum_{j=1}^{t-1} \phi^{-j} \prod_{k=1}^{j} \sigma(k) \right\}.$$

We now claim that a necessary and sufficient condition for existence of an equilibrium in which both currencies have value is that $\phi > \bar{z}$, where $\bar{z} \equiv \max(z_1, z_2)$.

We first establish sufficiency. Recall that $\sigma(k) \le \bar{z}$, all k. Then

$$\prod_{k=1}^{j} \sigma(k) \le \bar{z}^j.$$

The implication is that

$$\sum_{j=1}^{t-1} \phi^{-j} \prod_{k=1}^{j} \sigma(k) \le \sum_{j=1}^{t-1} \left(\frac{\bar{z}}{\phi} \right)^j = \frac{1 - (\bar{z}/\phi)^t}{1 - (\bar{z}/\phi)}.$$

Therefore

$$p_1(t) \ge \phi^{t-1} \left\{ p_1(1) - \frac{2M(1)}{N_1 \alpha_2 + N_2 \beta_2} \frac{1 - (\bar{z}/\phi)^t}{1 - (\bar{z}/\phi)} \right\}.$$

Then for any $p_1(1) > 2M(1)/(N_1 \alpha_2 + N_2 \beta_2)$, the sequence $\{p_1(t)\}$ is positive and increasing and satisfies all of the other conditions of an equilibrium.

To prove necessity we proceed by contradiction, that is, let $\bar{z} \le \phi$, and suppose that an equilibrium exists. From (a) we know that $\sigma(t)$ converges to $\bar{z}$. We want to argue that the term $\sum_{j=1}^{t-1} \phi^{-j} \prod_{k=1}^{j} \sigma(k)$ diverges, which in turn implies that $p(t)$ must be negative for some t. Denote $z(k) \equiv \sigma(k)/\phi$ and $w(t) \equiv \prod_{k=1}^{t} z(k)$. Then it is clear that

$$\sum_{j=1}^{t-1} \sigma^{-j} \prod_{k=1}^{j} \sigma(k) = \sum_{j=1}^{t-1} w(j).$$

The strategy is to show that $\lim_{j \to \infty} w(j) > 0$. This is sufficient to imply that the series diverges. Without loss of generality let $z_1 = \phi$ and let $z_2 = a\phi$ for some $0 < a \leq 1$. Then

$$\sigma(k) = \phi[\lambda(k) + a(1 - \lambda(k))]$$

$$z(k) = \frac{\sigma(k)}{\phi} = \lambda(k) + a[1 - \lambda(k)]$$

$$= \frac{(1/a)^k H_1(0) + aeH_2(0)}{(1/a)^k H_1(0) + eH_2(0)} = \frac{(1/a)^k + aeH_2(0)/H_1(0)}{(1/a)^k + eH_2(0)/H_1(0)}$$

$$= \frac{(1/a)^k + aB}{(1/a)^k + B},$$

where $B = \dfrac{eH_2(0)}{H_1(0)}$.

If $w(t) \to 0$ as $t \to \infty$, we must have that $\ln[w(t)] \to -\infty$ as $t \to \infty$, but

$$\ln[w(t)] = \sum_{j=1}^{t} \ln\left[\left(\frac{1}{a}\right)^j + aB\right] - \ln\left[\left(\frac{1}{a}\right)^j + B\right].$$

By concavity of the logarithmic function,

$$\ln\left[\left(\frac{1}{a}\right)^j + B\right] \leq \ln\left[\left(\frac{1}{a}\right)^j + aB\right] + \frac{B(1 - a)}{(1/a)^j + aB}.$$

Therefore

$$\ln[w(t)] \geq \sum_{j=1}^{t} \frac{B(a - 1)}{(1/a)^j + aB} = B(a - 1) \sum_{j=1}^{t} \frac{a^j}{1 + aBa^j}.$$

If $a = 1$, then $\ln[w(t)] \geq 0$, which implies $w(t) \geq 1$. [Actually in this case $w(t) = 1$ can be seen directly.] Suppose $0 < a < 1$. Then $a^j < 1$, all $j \leq 1$, and hence

$$\frac{a^j}{1 + aBa^j} \leq a^j.$$

Consequently

$$\ln[w(t)] \geq B(a - 1) \sum_{j=1}^{t-1} a^j$$

$$\lim_{t \to \infty} \ln[w(t)] \geq -B > -\infty.$$

Therefore there is no equilibrium.

ii. The result in (i) readily suggests a way of setting up conditions such that there is no equilibrium where country 2's currency is not valued. We can choose $z_2 \geq \phi > z_1$. If these conditions are satisfied, there is no equilibrium of the type analyzed in (i). If country 2's currency has no value, then $p_2(t)^{-1} = 0$, all t, and $M(t) = H_1(t)$, whereas now $\sigma(t) = z_1$, all t. It is straightforward to show that there exists a continuum of equilibria using the same approach as in (i). In particular the difference equation governing prices is given by

$$p_1(t + 1) = \phi p_1(t) - \frac{2H(t)}{N_1 \alpha_2 + N_2 \beta_2},$$

and the solution takes the form

$$p_1(t) = \frac{2}{\phi - z_1} \frac{H(t)}{(N_1 \alpha_2 + N_2 \beta_2)} + c\phi^t$$

for any $c \geq 0$. If $c = 0$, then $p_1(t + 1) = z_1 p_1(t)$, and real balances are constant.

d. Our argument in (c) has already proved this point. Recall that we can rephrase the existence result to read: given any e in the interval $(0, \infty)$, the conditions $\phi > 1$ and $\phi > \bar{z}$ are necessary and sufficient for existence of an equilibrium.

The feasibility of this procedure is clear from the fact that the existence argument relies on the limiting behavior of $\sigma(t)$ and that, although e affects $\sigma(t)$ for each t, it does *not* affect the limit. No matter what e is, we can therefore demonstrate the existence of an equilibrium for $\phi > \bar{z}$ and $\phi > 1$.

e. In this one-good world, a country is an exporter of the good if and only if it is an importer of the other country's currency. Therefore the balance of trade is simply the net imports of foreign currency.

Denote the trade balance of country i at t by X_t^i. Then $X_t^i = Y_t^i - C_t^i$, where Y_t^i is aggregate endowment and C_t^i is aggregate consumption at t, for $i = 1, 2$. Consider country 1. Per capita consumption of a young member of generation t is given by

$$c_t(t) = \alpha_1 - \frac{1}{2}\left[\alpha_1 - \frac{\alpha_2}{1 + r(t)}\right],$$

whereas per capita consumption of an old member of generation $(t - 1)$ is given by

$$c_{t-1}(t) = \alpha_2 + [1 + r(t - 1)]\frac{1}{2}\left[\alpha_1 - \frac{\alpha_2}{1 + r(t - 1)}\right].$$

Then per capita aggregate consumption at t is

$$c_t = \frac{1}{2}\left[c_t(t) + c_{t-1}(t)\right] = \frac{1}{2}\left\{\alpha_1 + \alpha_2 - \frac{1}{2}\left[\alpha_1 - \frac{\alpha_2}{1 + r(t)}\right]\right.$$
$$\left. + \left[1 + r(t-1)\right]\frac{1}{2}\left[\alpha_1 - \frac{\alpha_2}{1 + r(t-1)}\right]\right\}.$$

Per capita aggregate endowment is $(\alpha_1 + \alpha_2)/2$. The trade balance is then —
on per capita terms —

$$x_t^1 = \frac{1}{4}\left[\alpha_1 - \frac{\alpha_2}{1 + r(t)}\right] - \left[1 + r(t-1)\right]\frac{1}{4}\left[\alpha_1 - \frac{\alpha_2}{1 + r(t-1)}\right].$$

The balance of payments is always zero, that is, exports (or imports) of goods
are exactly compensated by imports (or exports) of currency.

EXERCISE 7.7   Asset Prices and Volatility

Consider an economy with overlapping generations of two-period-lived
agents. At time $t \geq 1$, there are born $N(t)$ young, each of whom is endowed
with w units of the one consumption good in the model in the first period of
life and zero units in the second period of life. The consumption good can be
productively invested under the following conditions: if $k(t)$ units of the
good are stored at t, then $(1 + \rho)k(t)$ units become available at time $(t + 1)$,
where $\rho \geq -1$. Each agent of each generation has the utility function $\ln$
$c_t(t) + \ln c_t(t + 1)$ where $c_t(s)$ is consumption of the s-period good of an agent
born in t.

In addition, there is a small and constant number T of "trees," all of which
are initially in the hands of the initial old at time $t = 1$. These trees live
forever. At time $t \geq 1$, each tree drops (pays dividends) d_t units of the consumption good to its owner as of the beginning of the period. Notice that d_t is
measured in units of time t consumption good per tree. Assume that $\{d_t\}_{t=1}^{\infty}$ is
a positive and bounded sequence. Let the price of trees at t be v_t, measured in
units of the consumption good at t per tree. Assume that the number of trees
is relatively small, in the sense that for any $\epsilon > 0$,

$$T \cdot \sum_{j=1}^{\infty}\left(\frac{1}{1 + \epsilon}\right)^j d_{t+j} < \frac{N(t)w}{2} \qquad \text{for all } t \geq 1.$$

a. Assume $N(t) = N$ and that $\rho > 0$ is constant for all time. Describe the
equilibrium of this economy. Show formally that the following formula

describes the evolution of the price of trees:

(1) $$v_t = \sum_{j=1}^{\infty} \left(\frac{1}{1+r}\right)^j d_{t+j},$$

where r is the real rate of interest. Prove that r is constant over time, and give a formula for it.

b. Assume now that $\rho = -1$, so that the consumption good is nonstorable. Derive a formula for v_t in this economy, and compare it with (1). How is the real rate of interest behaving in this economy? Describe an example in which dividends are constant ($d_t = d > 0$ for all $t \geq 1$) but in which v_t varies through time.

c. Prove that in model (b) the share price still obeys the following generalization of (a):

$$v_t = \sum_{j=1}^{\infty} \prod_{s=1}^{j} \left(\frac{1}{1 + r(t+s-1)}\right) d_{t+j},$$

where now the real rate $r(s)$ varies over time. Describe the way in which $r(s)$ varies over time.

SOLUTION

a. An agent faced with a rate of return $[1 + r(t)]$ solves the following problem

$$\max_{c_t^h(t), c_t^h(t+1), s_t^h(t)} u[c_t^h(t), c_t^h(t+1)]$$

subject to
$$c_t^h(t) + s_t^h(t) \leq w_t^h(t),$$
$$c_t^h(t+1) \leq w_t^h(t+1) + [1 + r(t)]s_t^h(t),$$

where $s_t^h(t)$ is interpreted as savings. In this economy a portfolio can include three assets: loans, $l_t^h(t)$, storage or capital, $k_t^h(t)$, and shares in trees, $\alpha_t^h(t)$. Therefore $s_t^h(t) = l_t^h(t) + k_t^h(t) + v_t \alpha_t^h(t)$. At time $(t+1)$ the return of this portfolio—its value in terms of time $(t+1)$ good—is given by $[1 + r(t)]l_t^h(t+1) + (1 + \rho)k_t^h(t) + (v_{t+1} + d_{t+1})\alpha_t^h(t)$. As usual, if all assets are held, their rates of return must be equal. Because there are no constraints on the sign of $l_t^h(t)$, we have that

$$1 + r(t) \geq 1 + \rho \quad \text{and} \quad 1 + r(t) \geq (v_{t+1} + d_{t+1})/v_t,$$

with equality whenever some agent holds either $k_t^h(t) > 0$ or $\alpha_t^h(t) > 0$, respectively.

Given the logarithmic utility function, it is straightforward to derive that

$s_t^h(t) = f^h[1 + r(t)] = \frac{1}{2}\{w_t^h(t) - w_t^h(t+1)/[1 + r(t)]\}$. In this economy with homogeneous agents, $f^h[1 + r(t)] = w/2$, all h. We want to argue that $\alpha_t^h(t) > 0$ for some h, that is, shares to trees are held. If not, then Td_t units of consumption available at t are not claimed by any agent, which cannot be an equilibrium with monotone preferences. Suppose that $K(t) \equiv \Sigma_{h=1}^{N(t)} k_t^h(t) > 0$, then

$$\frac{v_{t+1} + d_{t+1}}{v_t} = 1 + \rho = 1 + r(t).$$

Iterating "forward" on this first-order difference equation, we get

$$v_t = \sum_{j=1}^{\infty} (1 + \rho)^{-j} d_{t+j},$$

where we imposed that $\lim_{N \to \infty} v_N (1 + \rho)^{-N} = 0$. Notice that if we allow this limit to be positive, the resulting expression for v_t cannot be an equilibrium price, because $v_t T$ would go to infinity as t goes to infinity, contradicting the fact that the value of savings is bounded.

We now verify our conjecture, namely that $K(t) > 0$. Equilibrium in the savings market requires that

$$N(t)f[1 + r(t)] = K(t) + v_t T.$$

Then

$$K(t) = \frac{N(t)w}{2} - T \cdot \sum_{j=1}^{\infty} (1 + \rho)^{-j} d_{t+j}.$$

This expression, however, is positive by assumption. Therefore we have shown that the gross real rate of interest is constant over time and equal to $(1 + \rho)$.

b. In this new economy, the equilibrium condition is simply

$$\frac{N(t)w}{2} = v_t T.$$

Hence

$$v_t = \frac{N(t)w}{2T}.$$

The gross rate of return in this economy is given by $1 + r(t) = (v_{t+1} + d_{t+1})/v_t$. Hence

$$1 + r(t) = \frac{d_{t+1} + N(t+1)w/2T}{N(t)w/2T}.$$

It is clear that, even in the case $d_t = d$, if $N(t + 1) \neq N(t)$, $r(t)$ varies through time. If $\{N(t)\}$ displayed cyclical behavior, so would $r(t)$.

c. Recall that $1 + r(t) = (v_{t+1} + d_{t+1})/v_t$. If we again iterate forward on this difference equation, we get

$$\eta_t = \sum_{j=1}^{\infty} \prod_{s=1}^{j} \left[\frac{1}{1 + r(t + s - 1)} \right] d_{t+j},$$

where, as before, we have set $\lim_{N \to \infty} \prod_{s=1}^{N} [1 + r(t + s - 1)]^{-1} v_N = 0$, because otherwise the value of savings would exceed the value of endowments. The rate of interest is given by

$$1 + r(t) = \frac{d_{t+1} + N(t + 1)w/2T}{N(t)w/2T}.$$

EXERCISE 7.8   Unpleasant Monetarist Arithmetic

Consider an economy in which the aggregate demand for government currency for $t \geq 1$ is given by $[M(t)p(t)]^d = g[R_1(t)]$, where $R_1(t)$ is the gross rate of return on currency between t and $(t + 1)$, $M(t)$ is the stock of currency at t, and $p(t)$ is the value of currency in terms of goods at t (the reciprocal of the price level). The function $g(R)$ satisfies

(1) $g(R)(1 - R) = h(R) > 0$ for $R \in (\underline{R}, 1)$,
        $h(R) \leq 0$ for $R < \underline{R}$, $R \geq 1$, $\underline{R} > 0$.
        $h'(R) < 0$ for $R > R_m$
        $h'(R) > 0$ for $R < R_m$
        $h(R_m) > D$,   where D is a positive number to be defined shortly.

The government faces an infinitely elastic demand for its interest-bearing bonds at a constant over time gross rate of return $R_2 > 1$. The government finances a budget deficit D, defined as government purchases minus explicit taxes, that is constant over time. The government's budget constraint is

(2) $D = p(t)[M(t) - M(t - 1)] + B(t) - B(t - 1)R_2$, $t \geq 1$,

subject to $B(0) = 0$, $M(0) > 0$. In equilibrium,

(3) $M(t)p(t) = g[R_1(t)]$.

The government is free to choose paths of $M(t)$, $B(t)$, subject to (2) and (3).

a. Prove that, for $B(t) = 0$, for all $t > 0$, there exist two stationary equilibria for this model.

b. Show that there exist values of $B > 0$, such that there exist stationary equilibrium with $B(t) = B$, $M(t)p(t) = Mp$.

c. Prove a version of the following proposition: among stationary equilibria, the lower the value of B, the lower the stationary rate of inflation consistent with equilibrium. (You will have to make an assumption about Laffer curve effects to obtain such a proposition.)

This problem displays some of the ideas used by Sargent and Wallace (1981). Sargent and Wallace argue that, under assumptions like those leading to the proposition stated under (c), the "looser" money is today [that is, the higher $M(1)$ and the lower $B(1)$], the lower the stationary inflation rate.

SOLUTION

a. Because $B(t) = 0$, all t, the government budget constraint is

$$D = p(t)M(t) - \frac{p(t)}{p(t-1)} p(t-1)M(t-1)$$

where $\dfrac{p(t)}{p(t-1)} = R_1(t-1).$

Then, in equilibrium,

$$D = g[R_1(t)] - R_1(t-1)g[R_1(t-1)].$$

In any stationary equilibrium, $R_1(t) = R_1$, all t, in which case

$$D = g(R_1) - R_1 g(R_1) \equiv h(R_1).$$

The assumptions made on $h(R)$ imply that the function is continuous, increases for $R \le R_m$, and decreases for $R \ge R_m$. Because $D < h(R_m)$, it follows that there exist $\overline{R}_1$ and $\hat{R}_1$ with $\hat{R}_1 < \overline{R}_1$ such that $h(\hat{R}_1) = h(\overline{R}_1) = D$. See Figure 7.1.

b. For any such equilibrium we have

$$D = h(R_1) + (1 - R_2)B$$

or

(1) $D + (R_2 - 1)B = h(R_1),$

where $(R_2 - 1)B > 0$. We know, however, that if $D + (R_2 - 1)B \le h(R_m)$, there exist R_1 such that (1) is satisfied. Then, given R_2, the set of B consistent with equilibrium is the interval

$$\left(0, \frac{h(R_m) - D}{R_2 - 1}\right).$$

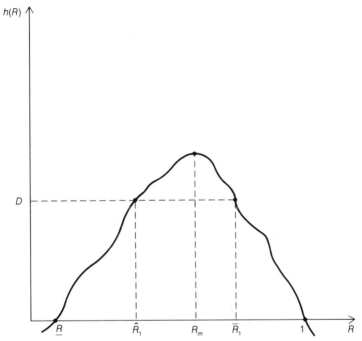

Figure 7.1. Seignorage as a function of the rate of return on currency

c. Let R_1^i be the largest rate of return on currency such that $D + (R_2 - 1)B^i = h(R_1^i)$, $i = 1, 2$. By the argument in (a) we know that $R_1^i > R_m$ and that over this range the $h(\cdot)$ function is decreasing. Letting $B^1 < B^2$, we have that

$$D + (R_2 - 1)B^2 > D + (R_2 - 1)B^1,$$

which implies that

$$h(R_1^2) > h(R_1^1) \text{ or } R_1^2 < R_1^1.$$

The rate of inflation, however, is simply $p(t)/p(t + 1) = R_1(t)^{-1}$. Consequently, inflation is higher in situation 2; that is, the more bonds outstanding, the higher the rate of inflation.

The reason for this result is that, because bonds pay a positive rate of interest, an increase in the amount of bonds increases the value of interest payments $(R_2 - 1)B^i$, which in turn requires an increase in the revenue from the inflation tax, $h(R)$. Over the range where the "Laffer curve" is decreasing, this requires an increase in the inflation tax.

EXERCISE 7.9   Grandmont

Consider a nonstochastic, one-good overlapping-generations model consisting of two-period-lived young people born in each $t \geq 1$ and an initial group of old people at $t = 1$ who are endowed with $H(0) > 0$ units of unbacked currency at the beginning of period 1. The one good in the model is not storable. Let the aggregate first-period saving function of the young be time invariant and be denoted $f[1 + r(t)]$ where $[1 + r(t)]$ is the gross rate of return on consumption loans between t and $(t + 1)$. The saving function is assumed to satisfy $f(0) = -\infty, f'(1 + r) > 0, f(1) > 0$.

Let the government pay interest on currency, starting in period 2 (to holders of currency between periods 1 and 2). The government pays interest on currency at a nominal rate of $[1 + r(t)] p(t + 1)/\bar{p}$, where $[1 + r(t)]$ is the real gross rate of return on consumption loans, $p(t)$ is the price level at t, and $\bar{p}$ is a target price level chosen to satisfy

(1) $\bar{p} = H(0)/f(1).$

The government finances its interest payments by printing new money, so that the government's budget constraint is:

(2) $H(t + 1) - H(t) = \left\{ [1 + r(t)] \dfrac{p(t + 1)}{\bar{p}} - 1 \right\} H(t), \qquad t \geq 1,$

given $H(1) = H(0) > 0$. The gross rate of return on consumption loans in this economy is $1 + r(t)$. In equilibrium, we have that $[1 + r(t)]$ must be at least as great as the real rate of return on currency

$$[1 + r(t)]p(t)/\bar{p} = [1 + r(t)] \frac{p(t + 1)}{\bar{p}} \frac{p(t)}{p(t + 1)}$$

with equality if currency is valued,

(3) $1 + r(t) \geq [1 + r(t)]p(t)/\bar{p}, \qquad 0 < p(t) < \infty.$

The loan market-clearing condition in this economy is

(4) $f[1 + r(t)] = H(t)/p(t).$

a. Define an equilibrium.
b. Prove that there exists a unique monetary equilibrium in this economy and compute it.

SOLUTION

a. We define an equilibrium as sequences $\{r(t)\}$, $\{p(t)\}$, and $\{H(t)\}$ and an allocation associated with the savings function $f(\cdot)$ such that

(1)
$$H(t+1) = [1 + r(t)]\frac{p(t+1)}{\bar{p}} H(t), \qquad t \geq 1,$$
$$H(1) - H(0) > 0$$

(2)
$$f[1 + r(t)] = \frac{H(t)}{p(t)}$$

(3)
$$1 + r(t) \geq [1 + r(t)]\frac{p(t)}{\bar{p}}$$

and
$$\left\{ 1 + r(t) - [1 + r(t)]\frac{p(t)}{\bar{p}} \right\} \frac{H(t)}{p(t)} = 0.$$

b. We want to argue that the unique equilibrium is given by $H(t) = H(0)$, $p(t) = \bar{p}$, and $r(t) = 0$, all t. That this is in fact an equilibrium can be verified by checking conditions (1)–(3). Given $1 + r(t) = 1$ and $p(t) = \bar{p}$, (1) implies that $H(t) = H(1) = H(0)$, all t. Because $f(1) > 0$, we have $f(1) = H(0)/\bar{p} > 0$. Finally condition (3) is satisfied with equality.

To prove that the equilibrium just discussed is unique within the class of valued-currency equilibria, notice that, in any such equilibrium, (3) must be met with equality. The implication is that $p(t) = \bar{p}$, all $t \geq 1$. At $t = 1$, we have from (2)

$$f[1 + r(1)] = \frac{H(1)}{\bar{p}} = \frac{H(0)}{\bar{p}} = f(1)$$

or $r(1) = 0.$

Hence

$$H(2) = [1 + r(1)]H(1) = H(0),$$

and consequently

$$r(2) = r(1) = 0.$$

Iterating upon this argument, it follows that $r(t) = 0$, all t, which establishes uniqueness.

EXERCISE 7.10   Bryant-Wallace

Consider an economy consisting of overlapping generations of two-period-lived agents. There is a constant population of N young agents born at each date $t \geq 1$. There is a single consumption good that is not storable. Each agent born in $t \geq 1$ is endowed with w_1 units of the consumption good when young and with w_2 units when old, where $0 < w_2 < w_1$. Each agent born at $t \geq 1$ has identical preferences $\ln c_t^h(t) + \ln c_t^h(t+1)$, where $c_t^h(s)$ is time s consumption of agent h born at time t. In addition, at time 1, there are alive N old people who are endowed with $H(0)$ units of unbacked paper currency and who want to maximize their consumption of the time 1 good.

A government attempts to finance a constant level of government purchases $G(t) = G > 0$ for $t \geq 1$ by printing new base money. The government's budget constraint is

$$G = [H(t) - H(t-1)]/p(t),$$

where $p(t)$ is the price level at t, and $H(t)$ is the stock of currency carried over from t to $(t+1)$ by agents born in t. Let $g = G/N$ be government purchases per young person. Assume that purchases $G(t)$ yield no utility to private agents.

a. Define a stationary equilibrium with valued fiat currency.

b. Prove that, for g sufficiently small, there exists a stationary equilibrium with valued fiat currency.

c. Prove that, in general, if there exists one stationary equilibrium with valued fiat currency, with rate of return on currency $1 + r(t) = 1 + r_1$, then there exists at least one other stationary equilibrium with valued currency with $1 + r(t) = 1 + r_2 \neq 1 + r_1$.

d. Tell whether the equilibria described in (b) and (c) are Pareto optimal, among those allocations that allocate among private agents what is left after the government takes $G(t) = G$ each period. (A proof is not required here: an informal argument will suffice.)

Now let the government institute a forced saving program of the following form. At time 1, the government redeems the outstanding stock of currency $H(0)$, exchanging it for government bonds. For $t \geq 1$, the government offers each young consumer the option of saving at least F worth of time t goods in the form of bonds bearing a constant rate of return $(1 + r_2)$. A legal prohibition against private intermediation is instituted that prevents two or more private agents from sharing one of these bonds. The government's budget constraint for $t \geq 2$ is

$$G/N = B(t) - B(t-1)(1 + r_2),$$

where $B(t) \geq F$. Here $B(t)$ is the saving of a young agent at t. At time $t = 1$, the government's budget constraint is

$$G/N = B(1) - \frac{H(0)}{Np(1)},$$

where $p(1)$ is the price level at which the initial currency stock is redeemed at $t = 1$. The government sets F and r_2.

Consider stationary equilibria with $B(t) = B$ for $t \geq 1$ and r_2 and F constant.

e. Prove that if g is small enough for an equilibrium of type (a) to exist, then a stationary equilibrium with forced saving exists. (Either a graphic argument or an algebraic argument is sufficient.)

f. Given g, find the values of F and r_2 that maximize the utility of a representative young agent for $t \geq 1$.

g. Is the equilibrium allocation associated with the values of F and $(1 + r_2)$ found in (f) optimal among those allocations that give $G(t) = G$ to the government for all $t \geq 1$? (Here an informal argument will suffice.)

SOLUTION

a. Consider the problem faced by agent h of generation $t \geq 1$.

$$\max_{c_t^h(t), c_t^h(t+1), s_t^h(t)} u^h[c_t^h(t), c_t^h(t+1)]$$

subject to
$$c_t^h(t) + s_t^h(t) \leq w_t^h(t),$$
$$c_t^h(t+1) \leq w_t^h(t+1) + [1 + r(t)]s_t^h(t),$$

where $s_t^h(t)$ is interpreted as savings at time t, and $1 + r(t)$ is the rate of return on savings. The solution to this maximization problem is a function $s_t^h(t) = f^h[1 + r(t)]$.

In this economy two assets can be used to transfer wealth between the first and second period of life, namely privately issued bonds and currency. Because there is no randomness, an arbitrage argument establishes that, if currency is held, $1 + r(t) = p(t)/p(t + 1)$.

We can now define equilibrium with valued fiat currency. It is a set of sequences $[\{r(t)\}, \{p(t)\}, \{H(t)\}]$ and an allocation $\{c_{t-1}^h(t)\}$, $h = 1, \ldots, N$, and $t \geq 1$, such that

(i) $1 + r(t) = p(t)/p(t + 1)$ all t. (Both assets are held.)
(ii) $G = [H(t) - H(t - 1)]/p(t)$. (The government budget constraint is satisfied.)

(iii) $\Sigma_{h=1}^{N} f^h[1 + r(t)] \equiv Nf[1 + r(t)] = H(t)/p(t)$, all $t \geq 1$. (This condition incorporates utility maximization and imposes market clearing.)

(iv) $c_t^h(t) = w_t^h(t) - f^h[1 + r(t)]$

$c_t^h(t + 1) = w_t^h(t + 1) + [1 + r(t)]f^h[1 + r(t)]$

for all $h = 1, \ldots, N$ and all $t \geq 1$.

Consumption of the old at $t = 1$ is given by the value of the currency they hold, $H(0)$, plus whatever endowment they have.

We say that an equilibrium is stationary if $c_t^h(t) = c_1^h$ and $c_t^h(t + 1) = c_2^h$, all $t \geq 1$. In this particular setup, in which there is no heterogeneity, consumption will not be indexed by h. Moreover, given the logarithmic utility function, it is easy to show that the individual and the average aggregate savings function take the form

$$f[1 + r(t)] = f^h[1 + r(t)] = \frac{1}{2}\left[w_1 - \frac{w_2}{1 + r(t)}\right].$$

In our setup stationary equilibria are necessarily associated with constant interest rates. This is the type of equilibrium we seek.

b. In any stationary equilibrium we have that

$$f(1 + r) = \frac{H(t)}{Np(t)}.$$

Then $H(t)/p(t)$ must be constant. The government budget constraint requires that

$$g = \frac{H(t)}{Np(t)} - \frac{p(t - 1)}{p(t)} \frac{H(t - 1)}{Np(t - 1)}$$

or $g = f(1 + r) - (1 + r)f(1 + r).$

We want to claim that, if there exists a rate of return $(1 + r)$ such that $f(1 + r) > 0$ and $1 + r < 1$, then there exists a range of g values that can be financed. To see this point, let $(1 + r)$ satisfy the assumptions. Because $(1 + r) < 1$, we have

$$(1 + r)f(1 + r) < f(1 + r).$$

Define $g = f(1 + r) - (1 + r)f(1 + r)$, and we have our result. For our particular economy it is easy to see that for any $w_2/w_1 < 1 + r < 1, f(1 + r) > 0$. Moreover, any g given by

$$0 < g = f(1 + r) - (1 + r)f(1 + r), \quad \frac{w_2}{w_1} < 1 + r < 1$$

can be financed.

To sum up, to describe the set of g that is feasible to finance we can follow these steps: first pick any gross interest rate in the interval $(w_2/w_1, 1)$. Then compute $f(1 + r) - (1 + r)f(1 + r)$. By construction, this quantity is positive. Set g equal to this value. Then the set of feasible g corresponds to the image of that expression for values of $(1 + r)$ in the interval $(w_2/w_1, 1)$. The key step in demonstrating existence is to establish that the interest rate at which aggregate savings equal zero (in this case w_2/w_1) is less than one.

c. This problem can be posed in the following alternative way: fix any g in the feasible interval. Then, in general, there are at least two r's, r_1 and r_2, such that

$$g = f(1 + r_1) - (1 + r_1)f(1 + r_1) = f(1 + r_2) - (1 + r_2)f(1 + r_2).$$

Let

$$h(1 + r) = f(1 + r) - (1 + r)f(1 + r).$$

We know $h(w_2/w_1) = h(1) = 0$. If $f(\cdot)$ is continuous and differentiable, these properties are inherited by $h(\cdot)$. Now if it can be established that $h'(w_2/w_1) > 0$ and $h'(1) < 0$, then it follows that any $g = h(1 + r)$ can be financed with at least two r's except possibly for $\bar{g} = \max_r h(1 + r)$. Now

$$h'(1 + r) = f'(1 + r) - (1 + r)f'(1 + r) - f(1 + r).$$

It follows that $f(1) > 0$ implies that $h'(1) < 0$. Also $h'(w_2/w_1) = (1 - w_2/w_1)f'(w_2/w_1) - f(w_2/w_1) = (1 - w_2/w_1)f'(w_2/w_1)$, because $f(w_2/w_1) = 0$. Thus, whenever savings increase with the rate of interest—a condition satisfied for the savings function derived from the logarithmic utility—we get the desired result.

d. We want to argue that the equilibrium is not Pareto optimal. To do so we show that there exist feasible allocations that improve the welfare of at least one individual, without reducing the utility level of the others. We first note that any allocation consistent with the government purchasing $G(t) = G > 0$ each period satisfies

$$\sum_{h=1}^{N} c_t^h(t) + \sum_{h=1}^{N} c_{t-1}^h(t) \leq Nw_2 + Nw_1 - G.$$

Any feasible allocation that treats all agents symmetrically and is stationary — in the sense of (b)—satisfies

$$c_1 + c_2 \leq w_1 + w_2 - g.$$

The allocation corresponding to a stationary equilibrium with valued currency $(\hat{c}_1, \hat{c}_2)$ also satisfies that constraint. Let (c_1^*, c_2^*) be the solution to

$$\max u(c_1, c_2)$$

subject to $c_1 + c_2 \leq w_1 + w_2 - g,$ $c_1 \geq 0, c_2 \geq 0.$

Such an allocation is feasible. We want to claim that it is Pareto superior to $(\hat{c}_1, \hat{c}_2)$. Suppose that $c_1^* > 0$ and $c_2^* > 0$. Then (c_1^*, c_2^*) satisfy

$$\frac{u_1(c_1^*, c_2^*)}{u_2(c_1^*, c_2^*)} = 1.$$

Denote

$$v(c_1, c_2) \equiv \frac{u_1(c_1, c_2)}{u_2(c_1, c_2)}.$$

We make the following assumptions about $v(c_1, c_2)$:

(i) $\forall\, c_2 > 0\ \lim_{c_1 \to 0} v(c_1, c_2) = \infty$

(ii) $\forall\, c_1 > 0\ \lim_{c_2 \to 0} v(c_1, c_2) = 0$

(iii) $v_1 < 0,\ v_2 > 0.$

The assumptions are satisfied by the logarithmic utility function. Recall that in a stationary equilibrium, utility maximization requires (for an interior solution) that $v(c_1, c_2) = (1 + r)$. Because $g > 0$ implies that $w_2/w_1 < (1 + r) < 1$, it follows that

$$v(\hat{c}_1, \hat{c}_2) < v(c_1^*, c_2^*) = 1.$$

Given that the feasibility constraint is satisfied with equality for both allocations, we can write

$$v(y - \hat{c}_2, \hat{c}_2) < v(y - c_2^*, c_2^*),$$

where $y \equiv w_1 + w_2 - g.$

Our assumptions on $v(\cdot)$ imply that the above inequality holds if and only if $\hat{c}_2 < c_2^*$. Then $c_1^* < \hat{c}_1$, and the old at $t = 1$ consume — on a per capita basis — $y - c_1^* > y - \hat{c}_1$. Consequently the old are better off. We now have to argue that the young born at $t \geq 1$ are not worse off, but this follows by construction, because $(\hat{c}_1, \hat{c}_2)$ satisfies the feasibility constraint and (c_1^*, c_2^*) is chosen to maximize utility subject to that constraint. Therefore

$$u(c_1^*, c_2^*) \geq u(\hat{c}_1, \hat{c}_2).$$

e. Consider the competitive problem faced by the young born at $t \geq 1$. Notice that the legal restriction permits no borrowing and lending among agents of the same generation. If that were not the case, a given agent would be able to share a bond by issuing private IOUs. The choice problem can be formulated as

$$\max u^h[c_t^h(t), c_t^h(t+1)]$$

$$\text{subject to} \quad c_t^h(t) + b_t^h(t) \leq w_t^h(t),$$
$$c_t^h(t+1) \leq w_t^h(t+1) + (1 + r_2)b_t^h(t)$$
$$F \leq b_t^h(t) \quad \text{and} \quad b_t^h(t) = 0 \quad \text{if } b_t^h(t) < F.$$

The optimal decision rule gives $b_t^h(t)$ as a function of $(1 + r_2)$ and F. Let

$$b(1 + r; F) \equiv \frac{1}{N} \sum_{h=1}^{N} b_t^h(t)$$

be the aggregate demand for bonds.

We can define a stationary equilibrium as a sequence $\{B(t)\}$, an allocation $\{c_{t-1}^h(t)\}$, and a vector of numbers $[F, r_2, p(1)]$ such that

(1) $$\frac{G}{N} = B(1) - \frac{H(0)}{Np(1)}, \qquad \frac{G}{N} = B(t) - B(t-1)(1 + r_2), \qquad t \geq 2$$

where $B(t) = b(1 + r_2, F)$

(2) $$c_t^h(t) = w_t^h(t) - b_t^h(t), \qquad t \geq 1,$$
$$c_t^h(t+1) = w_t^h(t+1) + (1 + r_2)b_t^h(t).$$

Notice that, because r_2 and F are constant, $B(t) = B$, all t, and $B = b(1 + r_2, F)$. Then to show existence we need to find numbers F, N_2, g such that, $b(1 + r_2, F)$ is given by

$$b(1 + r_2, F) \equiv \underset{b}{\mathrm{argmax}} \ u(w_1 - b, w_2 + (1 + r_2)b)$$

subject to $b \geq F$ and $b = 0$ if $b < F$,

g satisfies the government budget constraint, that is,

$$g = -r_2 b(1 + r_2, F) \quad \text{and finally} \quad -1 < r_2 < 0.$$

Given such values, $g = b - (1 + r_2)b > 0$ and $H(0)/Np(1) = (1 + r_2)b$ determines $p(1)$. The problem is to establish existence of the vector (r_2, F, g). This can be done analytically, but the argument turns out to be complicated. Instead we give a diagrammatic proof.

We fix g at the same level as in (a). [Clearly, we could pick $F = f(1 + r_1)$ and $1 + r_2 = 1 + r_1$ and trivially we have existence.] In Figure 7.2, the (a) equilibrium is shown. The budget constraint is represented by the line that passes through the endowment point w. Tangency of that line [which has slope $-(1 + r_1)^{-1}$] and an indifference curve occurs at the point A. Notice that, for this to be an equilibrium, the resulting allocation $(\hat{c}_1, \hat{c}_2)$ has to satisfy market clearing, that is, $\hat{c}_1 + \hat{c}_2 \leq w_1 + w_2 - g$; therefore, the tangency occurs on the feasibility locus denoted by TT'.

Consider now point B on TT', which also allows the government to consume g per capita. That this point exists and lies southwest of A is a key element of the argument. Notice that at A the indifference curve has slope $-1/(1 + r_1) < -1$, making it steeper than TT'. Moreover, as they have been drawn, the indifference curves are very flat near the axis. Therefore the same indifference curve $\hat{u}$ must cross also the locus TT' at a point like that labeled A'. Strict convexity implies that the slope at A' is, in absolute value, less than one. These two facts guarantee the existence of an indifference curve that yields a level of utility $u^* > \hat{u}$, which is tangent to TT' somewhere between A and A'.

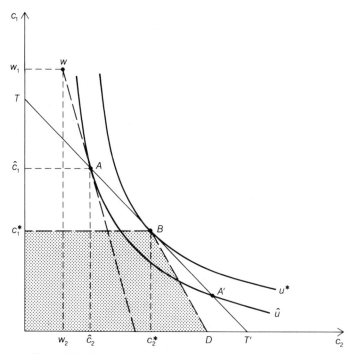

Figure 7.2. Government bonds as a revenue-raising device

If we set $F = w_1 - c_1^*$ and choose r_2 such that the slope of the line BD is $-(1 + r_2)^{-1}$, the budget constraint faced by a representative agent is the shaded area $c_1^* BD$ and the endowment point. Utility maximization occurs at B.

Notice that we apparently have some freedom in choosing r_2 in the sense that many different values would have resulted in the same choice of the same utility-maximizing bundle (c_1^*, c_2^*). This freedom is illusory, because it must also be true that $g = -r_2 F$, that is, $g = -r_2(w_1 - c_1^*)$, or

$$r_2 = \frac{g}{c_1^* - w_1}.$$

This equality satisfies $-1 < r_2 < 0$, because $c_1^* - w_1 < 0$ and $c_1^* + g < w_1$ as $c_2^* > w_2$.

f. We now find F and r_2 for our economy. First we want to determine (c_1^*, c_2^*). We have already argued in (d) what program this vector solves, namely,

$$\max_{c_1, c_2} \ln c_1 + \ln c_2$$

subject to $\quad c_1 + c_2 \le w_1 + w_2 - g.$

The solution is $c_1^* = (w_1 + w_2 - g)/2$, $c_2^* = (w_1 + w_2 - g)/2$. We choose

$$F^* = w_1 - c_1^* = \frac{w_1 - w_2 + g}{2} \quad \text{and} \quad r_2^* = \frac{2g}{w_2} - w_1 - g.$$

Then we verify that (c_1^*, c_2^*) is also the solution to

$$\text{argmax} \left\{ \max_{[c_1, c_2]} [\ln c_1 + \ln c_2], \ln w_1 + \ln w_2 \right\},$$

where the maximization inside the braces is subject to

$$c_1 + b \le w_1, \qquad c_2 \le w_2 + (1 + r_2^*)b, \qquad b \ge F^*.$$

To verify this point, notice that c_1^*, c_2^* are the optimizing values, given the less restrictive constraint for the previous programming problem. Then if they are feasible, they must also be the solution to this problem. Feasibility is guaranteed by construction. The last step is to make sure that the utility is higher than in autarky, that is,

$$2 \ln(w_1 + w_2 - g) - 2 \ln 2 \ge \ln w_1 + \ln w_2.$$

This requirement is clearly met for small g.

g. We can show directly that the allocation (c_1^*, c_2^*) would also be the equilibrium allocation for another economy with endowment patterns $\tilde{w}_1 = (w_1 + w_2 - g)/2$ and $\tilde{w}_2 = (w_1 + w_2 - g)/2$, which when we use the Balasko-Shell criterion is Pareto optimal (the gross interest rate is one). In terms of *feasible allocations* (though *not* in terms of individual endowments), however, both economies are identical. Because optimality is defined only in terms of preferences and aggregate endowments — or feasibility constraints — it must be the case that the allocation for our original economy is also Pareto optimal.

References and Suggested Readings

Aiyagari, S. Rao. 1985. Deficits, interest rates, and the tax distribution. *Federal Reserve Bank of Minneapolis Quarterly Review* 9(1):5–14.

Balasko, Y., and K. Shell. 1980. The overlapping-generations model I: the case of pure exchange without money. *Journal of Economic Theory* 23(3):281–306.

Barro, Robert J. 1974. Are government bonds net wealth? *Journal of Political Economy* 82(6):1095–1117.

Benhabib, Jess, and Richard H. Day. 1982. A characterization of erratic dynamics in the overlapping generations model. *Journal of Economic Dynamics and Control* 4(1):37–55.

Boyer, Russell. 1971. Nickels and dimes. University of Western Ontario, London, Ontario.

Bryant, J., and N. Wallace. 1979. The inefficiency of interest-bearing national debt. *Journal of Political Economy* 87(2):365–381.

——— 1984. A price discrimination analysis of monetary policy. *Review of Economic Studies* 51(2):279–288.

Fischer, Stanley. 1984. The economy of Israel. In *Monetary and Fiscal Policies and Their Applications,* Carnegie-Rochester Conference Series 20, ed. K. Brunner and A. H. Meltzer, pp. 7–52. Amsterdam: North-Holland.

Fisher, Irving. [1907] 1930. *The Theory of Interest.* London: Macmillan.

Friedman, Milton. 1960. *A Program for Monetary Stability.* New York: Fordham University Press.

Friedman, Milton, and Anna J. Schwartz. 1982. *Monetary Trends in the United States and the United Kingdom: Their Relation to Income, Prices, and Interest Rates, 1867–1975.* Chicago: University of Chicago Press.

Grandmont, Jean-Michel. 1985. On endogenous competitive business cycles. *Econometrica* 53(5):995–1046.

Kareken, J. H., and N. Wallace. 1981. On the indeterminacy of equilibrium exchange rates. *Quarterly Journal of Economics* 96(2):207–222.

Keynes, John Maynard. 1940. *How to Pay for the War: A Radical Plan for the Chancellor of the Exchequer.* London: Macmillan.

Koda, Keiichi. 1984. A note on the existence of monetary equilibria in overlapping generations models with storage. *Journal of Economic Theory* 34(2):388–395.

Lucas, Robert E., Jr. 1972. Expectations and the neutrality of money. *Journal of Economic Theory* 4(2):103–124.

—— 1976. Econometric policy evaluation: a critique. In *The Phillips Curve and Labor Markets,* Carnegie-Rochester Conference Series 1, ed. K. Brunner and A. H. Meltzer, pp. 19–46. Amsterdam: North-Holland.

Manuelli, Rodolfo. 1984. A note on the relationship between existence of monetary equilibrium and optimality of the nonmonetary equilibrium in stochastic overlapping generations models. Northwestern University, Evanston, Ill.

Mill, John Stuart. 1844. Review of books by Thomas Tooke and R. Toriens. *Westminster Review* 41(June):593.

—— [1848] 1965. *Principles of Political Economy.* New York: A. Kelley.

Millan, Teodoro. 1981. On the existence of optimal competitive equilibria in the overlapping-generations model. Ph.D. diss., University of Minnesota.

—— 1982. The role of currency reserve requirements in precluding the occurrence of inefficient equilibria. Working Paper 37. Universidad Autonoma de Barcelona. (Forthcoming in *Journal of Economic Theory.*)

Miller, P., and N. Wallace. 1985. The international coordination of macroeconomic policies: a welfare analysis. Federal Reserve Bank of Minneapolis *Quarterly Review* 9(2):14–32.

Nickelsburg, Gerald. 1980. Flexible exchange rates and uncertain government policies: a theoretical and empirical analysis. Ph.D. diss., University of Minnesota.

Peled, Dan. 1982. Information diversity over time and the optimality of monetary equilibria. *Journal of Economic Theory* 28(2):255–274.

Rolnick, A. J., and W. E. Weber. 1983. New evidence on the free banking era. *American Economic Review* 73(5):1080–1091.

—— 1984. The causes of free bank failures: a detailed examination. *Journal of Monetary Economics* 14(3):267–291.

—— 1985. Explaining the demand for free bank notes. Staff Report 97. Federal Reserve Bank of Minneapolis.

—— Forthcoming. Gresham's law. *Journal of Political Economy.*

Samuelson, Paul A. 1958. An exact consumption-loan model of interest with or without the social contrivance of money. *Journal of Political Economy* 66(6):467–482.

Sargent, Thomas J. 1979. *Macroeconomic Theory.* New York: Academic Press.

Sargent, Thomas J. and N. Wallace. 1981. Some unpleasant monetarist arithmetic. Federal Reserve Bank of Minneapolis *Quarterly Review* 5(3):1–17.

—— 1982. The real bills doctrine vs. the quantity theory: a reconsideration. *Journal of Political Economy* 90(6):1212–1236.

—— 1983. A model of commodity money. *Journal of Monetary Economics* 12(1):163–187.

—— 1984. Identification and estimation of a model of hyperinflation with a continuum of "sunspot" equilibria. Working Paper. Federal Reserve Bank of Minneapolis.

—— 1985. Interest on reserves. *Journal of Monetary Economics* 15(3):279–290.

Sebastian, Miguel. 1985. Fixed exchange rates and non-cooperative monetary policies. University of Minnesota, Minneapolis.

Shell, Karl. 1971. Notes on the economics of infinity. *Journal of Political Economy* 79(5):1002–1011.

Smith, Adam. [1776] 1937. *An Inquiry into the Wealth of Nations.* New York: Modern Library.

Sonnenschein, Hugo. 1973. Do Walras' identity and continuity characterize the class of community excess demand functions? *Journal of Economic Theory* 6(4):345–354.

Starrett, David A. 1972. On golden rules, the "biological theory of interest," and competitive inefficiency. *Journal of Political Economy* 80(2):276–291.

Varian, Hal. 1978. *Microeconomic Analysis.* New York: Norton.

Wallace, Neil. 1978. Models of overlapping generations: an exposition. University of Minnesota, Minneapolis.

——— 1980a. Integrating micro and macroeconomics: an application to credit controls. Federal Reserve Bank of Minneapolis *Quarterly Review* 4(4):16–29.

——— 1980b. The overlapping-generations model of fiat money. In *Models of Monetary Economies,* ed. J. H. Kareken and N. Wallace, pp. 49–82. Minneapolis: Federal Reserve Bank of Minneapolis.

——— 1981a. A Modigliani-Miller theorem for open market operations. *American Economic Review* 71(3):267–274.

——— 1981b. A hybrid fiat-commodity monetary system. *Journal of Economic Theory* 25(3):421–430.

——— 1983. A legal restrictions theory of the demand for "money" and the role of monetary policy. Federal Reserve Bank of Minneapolis *Quarterly Review* 7(1):1–7.

Wilson, Charles A. 1981. Equilibrium in dynamic models with an infinity of agents. *Journal of Economic Theory* 24(1):95–111.

8 | Government Finance in Stochastic Overlapping-Generations Models

EXERCISE 8.1 A Version of Kareken-Wallace Exchange Rate Indeterminacy

This problem concerns a two-country version of Wallace's model in his "A Modigliani-Miller Theorem for Open Market Operations." Residents in each country are free to hold assets issued by residents or the government of the other country. In each country, there is the same storage technology. If $k(t)$ units of the single good are stored at t, then $x(t + 1)k(t)$ become available at $(t + 1)$. It is assumed that $x(t + 1)$ for $t \geq 1$ is a positive and independently and identically distributed random variable. We assume that prob$\{x(t + 1) = x_i\} = f_i$. The same $x(t + 1)$ hits both countries. Agents have strictly increasing, strictly concave, and twice differentiable utility functions $u^h[c_t^h(t), c_{ti}^h(t + 1)]$. Agents maximize

$$\sum_{i=1}^{I} u^h[c_t^h(t), c_{ti}^h(t + 1)]f_i.$$

At time 1, old agents in the aggregate own $M^1(0)$ units of country 1's currency and $M^2(0)$ units of country 2's currency. Assume that there are $N_1(t)$ people born in country 1 and $N_2(t)$ born in country 2 at time t. Let $s(t)$ denote the vector of prices of one-period state-contingent commodities. Let $p^1(t)$ denote the value of country 1's currency at t (understood to be a function of the state of the economy at t) and let $p^2(t)$ denote the value of country 2's currency at t. Let superscripts denote country-specific values of the quantities defined in Wallace's paper. With this convention, the equilibrium conditions of the model can be expressed:

(1) $$c_t^{hc}(t) + s(t)c_t^{hc}(t+1) \le w_t^{hc}(t) + s(t)w_t^{hc}(t+1)$$
       for all h and $c = 1, 2$ (c denotes country)

(2) $$f_i u_2^{hc}[c_t^{hc}(t), c_{ti}^{hc}(t+1)] = s_i(t) \sum_{j=1}^{I} f_j u_1^{hc}[c_t^{hc}(t), c_{tj}^{hc}(t+1)]$$

(3) $$s(t)x(t+1) - 1 \le 0, \qquad = \text{ if } K^{p1}(t) + K^{p2}(t) > 0$$

(4a) $$p^1(t+1)s(t) - p^1(t) = 0$$

(4b) $$p^2(t+1)s(t) - p^2(t) = 0$$

(5) $$K^{gc}(t) + G^c(t)$$
       $$= T^c(t) + K^{gc}(t-1)x(t) + p^c(t)[M^c(t) - M^c(t-1)],$$
       $$c = 1, 2$$

(6) $$T_i^c(t) = Y^c(t) - \sum_h w_t^{hc}(t) - \sum_h w_{t-1,i}^{hc}(t) \qquad c = 1, 2$$

(7) $$\sum_c \sum_h [c_{ti}^{hc}(t+1) - w_{ti}^{hc}(t+1)] - [K^{p1}(t) + K^{p2}(t)]x_i$$
       $$= p_i^1(t+1)M^1(t) + p_i^2(t+1)M^2(t)$$

   subject to $M^1(0) > 0, \quad M^2(0) > 0, \quad K^{g1}(0) = 0, \quad K^{g2}(0) = 0.$

   a. Define an equilibrium for this economy.
   b. Define an equilibrium with two valued currencies for this economy.
   c. Assume that an equilibrium with two valued currencies exists, and let this equilibrium be denoted

   $$\{\overline{G}^1(t), \overline{G}^2(t), \overline{w}_t^{h1}(t), \overline{w}_t^{h2}(t), \overline{w}_t^{h1}(t+1), \overline{w}_t^{h2}(t+1), \overline{K}^{g1}(t),$$
   $$\overline{K}^{g2}(t), \overline{K}^{p1}(t) + \overline{K}^{p2}(t) > 0, \overline{s}(t), \overline{p}^1(t) > 0, \overline{p}^2(t) > 0, \overline{M}^1(t) > 0,$$
   $$\overline{M}^2(t) > 0, \overline{T}^1(t), \overline{T}^2(t)\} \quad \text{for } t \ge 1.$$

Furthermore, suppose that, in this equilibrium, $\overline{p}^1(t) = \overline{e}\overline{p}^2(t)$ for all t and states of the world, where $\overline{e} > 0$ is a scalar constant.

   Holding $M^1(0)$ and $M^2(0)$ fixed, prove that, for any $\hat{e} > 0$, there exists an equilibrium in which $\hat{p}(t) = \hat{e}\hat{p}^2(t)$, which is given by

   $$\{\overline{G}^1(t), \overline{G}^2(t), \overline{w}_t^{h1}(t), \overline{w}_t^{h2}(t), \overline{w}_t^{h1}(t+1), \overline{w}_t^{h2}(t+1), \overline{K}^{g1}(t),$$
   $$\overline{K}^{g2}(t), \overline{K}^{p1}(t) + \overline{K}^{p2}(t) > 0, \overline{s}(t), \overline{T}^1(t), \overline{T}^2(t);$$
   $$\hat{p}^1(t) > 0, \hat{p}^2(t) > 0, \hat{M}^1(t) > 0, \hat{M}^2(t) > 0\} \quad \text{for } t \ge 1.$$

   d. Are the allocations in the caret- and macron-bearing equilibria equal to one another? Does the answer depend on the distribution of $M^1(0)$ and $M^2(0)$ between old residents of countries 1 and 2?

e. State but do not prove a Modigliani-Miller-like theorem for government open-market operations in foreign currency. [Presumably you will have to modify (8.5) for one or both countries to state such a theorem.]

SOLUTION

a. We first define an equilibrium for this two-country world. As usual we must decide which are going to be the endogenous variables and which the exogenous variables. To some extent this choice is not crucial for the results, that is, we could change the set of variables that are called exogenous without changing either prices or the equilibrium allocation. We follow Chapter 8, *DMT,* and choose as exogenous the stochastic processes for

$$\{G^c(t),\ w_t^{hc}(t),\ w_{t-1}^{hc}(t),\ K^{gc}(t),\qquad c=1,2,\qquad t\geq 1\}.$$

Then, given the exogenous stochastic process, an equilibrium is a set of stochastic processes for

$$\{[c_t^{hc}(t),\ c_t^{hc}(t+1)],\ K^{pc}(t),\ s(t),\ p^c(t),\ e(t),M^c(t)$$
$$\text{and}\quad T^c(c),\qquad c=1,2,\qquad t\geq 1\},$$

such that

(i) Taking prices as given, agents choose $[c_t^{hc}(t),\ c_t^{hc}(t+1)]$ to maximize utility. This choice is reflected in the satisfaction of Equations (1) and (2).

(ii) All storage activities in which firms or agents can engage yield nonpositive profits. In other words, individual's budget constraints are bounded, a condition that is guaranteed by satisfaction of (3), (4a), and (4b).

(iii) The government budget constraint is satisfied, given the definition of taxes. This corresponds to (5) and (6) for $c=1,2$.

(iv) Equilibrium in the market for second-period consumption obtains, that (7) holds.

(v) If $p^c(t) \neq 0$, $c=1,2$, then $p^1(t) = e(t)p^2(t)$.

Notice that an equilibrium is a set of stochastic processes that satisfies (1) through (7).

b. An equilibrium in which both currencies are valued is an equilibrium [as defined in (a)] with the added requirement that $p^c(t) \neq 0$, $c=1,2$, all t.

c. We first note that our "candidate" for an equilibrium automatically satisfies constraints (1), (2), (3), and (6). Our job is to find sequences $\{\hat{p}^c(t)\}$ and $\{\hat{M}^c(t)\}$, $c=1,2$, such that (4), (5), and (7) are also satisfied.

First we take care of (4). Given any $\hat{p}_i^c(t)$, let $\hat{p}_j^c(t) = \hat{p}_i^c(t)$, all $i,j = 1,\ \dots\ ,$

I, and all *t*. In other words, we seek an equilibrium in which the price of money is not a function of the state $x(t)$, and if $\Sigma_{i=1}^{I} s_i(t) = r(t)$, we require that

$$\hat{p}^c(t+1) = r(t)^{-1}\hat{p}^c(t), \qquad c = 1, 2, \qquad t \geq 1.$$

Any price sequence satisfying this equation satisfies (4). Moreover, given any value of $\hat{p}^c(t)$, we can obtain the rest of the sequence. We now use (5) to generate the $\{\hat{M}^c(t)\}$ sequences. Given our conjecture about the equilibrium allocation, it must be true that

$$\hat{p}^c(t)[\hat{M}^c(t) - \hat{M}^c(t-1)] = \overline{p}^c(t)[\overline{M}^c(t) - \overline{M}^c(t-1)],$$
$$c = 1, 2, \quad \text{and} \quad t \geq 1.$$

Then let $\{\hat{M}^c(t)\}$ be given by the difference equation

$$\hat{M}^c(t) = \hat{M}^c(t-1) + \frac{\overline{p}^c(t)}{\hat{p}^c(t)}[\overline{M}^c(t) - \overline{M}^c(t-1)],$$

with initial condition $\hat{M}^c(0) = \overline{M}^c(0)$. This process for the money supply guarantees satisfaction of (5).

To specify an equilibrium fully, we must still find $\hat{p}^1(t^*)$ for some t^*. Then we shall take $\hat{p}^1(t^*) = \hat{e}\hat{p}^2(t^*)$. We must also verify that (7) holds for all $t \geq 1$. We claim that if (7) is satisfied for $t = \tau - 1$, then (7) is satisfied for $t = \tau$ and consequently for all $t \geq \tau$. To prove this claim, assume that (7) is satisfied for $t = \tau - 1$, that is,

(7') $\qquad \hat{p}^1(\tau)\hat{M}^1(\tau-1) + \hat{p}^2(\tau)\hat{M}^2(\tau-1)$
$\qquad\qquad = \overline{p}^1(\tau)\overline{M}^1(\tau-1) + \overline{p}^2(\tau)\overline{M}^2(\tau-1).$

Because

$$\hat{p}^c(\tau+1) = r(t)^{-1}\hat{p}^c(\tau), \qquad c = 1, 2,$$

it follows that

$$\hat{p}^1(\tau+1)\hat{M}^1(\tau) + \hat{p}^2(\tau+1)\hat{M}^2(\tau)$$
$$= r(t)^{-1}\{\hat{p}^1(\tau)\hat{M}^1(\tau) + \hat{p}^2(\tau)\hat{M}^2(\tau)\}.$$

Next, when we use the difference equation that generates $\{\hat{M}^c(t)\}$, the right-hand side is

$$= r(t)^{-1}\{\hat{p}^1(\tau)\hat{M}^1(\tau-1) + \overline{p}^1(\tau)[\overline{M}^1(\tau) - \overline{M}^1(\tau-1)]$$
$$+ \hat{p}^2(\tau)\hat{M}^2(\tau-1) + \overline{p}^2(\tau)[\overline{M}^2(\tau) - \overline{M}^2(\tau-1)]\}.$$

Imposing (7′) we get

$$= r(t)^{-1}\{\bar{p}^1(\tau)\overline{M}^1(\tau) + \bar{p}^2(\tau)\overline{M}^2(\tau)\}.$$

Because the original equilibrium satisfies (4), however, that is, $\bar{p}^c(t+1) = r(t)^{-1}\bar{p}^c(t)$, we get

$$= \bar{p}^1(t+1)\overline{M}^1(t) + \bar{p}^a(t+1)\overline{M}^a(t).$$

Our last step is to verify that, for *any* choice of $\hat{e}$, we can find $\hat{p}^2(1)$ such that (7) is satisfied for $t = 1$. Notice that once this has been done we have completed the argument, because we have generated sequences $\{\hat{p}^c(t)\}$ and $\{\hat{M}^c(t)\}$, $c = 1, 2$, such that the "remaining" equilibrium conditions, that is, (4), (5), and (7), are satisfied. Equation (7) at $t = 1$ is just

$$\hat{p}^1(2)\hat{M}^1(1) + \hat{p}^2(2)\hat{M}^2(1) = \bar{p}^1(2)\overline{M}^1(2) + \bar{p}^2(2)\overline{M}^2(2).$$

Using $\hat{p}^1(2) = \hat{e}\hat{p}^2(2)$, we get

$$\hat{p}^2(2)\{\hat{e}\hat{M}^1(1) + \hat{M}^2(1)\} = \bar{p}^1(2)\overline{M}^1(1) + \bar{p}^2(2)\overline{M}^2(1),$$

$$\hat{p}^2(1)r(1)^{-1}\left\{\hat{e}M^1(0) + \frac{\bar{p}^1(1)}{\hat{p}^2(1)}[\overline{M}^1(1) - M^1(0)] + M^2(0)\right.$$

$$\left. + \frac{\bar{p}^2(1)}{\hat{p}^2(1)}[\overline{M}^1(1) - M^1(0)]\right\}$$

$$= r(1)^{-1}\{\bar{p}^1(1)\overline{M}^1(1) + \bar{p}^2(1)\overline{M}^2(1)\}.$$

which, after we have rearranged terms, gives

$$\hat{p}^2(1)[\hat{e}M^1(0) + M^2(0)] = \bar{p}^1(1)M^1(0) + \bar{p}^2(1)M^2(0),$$

the desired expression.

d. In the part (c) equilibrium the allocations coincide for all generations born at $t \geq 1$. It is easy to see that consumption of the old at $t = 1$ depends on the choice of the exchange rate unless each agent holds a portfolio consisting of both currencies in similar proportions. Thus from the last equation in (c) and using $\bar{p}^1(1) = \bar{e}\bar{p}^2(1)$, we get

$$\frac{\hat{p}^2(1)}{\bar{p}^2(1)} = \frac{\bar{e}M^1(0) + M^2(0)}{\hat{e}M^1(0) + M^2(0)}.$$

Consider an agent that, at time 1, has the portfolio $[\alpha M^1(0), \beta M^2(0)]$, where $0 < \alpha, \beta < 1$. The value—in terms of time one good—is in each case

$$\bar{v} = \bar{p}^1(1)\alpha M^1(0) + \bar{p}^2(1)\beta M^2(0) = \bar{p}^2(1)[\bar{e}\alpha M^1(0) + \beta M^2(0)]$$

$$\hat{v} = \hat{p}^1(1)\alpha M^1(0) + \hat{p}^2(1)\beta M^2(0) = \hat{p}^2(1)[\hat{e}\alpha M^1(0) + \beta M^2(0)].$$

Therefore

$$\frac{\hat{v}}{\bar{v}} = \frac{\hat{p}^2(1)}{\bar{p}^1(1)} \left\{ \frac{\hat{e}\alpha M^1(0) + \beta M^2(0)}{\bar{e}\alpha M^1(0) + \beta M^2(0)} \right\}$$

$$= \left\{ \frac{\bar{e}M^1(0) + M^2(0)}{\hat{e}M^1(0) + M^2(0)} \right\} \left\{ \frac{\hat{e}\alpha M^1(0) + \beta M^2(0)}{\bar{e}\alpha M^1(0) + \beta M^2(0)} \right\}.$$

Then, unless $\alpha = \beta$, we have $\hat{v}/\bar{v} \neq 1$, and the different equilibria are associated with different allocations, that is, the distribution of $M^1(0)$ and $M^2(0)$ among the old of each country matters.

e. Without loss of generality, we assume that only country 1 engages in open-market operations in the foreign exchange market. This country's budget constraint is then given by the following version of (5):

(5a) $$K^{g1}(t) + G^1(t) + p^2(t)M_g^2(t)$$
$$= T^1(t) + K^{g1}(t-1)x(t) + p^1(t)[M^1(t) - M^1(t-1)]$$
$$+ p^2(t)M_g^2(t-1),$$

where $M_g^2(t)$ represents the government of country 1's holdings of currency issued by the government of country 2. The motivation for the theorem we are about to state is the following: suppose that the government of country 1 decides to increase its holdings of foreign currency and issues — for given prices — own currency for an amount equal to the value of the desired increase in holdings. The value of the currency held by private agents has not changed, although its composition has. Such a change in the structure of the portfolio should not matter, however, given that agents should not — and in fact do not — care which asset they hold, provided that the stream of future returns stay constant. The government budget constraint remains satisfied under such an exchange of assets. To state this point formally, let

$$\{\overline{G}^1(t), \overline{G}^2(t), \overline{w}_t^{h1}(t), \overline{w}_t^{h2}(t), \overline{w}_t^{h1}(t+1), \overline{w}_t^{h2}(t+1), \overline{K}^{g1}(t), \overline{K}^{g2}(t),$$
$$\overline{K}^{p1}(t) + \overline{K}^{p2}(t) > 0, \bar{s}(t), \bar{p}^1(t) > 0, \bar{p}^2(t) > 0, \overline{M}^1(t) > 0,$$
$$\overline{M}^2(t) > 0, \overline{T}^1(t), \overline{T}^2(t), 0 < \overline{M}_g^2(t) < \overline{M}^2(t)\}$$

for $t \geq 1$ be an equilibrium in which $\bar{p}^1(t) = \bar{e}\bar{p}^2(t)$, $\bar{e} > 0$, all t. Then we claim that there exists an equilibrium such that

$$\hat{M}_g^2(t) = \overline{M}_g^2(t) + \frac{\bar{p}^1(t)}{\bar{p}^2(t)} [\hat{M}^1(t) - \overline{M}^1(t)]$$

for any sequence $\{\hat{M}^1(t)\}$ such that

$$0 < \hat{M}^1(t) < \frac{\bar{p}^2(t)}{\bar{p}^1(t)} [\overline{M}^2(t) - \overline{M}_g^2(t)] + \frac{\overline{M}^1(t)}{\bar{p}^1(t)}.$$

The rest of the variables take on the same values as in the original equilibrium.

EXERCISE 8.2 The Term Structure of State-Contingent Claims

Consider the economy described in Wallace's "A Modigliani-Miller Theorem for Open Market Operations." Let $s^{(1)}(t, t + 1; j, i)$ denote the price at time t when $x(t) = x_j$ of a claim to one unit of consumption at date $(t + 1)$ when $x(t + 1) = x_i$ [this is Wallace's $s_i(t)$]. Now suppose that there is opened a market in two-period-ahead state-contingent claims. Let $s^{(2)}(t, t + 2; j, i)$ denote the price at time t when $x(t) = x_j$ of a claim to one unit of consumption at date $t + 2$ when $x(t + 2) = x_i$.

Use an arbitrage argument to prove that

$$s^{(2)}(t, t + 2; j, i) = \sum_{k=1}^{I} s^{(1)}(t, t + 1; j, k)s^{(1)}(t + 1, t + 2; k, i).$$

SOLUTION

The basic insight of the argument is that, unless the equality holds, it is possible to engage in trade in securities that results in a positive profit. This cannot be an equilibrium situation, because increasing the scale at which the trading is conducted would allow each agent to consume an infinite amount of each good. More precisely, suppose that

$$s^{(2)}(t, t + 2; j, 1) > \sum_{k=1}^{I} s^{(1)}(t, t + 1; j, k)s^{(1)}(t + 1, t + 2, k, i).$$

Then consider the following strategy: issue a security that promises to pay one unit of consumption at time $(t + 2)$ if $x(t + 2) = x_i$. The price—in units of time t consumption—is $s^{(2)}(t, t + 2; j, i)$. This amount equals the number of units of consumption that the agent gains at t selling this security, that is, it is the revenue from selling the contract.

We now compute the cost of covering the contract. The agent covers himself by planning at time $(t + 1)$ to purchase contingent claims to the good at time $(t + 2)$. The price—at $(t + 1)$ and in units of $(t + 1)$ good—of a claim to one unit of $(t + 2)$ good in state $x(t + 2) = x_i$—will be $s^{(1)}(t + 1, t + 2; k, i)$. In order to buy this contingent claim at $(t + 1)$, the agent-firm needs $s^{(1)}(t + 1, t + 2; k, i)$ units of time $(t + 1)$, state $x(t + 1) = x_k$ good. The price at time t of that quantity is simply $s^{(1)}(t, t + 1; j, k) s^{(1)}(t + 1, t + 2; k, i)$. Then this is the cost—in terms of time t good—of covering the contract if the state at $(t + 1)$ is $x(t + 1) = x_k$. In order to guarantee that the contract will be honored no matter what the state is at $(t + 1)$, the agent-firm must buy these one-period securities for all possible states. The total cost of doing so is simply the sum over states, that is,

$$\sum_k s^{(1)}(t, t + 1; j, k)s^{(1)}(t + 1, t + 2; k, i).$$

After having made the purchase, however, the agent-firm has made a profit, because the cost of buying securities that guarantees that the contract of time $(t + 2)$ can be honored is less than the revenue from selling such a contract. Then it is clear that if a contract to deliver N units is used, the profit increases linearly in N and goes to infinity as N goes to infinity. This situation cannot possibly be an equilibrium, because consumption must be bounded.

If the initial inequality is reversed, the trading strategy that achieves unbounded positive profits is exactly the opposite, namely, to buy rather than sell the same securities.

EXERCISE 8.3   Walras's Law: 1

In the model of Section 8.2, prove that (8.2), (8.3), and (8.7) imply that

$$\sum_h w_t^h(t) - \sum_h c_t^h(t) = K^P(t) + p(t)M(t).$$

Interpret this equality.

SOLUTION

Multiply Equation (8.7), *DMT*, by $s_i(t)$ and add over i to get

$$\sum_{i=1}^{I} \left\{ \sum_h [c_{ti}^h(t + 1) - w_{ti}^h(t + 1) - K^P(t)x_i] \right\} s_i(t)$$
$$= \left(\sum_{i=1}^{I} s_i(t)p_i(t + 1) \right) M(t).$$

By (8.4), *DMT*, $\sum_{i=1}^{I} s_i(t)p_i(t + 1) = p(t)$, whereas (8.3), *DMT*, implies that $K^P(t) \sum_{i=1}^{I} x_i s_i(t) = K^P(t)$. Finally (8.1), *DMT*, at equality implies that, for each h,

$$\sum_{i=1}^{I} s_i(t)[c_{ti}^h(t + 1) - w_{ti}^h(t + 1)] = w_t^h(t) - c_t^h(t).$$

Using this equation in the above expression and interchanging summation signs, we get

$$\sum_h [c_t^h(t) - w_t^h(t)] - K^p(t) = p(t)M(t).$$

EXERCISE 8.4   Walras's Law: 2

Verify that Equations (8.5) and (8.6) are satisfied for the caret-bearing equilibrium described in Theorem 8.1.

SOLUTION

We essentially impose (8.5) and (8.6), *DMT,* and show that it is satisfied. If (8.5) holds for the caret-bearing allocation and we subtract the corresponding version for the macron-bearing allocation, we get

$$\begin{aligned}
\hat{K}^G(t) - \overline{K}^G(t) = {}& \hat{T}_i^G(t) - \overline{T}_i^G(t) + x_i[\hat{K}^G(t-1) - \overline{K}^G(t-1)] \\
& + \hat{p}(t)\hat{M}(t) - \overline{p}(t)\overline{M}(t) \\
& - \hat{p}(t)\hat{M}(t-1) + \overline{p}(t)\overline{M}(t-1).
\end{aligned}$$

If we further impose (8.6) we get

$$\begin{aligned}
\hat{K}^G(t) - \overline{K}^G(t) = {}& \sum_h \overline{w}_t^h(t) - \sum_h \hat{w}_t^h(t) + \sum_h \overline{w}_{t-1,i}^h(t) - \sum_h \hat{w}_{t-1,i}^h(t) \\
& + x_i[\hat{K}^G(t-1) - \overline{K}^G(t-1)] + \hat{p}(t)\hat{M}(t) \\
& - \overline{p}(t)\overline{M}(t) - \hat{p}(t)\hat{M}(t-1) + \overline{p}(t)\overline{M}(t-1).
\end{aligned}$$

Next, by Equation (8.16), *DMT,* we have that

$$\hat{p}(t)\hat{M}(t) - \overline{p}(t)\overline{M}(t) = \hat{K}^G(t) - \overline{K}^G(t) + \sum_h \hat{w}_t^h(t) - \sum_h \overline{w}_t^h(t).$$

Using this, we reduce the previous equation to

(1) $$\begin{aligned}
0 = {}& \sum_h \overline{w}_{t-1,i}^h(t) - \sum_h \hat{w}_{t-1,i}^h(t) + x_i[\hat{K}^G(t-1) - \overline{K}^G(t-1)] \\
& + \overline{p}(t)\overline{M}(t-1) - \hat{p}(t)\hat{M}(t-1).
\end{aligned}$$

Next we use Equation (8.7), *DMT,* to show that

$$p(t)M(t-1) = \sum_h [c_{t-1,i}^h - w_{t-1,i}^h(t)] - x_i K^p(t-1).$$

This shows that (1) is equivalent to

$$\begin{aligned}
0 = {}& \sum_h [\overline{c}_{t-1,i}^h(t) - \hat{c}_{t-1,i}^h(t)] \\
& + x_i[\hat{K}^G(t-1) + \hat{K}^p(t-1) - \overline{K}^G(t-1) - \overline{K}^p(t-1)].
\end{aligned}$$

By equation (8.9), *DMT*, each of the terms in the first member, $\bar{c}_{t-1,i}^{h}(t) - \hat{c}_{t-1,i}^{h}(t)$, is zero, whereas Equation (8.11), *DMT*, guarantees that the aggregate capital stock is also constant. The second term is therefore also zero, and we have verified that (8.5) and (8.6) are satisfied.

EXERCISE 8.5   Constancy of Fiscal Policy

In Proposition 5.1, in what sense is fiscal policy being held constant across equilibria?

SOLUTION

In Proposition 5.1, *DMT*, the process for government consumption $\{g_t\}$ is being held constant. It is possible, however, to show that, for a fixed stochastic process for the money supply, infinitely many combinations of government bonds and taxes give rise to the same real equilibrium. Therefore if by fiscal policy is meant the mix of bonds and taxes used to finance a level of expenditure, this concept of fiscal policy is not constant. Notice that in the setup of this chapter the kind of policies that the government can pursue and that are consistent with neutrality is much more limited, basically because, although we may still think of the government as infinitely lived, private agents are alive for only two periods. Therefore if we require that the allocations remain constant, we need to guarantee that private agents face the same opportunity sets. In the setup of Chapter 5, *DMT*, the government also had to guarantee unaltered—in the present value sense—private budget sets. No restrictions, however, were imposed on any finite number of the flow budget constraints. In other words, the government could use infinitely many periods to compensate private agents for changes in their budget sets at time zero. No such opportunity is available in the model we study in this chapter. Consequently the class of policies consistent with neutrality is smaller.

EXERCISE 8.6   Altered Version of Logarithmic Preferences

Alter Example 8.1 as follows. Assume that

$$u^h[c_t^h(t), c_t^h(t+1)] = \ln[c_t^h(t) + \alpha] + \ln[c_t^h(t+1) + \gamma].$$

Assume that all other features of the example are the same.

   a. Show that there is a stationary equilibrium in which s_1 and s_2 continue to be given by (v) and pM and K are given by

(1) $$K = N\left[\frac{f_1x_1 + f_2x_2 - 1}{(1 - x_2)(x_1 - 1)}\right]\left(\frac{y}{2} + \frac{\gamma + \alpha}{2}\right)$$

(?) $$pM = N\left(\frac{y}{2} + \frac{\gamma + \alpha}{2}\right)x_1\,x_2\left[\frac{f_1x_1^{-1} + f_2x_2^{-1} - 1}{(1 - x_2)(x_1 - 1)}\right] - N\gamma$$

b. In what sense are α and γ parameters indexing "risk" aversion?

c. How are variations in risk aversion across economies, as indexed by α and γ, reflected in the equilibrium values of the risky asset (K) and the safe asset (pM) that are saved?

SOLUTION

a. The individual agent optimization problem is given by

$$\max \, ln[c_t^h(t) + \alpha] + f_1 ln[c_{t1}^h(t + 1) + \gamma] + f_2 ln[c_{t2}^h(t + 1) + \gamma]$$

$$\text{subject to} \quad c_t^h(t) + s_1 c_{t1}^h(t + 1) + s_2 c_{t2}^h(t + 2) \leq y,$$

where we already impose that the price of the consumption good contingent on tomorrow's realization of the productivity shock, s_i, is independent of the current realization.

The two available assets are capital (or storage) and currency. In a stationary equilibrium the price of currency, $p(t)$, is independent of the realization of x_2 and constant over time. The no-arbitrage conditions for this economy (or, equivalently, the requirement that none of the two productive activities — storage of capital and currency — yield a positive profit in equilibrium) imply

$$s_1 x_1 + s_2 x_2 - 1 \leq 0, \quad = 0 \quad \text{if } K > 0,$$
$$p(t + 1)[s_1 + s_2] - p(t) = 0.$$

Thus, given stationarity, the two conditions imply that in any equilibrium with positive storage we must have

$$s_1 x_1 + s_2 x_2 = 1, \qquad s_1 + s_2 = 1,$$

which implies

(1) $$s_1 = \frac{1 - x_2}{x_1 - x_2}, \qquad s_2 = \frac{x_1 - 1}{x_1 - x_2}$$

The first-order conditions of the agent's optimization problem are

$$(2) \qquad \frac{f_i}{s_i} \frac{1}{c_{ti}^h(t+1)+\gamma} = \frac{1}{c_t^h(t)+\alpha}, \qquad i = 1, 2.$$

Using these two conditions and the budget constraint, it follows that

$$c_t^h(t) = \frac{(y+\gamma-\alpha)}{2}.$$

Then (2) yields

$$c_{ti}^h(t+1) = \frac{f_i(y+\alpha+\gamma)}{2s_i} - \gamma.$$

In this economy there are two markets at each t: the market for consumption and the market for savings. By Walras's law we can ignore one; we choose to specify the equilibrium condition in the market for consumption. Total demand for consumption if state i occurs at $(t+1)$ is simply $Nc_{ti}^h(t+1)$. Total supply is given by $K_t x_i + pM$: the return to storage plus the value of real money balances. Thus the two equilibrium conditions can be written as

$$(3) \qquad Kx_1 + pM = \frac{N}{2} \frac{f_1(x_1-x_2)}{(1-x_2)} (y+\alpha+\gamma) - N\gamma,$$

$$\text{and} \qquad Kx_2 + pM = \frac{N}{2} \frac{f_2}{(x_1-1)} (x_1-x_2)(y+\alpha+\gamma) - N\gamma,$$

where we have used the result that s_i is given by (1). The system (3) is a system of two-linear equations in two unknowns: K and pM. Its solution is

$$(4) \qquad K = \frac{N}{2} \frac{f_1 x_1 + f_2 x_2 - 1}{(1-x_2)(x_1-1)} (y+\alpha+\gamma) = \frac{N}{2} A(y+\alpha+\gamma)$$

$$\text{and} \qquad pM = \frac{N}{2} \frac{f_1 x_1^{-1} + f_2 x_2^{-1} - 1}{(1-x_2)(x_1-1)} x_1 x_2 (y+\alpha+\gamma) - N\gamma$$

$$= \frac{N}{2} (1-A)(y+\alpha+\gamma) - N\gamma,$$

where A is between zero and one, because $EX^{-1} > 1$. It is easy to verify that per capita saving $[s_1 c_{t1}^h(t+1) + s_2 c_{t2}^h(t+1) = N^{-1}(pM+K)$ is given by

$$s = \frac{1}{2}(y+\alpha-\gamma).$$

b. The parameter θ in the utility function $u(c; \theta) = ln(c + \theta)$ indexes the level of relative and absolute risk aversion in the following sense: define the measures of absolute and relative risk aversion by

$$R_a(w; \theta) = \frac{-u_{11}(w; \theta)}{u_1(w; \theta)}, \qquad R_r(w; \theta) = \frac{-u_{11}(w; \theta)w}{u_1(w; \theta)}.$$

For this example we have

$$R_a(w; \theta) = \frac{1}{w + \theta}, \qquad R_r(w; \theta) = \frac{w}{w + \theta}.$$

Then as θ goes to infinity, both the absolute and relative levels of risk aversion go to zero. On the other hand, if θ goes to $-w$, these levels go to infinity. Therefore, in a loose sense, we can associate high θ with "low" risk aversion and low θ with "high" risk aversion.

The utility function in this example is given by the sum of two such functions. To make our analogy precise we should therefore define absolute and relative risk aversion in this multicommodity case. One way of doing so, following Kihlstrom and Mirman (1981), is to use as a basis the behavior implied by those functions. If we follow this approach, we can require that our characterization be such that "an increase in relative risk aversion decreases the proportion of savings allocated to the risky asset." For the standard constant relative risk aversion utility function $u(c; \theta) = c^{1-\theta}/1 - \theta$, $\theta > 0$, it is easy to verify that an increase in θ reduces the share of the risky asset. The problem we analyze, of course, is how to allocate a given level of wealth between two assets; one that is risky and one that is safe. In this exercise the two assets correspond to real currency balances (with a "safe" return of one) and capital or storage (with a "risky" return given by x). The intertemporal nature of the problem, however, implies that wealth (in our case savings) does not remain constant as we change the parameters of the utility function.

We now show that increases in γ correspond, in this interpretation, to a decrease in risk aversion, as our static analysis suggests. Changes in α, however, have ambiguous effects.

From the optimal choice of $k = K/N$ and $q = pM/N$, it follows that, if γ increases, so does K/N. On the other hand, savings decrease, and consequently the risky asset's share of the portfolio must increase. According to the criterion suggested above, this situation corresponds unambiguously to a decrease in risk aversion. On the other hand, an increase in α has the same interpretation if and only if

(5)
$$\frac{\partial k/\partial \alpha}{\partial s/\partial \alpha} > \frac{k}{s}.$$

To see this point, notice that

$$\frac{\partial(k/s)}{\partial \alpha} = \frac{(\partial k/\partial \alpha)s - k(\partial s/\partial \alpha)}{s^2}.$$

This quantity is positive if and only if (5) holds.

From (4) and the definition of s, it follows that

$$\frac{\partial k}{\partial s} = \frac{A}{2} \quad \text{and} \quad \frac{\partial s}{\partial \alpha} = \frac{1}{2}.$$

Thus (5) corresponds to

$$A > A \frac{y + \alpha + \gamma}{y + \alpha - \gamma}.$$

Therefore an increase in α increases k/s if and only if $\gamma < 0$. Because γ can be positive, there are some ambiguities regarding the relationship between α and risk aversion.

c. In this section we concentrate on the effects of changing γ to avoid ambiguities. From (4) it follows that the lower degree of risk aversion (higher γ), the higher the equilibrium level of K and the smaller the equilibrium level of real currency balances, pM. Total savings also decrease.

References and Suggested Readings

Barro, Robert J. 1974. Are government bonds net wealth? *Journal of Political Economy* 82(6):1095–1117.

Chamley, Christophe, and Heraklis Polemarchakis. 1984. Assets, general equilibrium, and the neutrality of money. *Review of Economic Studies* 51(1):129–138.

Friedman, Milton. 1971. Purchasing-power bonds. *Newsweek,* April 12. (Reprinted in M. Friedman, *An Economist's Protest,* pp. 84–85. Glen Ridge, N.J.: T. Horton, 1972.)

Kareken, John, and Neil Wallace. 1981. On the indeterminacy of equilibrium exchange rates. *Quarterly Journal of Economics* 96(2):207–222.

Kihlstrom, Richard E., and Leonard J. Mirman. 1981. Constant, increasing, and decreasing risk aversion with many commodities. *Review of Economic Studies* 48(2):171–180.

Koda, Keiichi. 1985. A note on the existence of monetary equilibria in overlapping generations models with storage. *Journal of Economic Theory* 53(5):995–1046.

Liviatan, Nissan. 1983. On equilibrium wage indexation and neutrality of indexation policy. In *Financial Policies and the World Capital Market: The Problem of Latin American Countries,* ed. P. Aspe-Armella, R. Dornbusch, and M. Obstfeld. Chicago: University of Chicago Press for the National Bureau of Economic Research, 1983.

Manuelli, Rodolfo. 1984. A note on the relationship between existence of monetary equilibrium and optimality of the nonmonetary equilibrium in stochastic overlapping generations models. Northwestern University, Evanston, Ill.

Modigliani, Franco, and Merton Miller. 1958. The cost of capital, corporation finance, and the theory of investment. *American Economic Review* 48(3):261–297.

Peled, Dan. 1980. *Government Issued Index Bonds—Do They Improve Matters?* Ph.D.diss., University of Minnesota, Minneapolis.

———— 1985. Stochastic inflation and government provision of indexed bonds. *Journal of Monetary Economics* 15(3):291–308.

Sargent, Thomas J. 1983. The ends of four big inflations. In *Inflation: Causes and Effects,* ed. Robert Hall. Chicago: University of Chicago Press, for the National Bureau of Economic Research.

Smith, Bruce D. 1985. Some colonial evidence on two theories of money: Maryland and the Carolinas. Working Paper 245. Federal Reserve Bank of Minneapolis. (Reprinted in the *Journal of Political Economy* 93(6):1178–1211.)

Tobin, James. 1958. Liquidity preference as behavior towards risk. *Review of Economic Studies* 25(2):65–86.

———— 1963. An essay on the principles of debt management. In *Fiscal and Debt Management Policies,* ed. William Fellner et al., pp. 143–318. Englewood Cliffs, N.J.: Prentice-Hall. (Reprinted in James Tobin, *Essays in Economics,* 2 vols., vol. 1, pp. 378–455. Amsterdam: North-Holland, 1971.)

Wallace, Neil. 1981. A Modigliani-Miller theorem for open-market operations. *American Economic Review* 71(3):267–274.

APPENDIX

Functional Analysis for Macroeconomics

EXERCISE A.1 Periodic Difference Equation

Consider the periodic linear difference equation

$$y_t = \lambda_1 y_{t+1} + x_t, \qquad t \geq 0, \qquad t \text{ odd}$$
$$y_t = \lambda_2 y_{t+1} + x_t, \qquad t \geq 0, \qquad t \text{ even}.$$

Suppose that $x_t \in l_\infty[0, \infty)$. Assume that $|\lambda_1 \lambda_2| < 1$.

a. Prove that the difference equation given above has a unique solution $\{y_t\}_{t=0}^\infty$ in $l_\infty[0, \infty)$.

b. Describe an algorithm for computing this solution.

c. Find the solution for $\{y_t\}_{t=0}^\infty$ that lies in $l_\infty[0, \infty)$.

SOLUTION

a. One way of solving the difference equation is first to transform it so that it can be put in a more familiar form. We assume that 0 is even. Then if t is even, we have $y_t = \lambda_2 y_{t+1} + x_t$. Then $y_{t+1} = \lambda_1 y_{t+2} + x_{t+1}$, however, because $(t + 1)$ must be odd. Substituting this equation into the first, we get

(1) $\qquad y_t = \lambda_1 \lambda_2 y_{t+2} + \lambda_2 x_{t+1} + x_t.$

Notice that (1) maps even values of t into even values of t. We can reflect this feature by an appropriate choice of subindex, namely

(2) $\qquad y_{2n} = \lambda_1 \lambda_2 y_{2(n+1)} + \lambda_2 x_{2n+1} + x_{2n}, \qquad n = 0, 1, 2, \ldots$

With this notation (2) looks like a standard difference equation. If we can find a solution for it, we can then generate all the odd values by simply using

$$y_{2n+1} = \lambda_1 y_{2(n+1)} + x_{2n+1}, \qquad n = 0, 1, \ldots$$

Therefore we concentrate on finding a solution to (2). We can regard this equation as being induced by a mapping T from $l_\infty[0, \infty)$ into $l_\infty[0, \infty)$ given by

$$(Ty)_n = \lambda_1\lambda_2 y_{2(n+1)} + \lambda_2 x_{2n+1} + x_{2n}, \qquad n = 0, 1, \ldots$$

A solution to (2) is then simply a fixed point of that mapping. To show that T has a unique fixed point, we verify that it satisfies Blackwell's sufficient conditions as presented in Theorems A.1 and A.2, *DMT*. First we show that it is monotone. Let w, z be two elements of $l_\infty[0, \infty)$ such that $w_{2n} \geq z_{2n}$ all n. Then

$$T(w)_n - (Tz)_n = \lambda_1\lambda_2(w_{2(n+1)} - z_{2(n+1)}).$$

If $\lambda_1\lambda_2 > 0$, then $(Tw)_n - (Tz)_n \geq 0$ and condition (a) of Theorem A.1 is satisfied. If $\lambda_1\lambda_2 < 0$, then condition (a) of Theorem A.2 is satisfied. Let a be an element of $l_\infty[0, \infty)$ that has all its coordinates equal to a. Then

$$Ty + a = Ty + \lambda_1\lambda_2 a.$$

If $\lambda_1\lambda_2 > 0$, pick $\beta = \lambda_1\lambda_2$ and condition (b) of A.1 is satisfied. If $\lambda_1\lambda_2 < 0$, set $a = -c$ to get $Ty - c = Ty - \lambda_1\lambda_2 c = Ty + \beta c$, where in this case we choose $\beta = -\lambda_1\lambda_2$ to satisfy (b) of Theorem A.2.

Notice that the crucial property is that $|\lambda_1\lambda_2| < 1$. This feature guarantees that our choice of β satisfies $0 \leq \beta < 1$. Because both the monotonicity and the discounting conditions are satisfied, T is a contraction mapping and has a fixed point.

As we indicated before, once we have a fixed point of t, say y, we have a sequence $\{y_0, y_2, \ldots\}$. We use these even values to generate the odd values. It is easy to verify that, given these odd values, our fixed point also satisfies the equation that generates the even values.

b. Because we have shown that T is a contraction mapping, we can find the fixed point by iterating on T, given an initial condition. In particular we know that the sequence $y_{2n}^N = (Ty^{N-1})_n$ converges to the fixed point y as $N \to 0$. Moreover we know that the rate of convergence is exponential. This statement holds for every $y^0 \in l_\infty[0, \infty)$.

c. We can take the approach suggested in (*b*) and use as our initial condition $y_{2n}^0 = 0$ for all n. Then we have

$$y_{2n}^1 = \lambda_2 x_{2n+1} + x_{2n}$$
$$y_{2n}^2 = \lambda_1 \lambda_2 y_{2(n+1)}^1 + \lambda_2 x_{2n+1} + x_{2n}$$
$$= \lambda_1 \lambda_2 (\lambda_2 x_{2(n+1)+1} + x_{2(n+1)}) + \lambda_2 x_{2n+1} + x_{2n}$$
$$y_{2n}^3 = \lambda_1 \lambda_2 y_{2(n+1)}^2 + \lambda_2 x_{2n+1} + x_{2n}$$
$$= \lambda_2 x_{2n+1} + x_{2n} + \lambda_1 \lambda_2 (\lambda_2 x_{2(n+1)+1} + x_{2(n+1)})$$
$$+ (\lambda_1 \lambda_2)^2 (\lambda_2 x_{2(n+2)+1} + x_{2(n+2)}).$$

In general, if we let $\phi_n \equiv \lambda_2 x_{2n+1} + x_{2n}$, we get

$$y_{2n}^N = \sum_{j=0}^{N-1} (\lambda_1 \lambda_2)^j \phi_{n+j}.$$

It is clear that

$$y_{2n} = \lim_{N \to \infty} y_{2n}^N = \sum_{j=0}^{\infty} (\lambda_1 \lambda_2)^j \phi_{n+j}.$$

Because the terms ϕ_n are all bounded [because $\{x_n\} \in l_\infty[0, \infty)$], the infinite sum is finite. Next we generate the odd elements of y using the corresponding equation. Notice that we can regard (2) as a regular difference equation of the form

$$v_n = a v_{n+1} + \phi_n,$$

where $a = \lambda_1 \lambda_2$. This is a first-order difference equation for which we do not have an initial condition. We can show that the requirement (often generated by the economic features of the problem) that the solution lie in a particular space is equivalent to choosing the "right" initial condition. To see this point, write the equation as

$$v_{n+1} = a^{-1} v_n - a^{-1} \phi_n$$

Then by iterating on this equation we get

$$v_1 = a^{-1} v_0 - a^{-1} \phi_0$$
$$v_2 = a^{-2} v_0 - a^{-2} \phi_0 - a^{-1} \phi_1$$
$$\cdot$$
$$\cdot$$
$$\cdot$$

(3) $$v_n = a^{-n} v_0 - \sum_{j=0}^{n-1} \phi_j a^{-(n-j)} = a^{-n} \left\{ v_0 - \sum_{j=0}^{n-1} a^j \phi_j \right\},$$

where v_0 is some initial condition. According to the solution we derived using the contraction mapping theorem $v_0 = \Sigma_{j=0}^{\infty} a^j \phi_j$. If we substitute in this condition we get the same solution. To show that it is the only solution that lies in $l_{\infty}[0, \infty)$, assume that $v_0^* = \Sigma_{j=0}^{\infty} a^j \phi_j + A$. Because A is arbitrary, our candidate for v_0 is totally general. Substituting v_0^* in (3), we get

$$v_n = a^{-n}\left\{ a^n \sum_{j=0}^{\infty} a^j \phi_{n+j} + A \right\} = \sum_{j=0}^{\infty} a^j \phi_{n+j} + a^{-n}A.$$

The first term is bounded for all n. The second, however, cannot converge. If $0 < \lambda_1 \lambda_2 < 1$, then it goes to infinity if A is positive and to minus infinity if it is negative. If $-1 < \lambda_1 \lambda_2 < 0$, the term alternates in sign but is unbounded. In either case the solution cannot lie in $l_{\infty}[0, \infty)$ unless $A = 0$, which coincides with the solution we discovered using the contraction mapping theorem.

EXERCISE A.2 Asset Pricing

Associated with Lucas's asset-pricing model (Chapter 3) is the functional equation

(1) $$w(x) = \beta \int w(x') \, dF(x', x) + g(x),$$

where $g(x)$ is a bounded and continuous function. We assume that $F(\cdot)$ is such that for every continuous and bounded function $h(x')$ the function $f(x) = \int h(x') \, dF(x', x)$ is a continuous function of x. This will be the case if, for example, the Markov process that x_t follows is generated by an equation of the form $x_{t+1} = g(x_t, \epsilon_{t+1})$, with ϵ_t a sequence of i.i.d. random variables and g a continuous function of x and a measurable function of ϵ.

a. Prove that the functional equation has a unique continuous and bounded solution $w(x)$.

b. Given a function $g(x)$, describe an algorithm for computing the unique continuous and bounded $w(x)$ that solves (1).

SOLUTION

a. Recall that the basic asset-pricing equation for Lucas's model is

$$u'[c(x)]p(x) = \beta \int u'[c(x')][p(x') + d(x')] F(dx', x),$$

where $c(x)$ is consumption when the state is x and $p(x)$ and $d(x)$ are, respectively, the price and the dividends or fruit corresponding to a given tree. If we define

$$w(x) \equiv u'[c(x)]p(x) \quad \text{and} \quad g(x) = \int u'[c(x')]d(x')F(dx', x),$$

we can rewrite the above equation as

(1) $$w(x) = \beta \int w(x')F(dx', x) + g(x).$$

Let the right-hand side of (1) define the operator T. We want to show that T has a unique fixed point in the space of continuous and bounded functions, $C(X)$. We first want to verify that T maps $C(X)$ into itself. This space with the supremum norm is a Banach space. Then we will show that Blackwell's sufficient conditions for a contraction mapping are satisfied. Then by Theorem A.1, *DMT,* it follows that T is a contraction mapping and that it has a unique fixed point.

To verify that T maps $C(X)$ into itself, let $f(x)$ be any continuous and bounded function. Then $(Tf)(x) = \beta \int f(x')F(dx', x) + g(x)$ is, given our assumptions, the sum of two continuous functions and therefore continuous. It also follows that

$$|(Tf)(x)| \leq \beta \int |f(x')|F(dx', x) + |g(x')|$$

$$\leq \beta \|f\|_\infty \int F(dx', x) + \|g\|_\infty = \beta \|f\|_\infty + \|g\|_\infty,$$

where $\|f\|_\infty = \sup_x |f(x)|$. Because f and g are both bounded, $\|f\|_\infty$ and $\|g\|_\infty$ are finite. Then if we take the supremum on the left-hand side of the previous inequality, we get

$$\|Tf\|_\infty \leq \beta \|f\|_\infty + \|g\|_\infty < \infty.$$

Next we verify Blackwell's conditions. First, it is easy to see that if $f(x) \geq h(x)$ for all x, then $(Tf)(x) \geq (Th)(x)$. Consequently the operator is monotone. Second, if a is any positive real number,

$$(Tf + a)(x) = \beta \int [f(x') + a]F(dx', x) + g(x)$$

$$= \beta \int f(x')F(dx', x) + g(x) + a\beta \int F(dx', x)$$

$$= (Tf)(x) + a\beta.$$

Because $0 \leq \beta < 1$, the second condition (discounting) of Theorem A.1, *DMT,* is satisfied.

b. Recall that the contraction mapping theorem says that, if T is a contraction and w is its unique fixed point, it follows that

$$w(x) = \lim_{n \to \infty} (T^n w^0)(x),$$

where w^0 is any arbitrary initial condition. Given this convergence result, we can choose $w^0 = 0$. Then w^1 is given by

$$w^1(x) = g(x).$$

We operate with T one more time to get

$$w^2(x) = \beta \int g(x')F(dx', x) + g(x).$$

In general, if we keep iterating on T, we get that

$$w^n(x) = \beta \int \left[\beta \int \left[\cdots \left[\beta \int g(s)F(ds, x_1) + g(x_1) \right] F(dx_1, x_2) \right. \right.$$
$$\left. \left. + g(x_2) \right] \cdots \right] F(dx_{n-1}, x) + g(x).$$

Then with knowledge of $g(\,\cdot\,)$ and $F(\,\cdot\,)$ we can repeatedly integrate to get a sequence of functions w^n that the contraction mapping theorem guarantees converges to the fixed point.

References and Suggested Readings

Blackwell, David. 1965. Discounted dynamic programming. *Annals of Mathematical Statistics* 36(1):226–235.

Hansen, Lars P., and Thomas J. Sargent. 1980. Formulation and estimating dynamic linear rational expectations models. *Journal of Economic Dynamics and Control* 2(1):7–46. (Reprinted in *Rational Expectations and Econometric Practice*, ed. R. E. Lucas, Jr., and T. J. Sargent, pp. 91–125. Minneapolis: University of Minnesota Press, 1981.)

——— 1981. Linear rational expectations models for dynamically interrelated variables. In *Rational Expectations and Econometric Practice*, ed. R. E. Lucas, Jr., and T. J. Sargent, pp. 127–156. Minneapolis: University of Minnesota Press.

Lucas, Robert E., Jr., Edward C. Prescott, and Nancy Stokey. Recursive methods for economic dynamics. Forthcoming.

Luenberger, David G. 1969. *Optimization by Vector Space Methods*. New York: Wiley.

Naylor, Arch, and George Sell. 1982. *Linear Operator Theory in Engineering and Science*. New York: Springer.

Sargent, Thomas J. 1981. Lecture notes on filtering, control, and rational expectations. University of Minnesota, Minneapolis. Unpublished.

—— 1986. *Macroeconomic Theory*, 2nd ed. New York: Academic Press.

Index